the Geography of NOWHERE

The Rise

and Decline

of America's

Man - Made

Landscape

JAMES HOWARD KUNSTLER

A Touchstone Book

Published by Simon & Schuster

NEW YORK

LONDON

TORONTO

SYDNEY

TOUCHSTONE
Rockefeller Center
1230 Avenue of the Americas
New York, New York 10020

First Touchstone Edition 1994

Designed by SONGHEE KIM
Manufactured in the United States of America

20   19   18

Library of Congress Cataloging-in-Publication Data
Kunstler, James Howard.
The geography of nowhere: the rise and decline of
America's man-made landscape/James Howard
Kunstler.
p.   cm.
Includes index.
1. Architecture—Environmental aspects—United States.
2. Architecture and society—United States.   I. Title.
NA2542.35.K86   1993
720'.47—dc20   93–20373
                                                      CIP

ISBN: 0-671-70774-4
       0-671-88825-0 (Pbk.)

For Amy—
wife, muse, 'possum

CONTENTS

Chapter One

SCARY PLACES

There is a marvelous moment in the hit movie *Who Framed Roger Rabbit?* that sums up our present national predicament very nicely. The story is set in Los Angeles in 1947. The scene is a dreary warehouse, headquarters of the villain, Judge Doom, a cartoon character masquerading as a human being. The hallucinatory plot hinges on Judge Doom's evil scheme to sell off the city's streetcar system and to create just such a futuristic car-crazed society as Americans actually live and work in today.

"It's a construction plan of epic proportions," he intones. "They're calling it [portentous pause] a freeway! Eight lanes of shimmering cement running from here to Pasadena! I see a place where people get on and off the freeway, off and on, off and on, all day and all night. . . . I see a street of gas stations, inexpensive motels, restaurants that serve rapidly prepared food, tire salons, automobile dealerships, and wonderful, wonderful billboards as far as the eye can see. My god, it'll be beautiful!"

In short order, Judge Doom is unmasked for the nonhuman scoundrel he is, dissolved by a blast of caustic chemical, and flushed into the Los Angeles sewer system, while the rest of the cute little cartoon creatures hippity-hop happily into the artificial sunset.

"That lamebrain freeway idea could only be cooked up by a 'toon," comments the movie's gumshoe hero, Eddie Valiant, afterward.

The audience sadly knows better. In the real world, Judge Doom's vision has prevailed and we are stuck with it. Yet the movie's central metaphor—that our civilization has been undone by an evil cartoon ethos—could not be more pertinent, for more and more we appear to be a nation of overfed clowns living in a hostile cartoon environment.

Thirty years ago, Lewis Mumford said of post-World II development, "the end product is an encapsulated life, spent more and more either in a motor car or within the cabin of darkness before a television set." The whole wicked, sprawling, megalopolitan mess, he gloomily predicted, would completely demoralize mankind and lead to nuclear holocaust.

It hasn't come to that, but what Mumford deplored was just the beginning of a process that, instead of blowing up the world, has nearly wrecked the human habitat in America. Ever-busy, ever-building, ever-in-motion, ever-throwing-out the old for the new, we have hardly paused to think about what we are so busy building, and what we have thrown away. Meanwhile, the everyday landscape becomes more nightmarish and unmanageable each year. For many, the word *development* itself has become a dirty word.

Eighty percent of everything ever built in America has been built in the last fifty years, and most of it is depressing, brutal, ugly, unhealthy, and spiritually degrading—the jive-plastic commuter tract home wastelands, the Potemkin village shopping plazas with their vast parking lagoons, the Lego-block hotel complexes, the "gourmet mansardic" junk-food joints, the Orwellian office "parks" featuring buildings sheathed in the same reflective glass as the sunglasses worn by chain-gang guards, the particle-board garden apartments rising up in every meadow and cornfield, the freeway loops around every big and little city with their clusters of discount merchandise marts, the whole destructive, wasteful, toxic, agoraphobia-inducing spectacle that politicians proudly call "growth."

The newspaper headlines may shout about global warming, extinctions of living species, the devastation of rain forests, and other worldwide catastrophes, but Americans evince a striking complacency when it comes to their everyday environment and the growing calamity that it represents.

I had a hunch that many other people find their surroundings as distressing as I do my own, yet I sensed too that they lack the vocabulary to understand what is wrong with the places they ought to know best. That is why I wrote this book.

The sentimental view of anything is apt to be ridiculous, but I feel that I have been unusually sensitive to the issue of place since I was a little boy. Before I was old enough to vote, I had lived in a classic postwar suburb, in the nation's greatest city, and in several classic small towns, and along the way I acquired strong impressions about each of these places.

One September day in 1954 my father and mother and I drove twenty miles east out of New York City in our Studebaker on the Northern State Parkway to meet the movers at our new house "in the country," as my mother would refer forever to any place where you cannot walk out your front door and hail a taxi. Until that time, Long Island had been one of the most beautiful places in the United States, and our house was one small reason it would not remain that way much longer.

It was in a "development" called Northwood. The name had only a casual relation to geography. Indeed, it was *north* of many things—the parkway, the land of Dixie, the Tropic of Capricorn—but the *wood* part was spurious since the tract occupied a set of former farm fields, and among the spanking new houses not a tree stood over ten feet tall or as thick around as my father's thumb. The houses, with a few exceptions, were identical boxy split-levels, clad in asphalt shingles of various colors, with two windows above a gaping garage door, affording the facades an aspect of slack-jawed cretinism. Our house was an exception. The developers, I'm told, had started out with different models before they settled on the split-levels, which were absolutely the latest thing and sold like hotcakes.

Our house was a ranch clad in natural cedar shingles. It had a front porch too narrow to put furniture on and shutters that didn't close or conform to the dimensions of the windows. It sported no other decorative elaborations beside an iron carriage lamp on the front lawn that was intended to evoke ye olde post road days, or something like that. What it lacked in exterior grandeur, it made up in comfort inside. The three bedrooms were ample. We had baths galore for a family of three, a kitchen loaded with electric wonders, wall-to-wall carpeting through-out, and a real fireplace in the living room. The place cost about $25,000.

Our quarter-acre lot lay at the edge of the development. Behind our treeless back yard stood what appeared to my six-year-old eyes to be an endless forest like the wilderness where Davey Crockett slew bears. In fact, it was the 480-acre estate of Clarence Hungerford Mackay, pres-ident and major stockholder of the Postal Telegraph Cable Company—the precursor of Western Union. Mackay was long gone by the 1950s, his heirs and assigns scattered to the winds, and "Harbor Hill," as his property had been named, was in a sad state of abandonment and decay. It took me and my little friends some time to penetrate its glades and dells, for there was much news on the airwaves that fall about the exploits of George Metesky, New York City's "Mad Bomber," and we had a notion that the old estate was his hideout.

A lacework of gravel carriage drives overgrown by dogwood and rhododendron criss-crossed the property. At its heart stood the old mansion. I don't recall its style—Shingle? Queen Anne? Railroad Ro-manesque? But it was much larger than any Northwood house. Juvenile delinquents had lit fires inside, and not necessarily in the fireplaces. Yet for its shattered glass, musty odors, and bird droppings, the mansion projected tremendous charm and mystery. Even in ruin, it felt much more authentic than our own snug, carpeted homes, and I know we regarded it as a sort of sacred place, as palpably a place apart from our familiar world. We certainly spent a lot of time there.

One week in the spring of 1956, the bulldozers appeared in the great woods behind our house. Soon they had dug a storm sump the size of Lake Ronkonkoma back there, a big ocher gash surrounded by chain-link fencing. In the months that followed, the trees crashed down, the mansion was demolished, new houses went up, and Clarence Hunger-ford Mackay's 480 acres was turned into another development called—what else?—Country Estates!

A year later my parents landed in divorce court, and I moved into Manhattan with my mother. On the whole I did not like the city at first. My mother enrolled me in an organized after-school play group to keep me out of trouble. Our group made its headquarters in a little meadow near the Ramble in Central Park where we played softball and "kick the can." Unlike the wilderness of Clarence Mackay's estate, the park seemed cluttered with bothersome adults, strolling lovers, nannies pushing prams, winos—everyone *but* George Metesky. By and by, I made city friends. We played in the Metropolitan Museum of Art, because it was a block away from my elementary school at 82nd and Madison. This was in the days before art became just another form of show biz, and on weekday afternoons the great halls of the Met were practically deserted. My other chief recreation was throwing objects off the terrace of a friend's fifteenth-story penthouse apartment—snowballs, water balloons, cantaloupes—but the less said about this the better.

Summers I was sent away to a boys' camp in New Hampshire, where I got my first glimpse of what real American towns were like. From age twelve up, we were trucked one night a week into the town of Lebanon (pop. 8000) where we had the choice of attending a teen street dance or going to see a movie at the old opera house. There was a third, unofficial, option, which was to just wander around town.

Lebanon had a traditional New England layout. A two-acre square occupied the center of town. Within it stood a bandshell and a great many towering elms. Around the square stood various civic buildings of agreeable scale—the library, the town hall, the opera house—whose dignified facades lent Lebanon an aura of stability and consequence. At the west end of the square lay a commercial district of narrow shop-lined streets wending downhill to a mill district. Here I bought fishing lures and the latest baseball magazines.

Off the square's east end stood the town's best residential streets, lined with substantial-looking houses mainly of nineteenth-century vintage. They were set rather close together, and lacked front lawns, but they seemed the better for that. Instead, the capacious porches nearly met the sidewalks. Big trees lined the streets and their branches made a graceful canopy over it like the vaults inside a church. In the soft purple twilight with the porch lamps glowing, and the sights and sounds of family life within, these quiet residential streets made quite an impression on me.

I was charmed and amazed to discover that life could be physically arranged the way it was in Lebanon, New Hampshire. As I thought about it, I realized that a town like Lebanon was what a place like Northwood could only pretend to be: that Northwood, lacking any center, lacking any shops or public buildings, lacking places of work or of play, lacking anything except the treeless streets of nearly identical houses set on the useless front lawns, was in some essential way a mockery of what Lebanon really was.

As a teenager I visited my old suburban chums back on Long Island from time to time and I did not envy their lot in life. By puberty, they had entered a kind of coma. There was so little for them to do in Northwood, and hardly any worthwhile destination reachable by bike or foot, for now all the surrounding territory was composed of similar one-dimensional housing developments punctuated at intervals by equally boring shopping plazas. Since they had no public gathering places, teens congregated in furtive little holes—bedrooms and basements—to smoke pot and imitate the rock and roll bands who played on the radio. Otherwise, teen life there was reduced to waiting for that transforming moment of becoming a licensed driver.

The state college I went off to in 1966 was located in a small town of 5000 in remote western New York state. To a city kid, Brockport was deeply provincial, the kind of place where the best restaurant served red wine on the rocks. Yet I enjoyed it hugely. At a time when small towns all over America were dying, little Brockport remained relatively robust. Its little Main Street had a full complement of shops, eating places, and, of course, drinking establishments, for this was back in the days when eighteen-year-olds could buy liquor. There was an old single-screen movie theater downtown with an Art Deco facade and a marquee edged in neon lights.

The reason for the town's healthy condition was obvious: the college. It furnished jobs and a huge volume of customers for Main Street's businesses. It gave the place some intellectual life—totally absent in neighboring burgs where all the lesser institutions of culture had been replaced by television. The students enlivened the town by their sheer numbers. Many of them had come from boring one-dimensional suburbs like Northwood, and they appreciated what life in a real town had to offer. It was scaled to people, not cars. It had the variety that comes from a mixed-use community. Its amenities lay close at hand. It offered ready access to genuine countryside, mostly farms and apple orchards.

We loved our off-campus apartments in the nineteenth-century houses on tree-lined streets or above the shops in the business blocks downtown. We loved rubbing elbows on the streets, meeting friends as we walked or biked to class. We loved the peace and quiet of a small town at night. The campus itself—a miserable island of androidal modernistic brick boxes set in an ocean of parking—was quite secondary to the experience of life in the town.

I suppose that my experiences in suburb, city, and town left me biased in favor of town life—at least insofar as what America had to offer in my time. That bias is probably apparent in the chapters ahead. But all places in America suffered terribly from the way we chose to arrange things in our postwar world. Cities, towns, and countryside were ravaged equally, as were the lesser orders of things within them— neighborhoods, buildings, streets, farms—and there is scant refuge from the disorders that ensued.

The process of destruction that is the subject of this book is so poorly understood that there are few words to even describe it. Suburbia. Sprawl. Overdevelopment. Conurbation (Mumford's term). Megalopolis. A professor at Penn State dubbed it the "galactic metropolis." It is where most American children grow up. It is where most economic activity takes place. Indeed, I will make the argument that this process of destruction, and the realm that it spawned, largely *became* our economy. Much of it occupies what was until recently rural land—destroying, incidentally, such age-old social arrangements as the distinction between city life and country life. To me, it is a landscape of scary places, the geography of nowhere, that has simply ceased to be a credible human habitat. This book is an attempt to discover how and why it happened, and what we might do about it.

⬆

Chapter Two

AMERICAN SPACE

The settlement of the New World was a transforming event in human history. For Christian Europe, already burdened by its past, the New World was a vast stage upon which to act out, at the scale of nations, the romance of redemption, of a second chance at life. In the first two centuries of the settlement saga, this state of mind was as significant as the vast new supply of virgin land.

The Puritan pilgrims who came to the wild coast of North America in 1620 must have wondered, from one moment to the next, whether they had landed in the Garden of Eden or on Monster Island. The Biblical scripture that formed the bulk of their intellectual cargo was full of confusing notions. The wilderness of Hebrew folklore had been the abode of evil presided over by the arch-demon Azazel.[1] Yet the wilderness was also a place where the Hebrew prophets went to commune with God, to be tested by him, and purify themselves.

The Bible describes the Garden of Eden only sketchily, sidestepping many particulars. It was "well-watered." It contained "every tree that is pleasant to sight and good for food." The climate is not avouched. Regarding animal life the text is vague. The "beasts of the field" and "fowls of the air" were present, but there is no mention of wolves, lions, bears, crocodiles, rats, tarantulas, and other less tractable creatures. One snake is reported. Man was put into the garden "to dress it and to keep it," as a sort of custodian, one who works for a very tough landlord. The Garden of Eden was never a place to which Adam and Eve ever held any proprietary rights, and the first time they misbehaved, the landlord evicted them.

America in the minds of the earliest settlers was therefore a place fraught with paradox. Viewed as a wilderness, it was possibly wicked, possibly holy. If it was the Garden of Eden, then it was a place to which sinful man really had no rightful claim. There was a third point of view consistent with scripture: like other persecuted people, the Puritans identified with the Israelites, with their sojourn in the wilderness and their arrival in the Promised Land of Canaan. This was finally the myth they embraced to understand themselves, though it took some strenuous intellectual stretching to pull together all these ideas.

In 1607 a group of Puritans from Scrooby, a village not far from York, fled the Babylon of England for Holland. There they were exploited in the cloth industry, as foreign workers are apt to be, while their children became Dutchified. After ten years of this they decided to make a fresh start in the wild country of America, with the hopes of establishing a profitable fishing and trading settlement in the Virginia Company's grant under English Protection. It took them several more years to make the arrangements. The enterprise was eventually financed by Thomas Weston, a Puritan merchant of London. History is not clear as to who may have been using whom. As a practical matter, the Puritans needed financial backing to get to America; and the Virginia Company needed colonists to begin the commercial exploitation of the New World.

Weston engaged two ships, the *Speedwell* and the *Mayflower*, and drew up terms for a joint stock venture which the Holland group accepted. They soon quarreled with Weston over the details. He withdrew his support, but the fully provisioned ships sailed anyway. The *Speedwell* was abandoned in Devon as unseaworthy and the *Mayflower* continued alone across the Atlantic with as many as it could hold. Once Cape Cod was sighted, a rash of impromptu changes were made in the plan. The pilgrims understood from their navigational instruments that the region lay north of the Virginia Company's patent, but decided to settle in Massachusetts anyway, without legal rights—Virginia's only existing settlement at Jamestown was inhabited by non-Puritans and the pilgrims may have wanted to keep a distance. Since quarreling with their backers, the spiritual purpose of the voyage had come to override the commercial considerations.

The eighty-seven pilgrims—plus fourteen servants and workmen, and the forty-eight-man crew of the hired *Mayflower*—who landed at Plymouth Harbor faced a chilling prospect. It was December and the fathomless forest they confronted must have looked like anything but a Promised Land. They had believed in the literal reenactment of Biblical events. William Bradford, one of their leaders, was deeply disappointed when a search around the vicinity of Massachusetts Bay failed to turn up Mount Pisgah, the prospect from which Moses had first sighted the land of Canaan.

Under the circumstances, they made an astonishing mental leap. They stepped outside their myth-clogged mental lives to grasp something essential about the real world: that the wilderness could become a land of milk and honey, that one was the raw material of the other, and that a land of milk and honey was a fair approximation of Eden. In fact, they might all be one and the same thing. This insight didn't dispose them to fear the wilderness any less, but it spawned the utilitarian hope that something could be done with it, that it could be conquered, vanquished, and ultimately redeemed by godly men. They immediately went to work building a settlement, their "city on a hill." Before spring came, forty-four of their number had died.

Though the Puritans had exiled themselves spiritually and geographically from England, they still thought of themselves as English, carrying with them English laws and customs. Within a year of their fateful landing they came to terms with the London financiers and received a charter that gave legal birth to Plymouth Plantation. The Puritan foothold in the New World was greatly fortified by the creation of the Massachusetts Bay Company in 1629. It began as a commercial venture but almost immediately shifted its focus from trade to religion. A large number of its stockholders, Puritans disgusted with the libertine regime of Charles I, sailed off to America. The company's organizational structure became the colonial government with a governor at the top, and the General Court of stockholders became the legislature. Now they set about building real towns.

Despite the cultishness of the enterprise, as well as the need for communal labor, a system of private property ownership prevailed from very near the start. The first towns naturally enough were modified versions of the late medieval English towns—though the supply of land was enormous by English standards. In England, farmers lived neatly clustered together in villages with their fields located all around on the outskirts. Typically, an early Massachusetts town was organized with individually owned home lots around a fenced common used to pen livestock. Townships were granted to whole congregations who crossed the ocean as a group, bringing with them highly localized customs and farming practices. Where a minority couldn't abide the way a town was run, they could resolve their problem by "hiving out" to some unsettled area—always in a group—and creating a way of life with which they were at ease.[2]

The founding families of a town formed a covenanted corporation that held title to all the land and then dealt out home lots based on family needs and social standing. The land was not paid for per se with money, but each signatory to the covenant was obliged to erect a house within two or three years, to pay taxes, and to help support a church. A family with many children got a larger lot, bachelors got smaller ones, men with desirable skills, such as blacksmiths, millers, and ministers, were attracted by offering double and triple allocations.[3] The Puritans were not egalitarian. The idea of a social order based on hierarchy of position was natural to them. Wealthy or exalted persons got bigger allocations. Even so, the distribution of home lots in this early phase of settlement was most equitable by later standards. For in laying out the physical plan of their towns they were also laying the foundation of an economic system that they hoped would be stable and enduring.

The home lot in a Puritan village held the family's house and barn, kitchen gardens, and fruit trees. A family normally received 120 acres of land outside the village, often scattered around the township so that no one could consolidate his holdings on a single parcel. Much of the acreage was left in rough pasture and woodlot. Wheat and rye were grown in one or two common fields in which each family was given a strip proportionate in size with its home lot. Since tools were scarce, plowing was often a community project, but after plowing, each farmer was expected to work his own fields.[4]

The object of this way of life was not to grow surplus crops for market, but to achieve a sort of drowsing medieval stability based on self-sufficiency and a dour preoccupation with getting to heaven. The church, or meeting house as they called it, was the center of civic as well as spiritual life, the adhesive that held the town together. At times it was even used as a granary or a warehouse. Everyone had to belong to the congregation and attend its services. Massachusetts passed a law in 1635 forbidding settlers to establish homes more than a half mile from the meeting house. (Five years later the General Court repealed the much-flouted law.)

Roads were practically nonexistent between towns. Towns were generally sited near water, and goods and people moved by boat when they moved at all. For a couple of generations, the pattern held. In contrast to today's heedless lust for "growth" at any price, the Puritan towns observed agreed-upon limits. A consensus emerged within each town when it had reached optimum size and then no more lots were granted. Of course, this did not stop settlers from coming to Massachusetts. Through the first two generations, the General Court solved the problem by simply chartering new towns as required.

This too eventually reached a limit. The medieval pattern, the model of changelessness itself, based on an ever-stable population with births equaling deaths, could not survive the relentless pressure of immigration. At any distance from the seacoast it was more difficult to establish viable towns, and the resident Indian tribes were not easily dislodged. Instead, new villages began to form within larger existing coastal townships, each with its own church congregation. This led to conflicts in town management. During this period, the mid-1600s, a theological uproar gripped England and exotic new sects, Quakers and Baptists, began to arrive in America seeking the same kind of religious liberty that the Puritans enjoyed. But their presence irritated the Puritan theocracy and challenged their authority, and not a few of the newcomers were hanged.

During the Cromwellian usurpation, England had left Massachusetts to its own devices. But with the monarchy restored in 1660, agents of the Crown finally came to inspect their neglected Puritan colonies in

America. Having only recently disposed of an obnoxious Puritan dictatorship at home, the royal commissioners were not pleased by the church's stranglehold on the colony's civil affairs. And certain colonial practices, like coining their own money, smacked of rather too much independence from the mother country. The Puritan colonists, for their part, proved uninterested in reform.

In 1684, after twenty years of bootless negotiation, the Crown revoked the Massachusetts Bay Company's charter. In the future it would be run by the King of England and parliament. This shattered the integrity of the Puritan townships. Future settlement would happen under a new set of rules, in a far more random, less deliberate fashion. Connections between towns improved, trade increased, the standard of living rose, and the way of life in New England began to steadily creep up from the medieval murk. Settlers now advanced into the wilderness on single-family farms, making for a very sparse, scattered, individualistic settlement pattern. These farms were necessarily small because each family did its own labor with a few hand tools.

✦

The other colonies along the Atlantic seaboard evolved in strikingly different patterns. Four years after the English Puritans landed at Plymouth Harbor, the Dutch West India Company founded New Netherland without the adhesive of a cultish religion. Theirs was a much more unalloyed commercial venture, looking mainly to the lucrative trade in beaver furs. They set up their first trading post, Fort Orange, near the place where the Mohawk and Hudson rivers converge—today called Albany, New York—because these were the main highways of the Indians, who procured the masses of beaver pelts in exchange for European goods. The Dutch were bedeviled by Indian trouble, a geographical misfortune, since the Hudson marked the boundary between the Iroquois and their Algonquin enemies. In 1626, a series of incidents prompted Peter Minuit to move most of the Fort Orange families to Manhattan, recently purchased from the Wampanoags for sixty guilders in trinkets.

Colonists who wished to farm were allotted free land on isolated parcels up and down the Hudson Valley, but they were obliged to stay there for six years, and the Dutch West India Company took a large share of their crops. A yet more lowly caste of indentured serfs worked company farms under harsher restrictions. In 1629, the company began granting vast estates called patroonships to members who could found settlements of fifty persons within four years. A patroon might claim as much land as he wanted, in one case twenty-four miles along the bank of the Hudson. But it was an impractical system. All the patroonships failed with the exception of Rensselaerwyck, located near Fort Orange. They lacked skilled managers and able tenants. The colony as a whole sorely lacked recruits, for why should men and women leave Holland with its stable republican government, its religious tolerance, and its robust economy, to struggle for existence in the wilderness?[5]

The seaport of New Amsterdam at the tip of Manhattan island fared better. A solid burgher aristocracy built large brick houses with tiled roofs and spacious tulip gardens, and a middle class of merchants, sailmakers, carpenters, and tavern-keepers lent the town stability and verve. New Amsterdam's focus lay outward to coastal trading, not inland to the struggle for settlement. But Charles II, the newly restored English king, had made up his mind to monopolize shipping along the Atlantic coast. Massachusetts and now Connecticut—which had received the overspill of settlers from Massachusetts—were pressing claims beyond the Hudson Valley. New Netherland was something of a foreign carbuncle on what was becoming a solid body of English colonies lining the North American coast. So in 1664 the king elected to remove it by sending four warships into the upper bay. Persuaded that his situation was hopeless, Governor Peter Stuyvesant surrendered without a shot.

✦

In 1681, William Penn accepted a grant for territory along the Delaware River in place of a 16,000 pounds cash debt owed to his father by the crown. Penn was a youthful and enthusiastic convert to Quakerism, and in his fertile eponymous patent, he undertook to create a settlement of fellow Quakers who were being persecuted more cruelly in Massachusetts than they had been in England. In Penn's tolerant colony, the welcome mat was out for other European sects. German Mennonites, who came to Pennsylvania as early as 1683, established settlements more efficiently than had the English Puritans. They bred larger horses, built better wagons, and produced firearms with rifled barrels. Barn-raising was a Mennonite social innovation. Their axes were better-designed, allowing them to clear forests faster. David Hawke says, "Within a few years of settlement, the [Pennsylvania] Germans were plowing cleared fields while colonists elsewhere were still grubbing out tree stumps and turning up the soil with hoes."[6]

Initially, William Penn had hoped to settle the countryside in a tidy pattern of hamlets, each approximately 5000 acres, with farms divided into pie-shaped wedges. The settlers, he hoped, would erect their home-steads where the wedges converged, so as to form nuclear villages. But the idea fizzled. Instead, farmers scattered around the countryside, in family units, and the towns that soon sprang up were from the very beginning strictly market towns.

In the south, the individual, not the group or even the family, became the primary unit of settlement, bound neither by religion, kinship, nor community. The Virginia Colony, from Jamestown on, was an enter-prise of freebooting egoists. Single young men outnumbered females nearly twenty to one. Many expected to get rich, return to England, and live out the rest of their lives in leisure and luxury. Hawke calls it "an abnormal society," in which "manners and morals collapsed."[7] Looking to make their quick fortune, men carved tobacco plantations along the shores of Chesapeake Bay and the Potomac, York, James, and Rappa-hannock estuaries. Their agricultural practices were ruinous and after exhausting one piece of land in five or six years' time, they would move to another. With so much coastline available—2000 miles of indented shore along immense Chesapeake Bay alone—anyone could start his tobacco plantation near the water's edge, and ship out a crop—packed into half-ton hogsheads—from his own landing. This obviated the need for trading centers. Two notable exceptions we will discuss ahead were the ports of Savannah and Charleston.

The Virginians had started the tradition of importing African slaves at Jamestown in 1619. By the time settlement spread inland through the 1700s, the slavery system had reached a level of refinement that allowed many plantations to operate as little worlds unto themselves, complete with a workforce of slave artisans who did the very things that free men increasingly carried on as gainful occupations in northern towns: carpenters, coopers, wheelwrights, millers, blacksmiths, tinsmiths.

♟

In prerevolutionary America, land was plentiful and the colonies were so eager to have it settled that almost anyone who wanted land could get some. However, in this age before industrial manufacturing, land was also one of the few outlets for capital investment. Stock ventures of that time were mainly schemes cooked up to promote large-scale trade in natural resources, and raw land was the ultimate resource. As soon as the Revolutionary War was over, companies like the Georgiana, the Wabash, the Vandalia, the Loyal, the Ohio, and the Indiana were organized to speculate in vast tracts of interior land that had been claimed by the seaboard states. Leading citizens engaged in speculation. For instance, George Washington owned land in Virginia, Pennsylvania, and the Ohio country. Banker Robert Morris, who almost single-handedly financed the war, acquired enormous tracts in western New York.

The Revolution swept away the prerogatives of the Crown associated with English land tenure in America. In America, ownership meant freedom from the meddling of nobles, the right to freely dispose of land by sale at a profit, the ability to move from one place to another without hindrance, to enjoy the social respect of other small holders, and to have a voice in matters of community interest. The Revolution also got rid of such obnoxious English traditions of inheritance as primogeniture, the law that awarded all of a man's estate to his eldest son, and the right of entail, which allowed a landowner to forbid by will the future sale of his property by his descendants.

After the Revolution, Americans adopted what came to be called *fee simple* land ownership. The term derives from feudal times, when all land ultimately belonged to the Crown. Those who lived on it, from lord to churl, were obliged to perform services (e.g., fight in the crusades) and pay fees (in crops or money) as a condition of their occupancy. Land held with the fewest strings attached came to be known as fee simple—the fee being simple cash payment.[8] But in England, fee simple ownership would remain relatively uncommon until the rise of an industrial plutocracy in the mid-nineteenth century.

American land law was predicated on the paramount principle that land was first and foremost a commodity for capital gain. Speculation became the primary basis for land distribution—indeed, the commercial transfer of property would become the basis of American land-use planning, which is to say hardly any planning at all. Somebody would buy a large tract of land and subdivide it into smaller parcels at a profit—a process that continues in our time.

Other Old World values toppled before this novel system—for example, the idea of land as the physical container for community values. Nearly eradicated in the rush to profit was the concept of stewardship, of land as a public trust: that we who are alive now are responsible for taking proper care of the landscape so that future generations can dwell in it in safety and happiness. As historian Sam Bass Warner put it, the genius of American land law and the fanatical support it engendered "lay in its identification of land as a civil liberty instead of as a social resource."[9]

This is embodied today in the popular phrase, "You can't tell me what to do with my land." The "you" here might be a neighbor, the community, or the government. The government's power to regulate land use was limited under the Fifth and Fourteenth Amendments to the Constitution. The Fifth states that private property cannot be taken for public use without due process of law and just compensation—the right to public hearings and payment at market value—and the Fourteenth reiterates the due process clause. All subsequent land-use law in America has hinged on whether it might deprive somebody of the economic value of their land.

America's were the most liberal property laws on earth when they were established. The chief benefits were rapid development of the wilderness, equal opportunity for those with cash and/or ambition, simplicity of acquisition, and the right to exploitation—such as chopping down all the virgin white pine forests of Michigan (they called it "mining trees"). Our laws gave the individual clear title to make his own decisions, but they also deprived him of the support of community and custom and of the presence of sacred places.

The identification of this extreme individualism of property ownership with all that is sacred in American life has been the source of many of the problems I shall describe in the pages that follow. Above all, it tends to degrade the idea of the public realm, and hence of the landscape tissue that ties together the thousands of pieces of private property that make up a town, a suburb, a state. It also degrades the notion that the private individual has a responsibility to this public realm—or, to put it another way, that the public realm is the physical manifestation of the common good.

Tocqueville observed this when he toured America in 1831. "Individualism," he wrote, "at first, only saps the virtues of public life; but in the long run it attacks and destroys all others and is at length absorbed in selfishness."

Chapter Three

LIFE ON THE GRIDIRON

With the Revolution, the new nation acquired an immense amount of unincorporated formerly English land that stretched all the way to the Mississippi. The territory would more than double when Jefferson purchased Louisiana from Bonaparte just twenty years later. And it was extraordinary land. Retreating glaciers had laid down deep, rich loam in the area that we call the Midwest. It was not studded with boulders like much of the land in New England. Most of it was flat, too, easy to work, watered by dozens of pristine rivers, and thickly timbered to the Missouri.

The American government was most effective at getting settlers into this land. Every day, ships filled with land-hungry newcomers docked in Boston, New York, Philadelphia, Baltimore, and Charleston, but New Englanders were just as eager to give up their stony hill farms for the frontier. There was little question that even distant territories would attract settlers. The government all but gave land away. A price of $2 an acre was set by Congress in 1796, with a year's credit allowed on half the total. By 1800 they reduced it to 25 percent down on four years credit. A settler could buy a gigantic farm by European standards for a very reasonable sum.[1] Still, there was so much raw land to dispose of that the price steadily dropped and by the 1820s an acre could be bought for $1.25.

A system was needed to divide it up for sale. The answer was the national grid. The grid was a product of the era's neoclassical spirit, at once practical and idealistic. It was rational, mathematical, and democratic. It was fair and square, and easy to understand. The federal survey platted the raw land of the Middle West into square township units measuring six miles on each side. These were divided into thirty-six square-mile "sections" of 640 acres each. At first, only full sections were sold, but eventually the quarter section (160 acres) became the standard, since it was considered the ideal size for a family farm. Over five million farms were platted on public lands between 1800 and 1900.[2]

Expeditious as it was—indeed, it is hard to imagine a more rational method—the national grid had some serious drawbacks. It failed to take account of topography. The relentlessly straight section lines followed the compass, marching through swamps, across rivers, and over hilltops, "a transcontinental triumph of the abstract over the particular," in the words of architect Daniel Solomon.[3] In terms of rural life, the grid institutionalized the trend toward scattered farms, rather than agricultural villages, giving physical expression to the powerful myth that only lone individuals mattered in America. The new towns of the Middle West were more often than not laid out on grids that echoed the larger U.S. survey grid of the surrounding countryside, with some unfortunate results. The grid was primarily concerned with the squares of private property that lay within the gradients, not with gradients themselves, or how the two related with one another. This dictated a way of thinking about the community in which private property was everything and the public realm—namely, the streets that connected all the separate pieces of private property—counted for nothing. This spawned towns composed of blocks unmodified by devices of civic art, checkerboard towns without visible centers, open spaces, odd little corners, or places set aside for the public's enjoyment.

The grid had some salient advantages as a planning scheme for cities. Rectangular lots made for good economy of building. The grid made orientation easy. For example, in New York one was obviously going either up or downtown on numbered streets, and the east-west fix was pretty easy too. The four-way intersections at every block allowed for flexible traffic patterns, particularly with slow-moving horses and wagons.

Where the grid's tendency to dulling regularity was modified by planned open space and the siting of civic buildings, the result could be felicitous. In carving Savannah out of the Georgia pine woods, James

Oglethorpe designed a city based on a grid of twenty-four public squares surrounded by blocks of building lots. Each parklike square was to serve as the focus of a neighborhood. The scheme worked so well that twenty of the twenty-four public squares still stand in the old part of the city, just as Oglethorpe laid them out in 1733.

Williamsburg, which sprang up only a few miles from the abandoned settlement at Jamestown, was another fine town that modified the grid in a way that made the most of its formal strengths—coherence, orderliness—while mitigating its worst weakness—the straight line repeated over and over. It achieved this by setting two important focal points—the capitol building and the governor's palace—at the ends of its two main axial streets. So instead of dribbling off into the gloaming, as many gridded main streets in American towns would later do, these streets resolved in celebrations of civic architecture—the eye had something to rest on other than the vacant horizon, and the spirit was soothed by a sense of enclosure. Later, the College of William and Mary would further enhance the scheme by anchoring the other end of Duke of Gloucester Street, opposite the state house.

Philadelphia began as an experiment in town planning that curiously anticipated Levittown in its attempt to create a city out of individual houses on large lots. William Penn's initial idea for a utopian metropolis called for 10,000 acres divided into 10,000 one-acre lots, upon which were to sit 10,000 single-family dwellings, each one to be surrounded by its own gardens and orchards. The transportation problems presented by such a sprawling pattern seem not to have occurred to Penn. The surveyor he sent over found a suitable site on a tongue of land lying between the Delaware and Schuylkill rivers that offered excellent potential as a seaport. On the downside, the site comprised only 1300 acres, but Penn went ahead anyway.

His "Holy Experiment" quickly proved too fanciful and abstract. No sooner had Penn doled out the first one-acre parcels than their owners subdivided them and sold them off. Blocks of row houses and warehouses began to go up along the busy waterfront. Penn quickly revised his scheme to include a central square and four other parklike squares geometrically disposed on a grid so that however the inhabitants pleased to build the city, it would always have some feeling of "a green country town."[4] In a few decades, blocks of three-story row houses, standing shoulder-to-shoulder, filled in the land between the two rivers. Today, Philadelphia is still primarily a city of three-story row houses.

The city of Washington was built from scratch on the theory that a new nation ought to have a spanking new capital. Pierre L'Enfant's 1791 plan was a huge grid, larger than Paris, elaborated by a network of radial boulevards that cut through the city diagonally, meeting at frequent rotary intersections. Picture a linked series of spiderwebs imposed over a checkerboard. These diagonal boulevards were supposed to provide sightlines between architectural landmarks, and incidentally to act as shortcuts for crosstown trips. For all its baroque rigidity, the plan tried to pay some respect to the topography of the site. For instance, L'Enfant sited the Capitol building on a hill, affording it visual grandeur appropriate to the idealism of a young democracy. But as Robert A. M. Stern points out, the arrangement as a whole resulted in too many oddly shaped and awkward building sites that hindered property development, and tended to disorient the pedestrian.[5] Lewis Mumford said that the huge proportion of area given over to boulevards compared to the area reserved for public buildings was "absurd," and on a par with the later efforts of freeway engineers. Finally, for all its shortcomings, much of L'Enfant's plan actually got built. Washington grew into a major city very slowly and painfully. Until after World War II it was widely regarded as an overgrown country town.

New York City both benefited and suffered from the imposition of a relentless grid of rectangular blocks—except for the diagonal slash of Broadway, which was already built up and had to be accommodated. An 1811 plan platted the blocks up to 155th Street. Nothing on the order of Central Park was then conceived, but modest parklike squares were staggered at about twenty-block intervals.[6] The scheme accelerated the city's already rapid growth, but in doing so it wiped out the geographical features—hills, dales, and ponds—that characterized rugged Manhattan island, and replaced them with an unrelievedly mechanistic layout of linear streets and avenues that did not lend itself to memorable cityscape—one block was the same as any other block, and, indeed, when built up they would appear interchangeable.

As New York became the hub of American business activity in the years before the Civil War, the blocks on numbered streets marched implacably north, mile after mile, each one subdivided into standard

25-by-100-foot lots. The deadening uniformity finally became intolerable. William Cullen Bryant, editor of the *New York Evening Post*, led a campaign that culminated in the creation of the 840-acre Central Park, designed by Frederick Law Olmsted and Calvert Vaux, a romantic eruption of green foliage and water amid the cartesian monotony of the grid.

In a nation where the opportunity for personal profit knew no natural limit, unbridled economic forces were free to damage both nature and culture, and they accomplished this most visibly by degrading the urban setting. The great cities of Europe, long abuilding, were at once centers of political, commercial, ecclesiastical, and military power, and they showed it not just in their finely grained urban fabrics—their plazas, forecourts, esplanades, and galleries—but in the overarching civic consciousness with which buildings and spaces were tied together as an organic whole, reflecting the idea of civilization as a spiritual enterprise.

American cities flourished almost solely as centers for business, and they showed it. Americans omitted to build the ceremonial spaces and public structures that these other functions might have called for. What business required was offices, factories, housing for workers, and little else. Beyond advertising itself, business had a limited interest in decorating the public realm. Profits were for partners and stockholders. Where architectural adornment occurred, it was largely concerned with the treatment of surfaces, not with the creation of public amenity. The use of the space itself, of the real estate, was a foregone conclusion: maximize the building lot, period.

On the theory that politicians should not be subject to the blandishments of business interests, many states with big cities exiled their capitals to the provinces—New York to Albany, Illinois to Springfield, California to Sacramento—so the monumental architecture of government went up in cow towns where the great new capitol buildings looked bombastically out of proportion and served little civic purpose, while depriving the bigger cities of monuments and the large public gathering spaces that go with them. Historically, Americans considered the professional military to be an expensive and dangerous nuisance, to be kept at a safe distance in wilderness outposts. So, except in Washington, the architectural trappings of the army were kept to a minimum in the urban setting.[7] The church's influence on the development of American cities was practically nil, except for the Mormons in Utah, and their secular culture was at least as materialistic as the mainstream's, so that the city they built is now indistinguishable, in its man-made elements, from Omaha or Spokane.

Without a secure aristocracy to patronize them, the fine arts barely existed before 1865, and not in any organized way like the ateliers of Paris or Venice that gave respectability as well as steady employment to the artists. Our art was for the most part a hardscrabble merchandise folk art: ships' figureheads, tavern signs, crude portraits of businessmen and their wives painted by impoverished itinerants. And our architecture, until well into the nineteenth century, was with some notable exceptions strictly impromptu.

✦

Before the Civil War, American city life was a welter of small-scale activities. Zoning did not exist. "Downtown" in New York, Baltimore, Boston, or Philadelphia of the late 1830s was an agglomeration of small offices, dwellings, shops, warehouses, saloons, and little factories that turned out a fantastic array of mostly handmade products from pianos to teakettles to chocolate. Quite a few of the mingled enterprises gave off obnoxious effluents and odors: slaughterhouses, soap factories, glue works. John R. Stilgoe mentions an indoor dairy in Brooklyn housing 500 cows who never saw the light of day and were fed on distillery slops.[8]

The wealthy lived very close to downtown on streets of fashion. The poor were not a permanent class of subsidized indigents but rather working people who made less money. As factories multiplied, and the streets where they stood became less desirable places to live, older, single-family houses were bought by enterprising landlords and chopped up into warrens for the poor. But a great many more of the working poor lived among middle-class families, in rented rooms, apartments, basements, and in back-alley dwellings scattered fairly evenly throughout the city.

In the first phase of industrialism, the dimensions of city life remained at a human scale. While the canal system and then the railroads vastly improved the transport of goods *between* towns and cities, the movement of anything bulky within the city itself was still arduous. Freight moved by hand cart or horse cart, and it did not move easily.

Elevators did not exist. No buildings were higher than six stories. Church steeples and the masts of ships along the waterfront made up the skyline. Denizens of the cities moved about mainly on foot.

In the second half of the nineteenth century, city life changed more dramatically than any time since the Renaissance. The American city had embarked on a pattern of growth that would ultimately consume it. "Industrialism, the main creative force of the 19th century," wrote Lewis Mumford, "produced the most degraded human environment the world had yet seen."[9] Extraordinary changes of scale took place in the masses of buildings and the areas they covered. Huge new factories employing thousands of workers congregated in clusters along rivers and the rail lines that followed rivers. Not uncommonly, houses stood right up against gasworks, rolling mills, and paint factories, exposed to round-the-clock noise and poisonous discharges. The railroad brought the ambiance of the coal mine straight to the heart of the city.[10]

The armies of workers required by large-scale manufacturing were recruited from the American countryside and from distant lands across the seas. The housing built for them was a new and specialized type of building: the tenement, an instant slum. There were no legal minimum standards of decency. The buildings were not required by law to provide air or light, so valuable building-lot space did not have to be wasted with air shafts. Running water was not required, though the technology of modern plumbing had been all but perfected by the mid-nineteenth century. Water mains had been laid in many cities, but they did not necessarily connect to houses. Privies were in basements or rear yards. Under such circumstances, personal hygiene and rudimentary household cleanliness were impossible. Filth accumulated. Typhus, tuberculosis, and other diseases raged, affecting the rich as well as the slum dwellers.

It took most of the century to overcome the sanctity of private property in order to pass public health laws. As Sam Bass Warner points out, a city could only admonish, harass, and fine a slumlord who refused to install plumbing, but they couldn't barge into his property and install it themselves. And the law did not permit a tenant to withhold rent or sue for damages when his landlord failed to comply with regulations. Our property laws ignored the social dimensions of ownership as though they didn't exist.[11] Property ownership was the keystone of liberty, and who was the slumlord but that quintessential American, the property owner? *Don't tell me what to do with my land!*

Tenements were thrown up as surefire real estate investments. They could be built cheaply with practically no risk of failure. The demand for slum housing was bottomless; no matter how swinish the accommodations were, the slumlord never ran out of eager customers fresh off the boat. One family to a room was typical, though worse crowding was not uncommon. Tenements came to occupy vast districts. In New York City, where the population ballooned from 696,115 in 1850 to 3,437,202 in 1900, the slums marched north up Manhattan island in successive waves, driving the better-off before them.

Yet through the nineteenth century, the standard of city housing declined steadily for all classes. In a curious process described by Lewis Mumford, the homes of the middle classes and then even the well-off in New York began to emulate the architectural pattern of the tenement. As the value of real estate climbed, speculative builders tried more than ever to maximize the coverage of their building lots, and soon the "chocolate-colored" sandstone row houses that Edith Wharton so deplored came to blanket the whole city. Rear gardens were reduced to dingy, lightless courts only good for hanging wash.[12] Houses were built more than the traditional two rooms deep—the pattern of the "railroad" flat with a train of windowless inside rooms strung from front to rear—and crowded in upon each other, depriving even their outer rooms of light and ventilation. You could be in a second-floor dining room and feel as though you were in a cellar.

⁂

City life in the Western world had gone through many historical cycles of commodity and wretchedness before the transformations of industrialism. Hellenic Athens informed mankind that a city could be something greater than a slave labor supply depot for the aggrandizement of kings. The corpse-filled carnaria that surrounded classical Rome were an early version of our toxic waste dumps and that city's insulae the first speculator-built tenement slums. The cutpurses, whores, and gin fiends who infested Hogarth's London were the hopeless underclass of their day. So the squalor of the industrial city was not exactly a new thing, but the scale and intensity of it was: the roar of furnaces, the clank of machinery, the shrill steam whistles, the speed of locomotives, the coal smoke and the soot that fell like black snow everywhere, the frightening new size of new buildings, and the mushrooming population which strained the physical boundaries of cities everywhere. That American cities were newer than those of Europe did not necessarily lessen their problems, for as we have seen, the worst slums could be brand-new and American smoke was just as dirty as the English kind.[13]

The spread of slums, the hypergrowth and congestion of manufacturing cities, the noise and stench of the industrial process, debased urban life all over the Western world and led to a great yearning for escape. In England, this yearning expressed itself in the colonialist quest for the exotic, an adventure open chiefly to the educated upper classes, who fled smog-choked London for far-flung administrative duties in sunny India and Africa. (The lower classes were welcome to tag along if they joined the army or navy.) In Germany, the debasements of industrial growth were channeled into a romantic, technocratic militarism that flared with increasingly catastrophic results from 1870 to 1945 and climaxed in the morbid ingenuity of mass extermination. In France, it found expression partly as a colonialist romp, but even more in a surprisingly successful quest for civic amenity that transformed Paris from an overgrown medieval rat maze into a city of wide boulevards, greenery, and light—permitting the French to develop a coherent idea of the good life that was at once metropolitan, middle class, and respectful of the arts. In America, with its superabundance of cheap land, simple property laws, social mobility, mania for profit, zest for practical invention, and Bible-drunk sense of history, the yearning to escape industrialism expressed itself as a renewed search for Eden. America reinvented that paradise, described so briefly and vaguely in the book of Genesis, called it Suburbia, and put it up for sale.

Chapter Four

EDEN UPDATED

The suburban "developments" of today and the shopping smarm that clutters up so much of the landscape in between them, arose from the idea, rather peculiar to America, that neither the city nor the country was really a suitable place to live.

Historians speak of an anti-urban bias in American life. In fact, American cities did not develop the same way as those in the Old World, by slow stages over a long period of time. Until after the Revolution, few towns were worthy of the term *city*. Those that burgeoned rapidly in the early 1800s were soon beset by the horrors of industrialism. The urban culture that this rapid development spawned was provisional and insecure.

The devices in civic design that had adorned Europe—derived chiefly from the notion that the space between buildings was as important as the buildings themselves—did not jibe with American property-ownership traditions, which put little value in the public realm. Rome had the Campidoglio, Paris had the joyful Place de Vosges, and New York got the marshaling yards of the New York Central Railroad.

The yearning to escape the new industrial cities for a better life elsewhere was a reenactment of the same drama that had brought the Pilgrims to Plymouth Harbor: the flight from human wickedness and rottenness into nature, the realm of God. However, there had been some significant psychological shifts since the 1600s in the way that nature was perceived.

The Age of Reason had interposed with its program for organizing knowledge and demonstrating the truths of science—platting a grid of the human mind—so that an exemplary man of that age, such as Jefferson, could view the vast wilderness that lay beyond the Mississippi River not as a death-haunted wasteland filled with yowling devils but rather as so much wonderful raw material to be catalogued for the American Philosophical Society. Inevitably, the Age of Reason inspired a revolt. What came to be known as Romanticism sprang up in the late 1700s in Europe as a movement in literature and the arts that championed emotion over reason, distrusted science, rejected the mathematical regimentation that it imposed on the life of the mind, and sought a superior order in the organic patterns of nature.

In America, where there was little literature or art until the nineteenth century, the Romantic revolt was postponed by the War for Independence, itself a political climax to the Age of Reason, while paradoxically a great romantic enterprise on its own terms. When a native-born American art began to flower in the 1830s and 40s, it coincided exactly with the industrial transformation—by 1840, 2800 miles of railroad track were in operation—and was in large part a response to its grim portents.

To the writers Thoreau and Emerson, and the painter Thomas Cole, the wilderness was the seat of all transcendent values—that is, of godliness—though the juggernaut of settlement was just then busy overrunning that wilderness. Thoreau lived outside Concord, a satellite community of Boston, at Walden Pond, and gnashed his teeth whenever the train from Boston to Lowell passed within a few hundred yards of his cabin. Emerson sought in nature the spiritual authenticity that the new world of factories and business offices threatened to extirpate with its relentless mechanical routines. Cole, and the group of American painters who followed his lead—Durand, Church, Heade, Kensett, Cropsey—celebrated the American landscape as a repository of the sublime.

Cole was consumed with images of transformation and expressed these repeatedly in landscape terms. He was fond of working a theme into a series of paintings, and perhaps the best known of these, "The Course of Empire," portrays the entire rise and fall of Rome in five canvases. They show the same rugged landscape viewed from the same vantage point changing, in sequence, from stormy wilderness, to pastorale, to an Augustan city of huge temples and fora filled with feasting grandees, to the fiery destruction of that city and its populace, and finally to the silent repose of ruin in which vines and creepers have overcome the toppled monuments and all the people are gone. Cole had traveled extensively in Italy, painting ruins wherever he went, and must have been very impressed with the impermanence of mankind's most grandiose works. The moralistic streak in him wanted to post a warning for America, which was just then adopting the architectural trappings of classical Greece while bethinking itself a rising great empire. In fact, around the time he painted the series, Cole wrote that he feared for the stability of his country, fretting that vices and material lusts would overcome the American people.[1] He should have lived to see Las Vegas.

Despite his weakness for historical allegory, Cole also painted a lot of contemporary landscape scenes, and many of these portray a wilderness in the active process of being vanquished. His panorama "The Oxbow," laden with symbolism, depicts the Connecticut River Valley near Holyoke as viewed from the heights above. The heights in the foreground (roughly half the painting) show a terrain of bare rocks and gnarled tree limbs mingled with stormy clouds—a wilderness close to God. Far below, bathed in yellow sunshine, the valley is divided into neat little oblong farm fields along the winding river. Plumes of woodsmoke rise here and there from the farmhouse chimneys. Ominously, in the deep background, clearings on a distant wooded hillside appear to dimly spell the Hebrew letters *Noah*, as though a warning.

In the last decade of his short life—he died at forty-eight—Cole more and more portrayed a landscape almost housebroken in its secure domesticity. In his painting "River in the Catskills," he shows the wilderness in full retreat before the prosperous farms of the Hudson Valley. There is even a puffing train in the middle distance. Cole did not approve of this—in 1840 he asked for a debate at the Catskill Lyceum on the question "Are railroads and canals favorable or unfavorable to the morality and happiness of the present generation in the United States?" His last works are steeped in sentimental artificiality, as though he despised what the wilderness was becoming.

What it had become, in most of the East at least, was an agricultural landscape divested of wild Indians and panthers, something no longer to be feared, drained of mystery, and very different from the Eden/Hell duality that had befuddled the Puritans. This rural landscape was still the abode of nature, but a new version of nature, neither a wild untamed force nor a cold scientific curiosity. It was a safe, green, warm, sheltering, life-giving realm, full of fruit, grains, flocks of sheep and fowl, its hills and valleys feminine in their voluptuousness and ability to nurture. It was a sweet homeland, at last. Most of all, it was an antidote to the atrocious new place called the industrial city.

A Romanticism for popular consumption mixed this new view of the landscape with the yeast of political idealism and cooked it all up into the dream of Arcadia. Arcadia was the mountainous district of ancient Greece that had been the abode of a contented race of shepherds who enjoyed a drowsing, changeless life of peace. Cole treated the allegory of Arcadia in many paintings. It was also visibly objectified everywhere in the new Grecian temple architecture that was suddenly the rage. Banks, courthouses, schools, waterworks, taverns, and farmhouses all echoed the Arcadian theme, as though Americans explicitly believed that the new nation would become this fabled land of peace and plenty. There was a certain wacky pragmatism to their belief. Arcadia didn't pretend to be heaven. You didn't have to die to go there. And best of all, it was democratic. Anyone could get in. At least in theory.

↑

Democracy itself, the supposed lack of class distinctions, soon proved problematic when it came to country living. Americans might have dreamed of Arcadia, but their social traditions were English, not Greek, and the model for country living that prosperous Americans chose to emulate was that of the English Lord of the Manor. This style of life was possible at first only for those who, like Washington and Jefferson, owned slaves—which is to say, those who lived in a society of severe class distinctions with two basic classes: free whites and enslaved Africans. Or for the rare northerner like James Fenimore Cooper, whose father had carved an empire out of the central New York wilderness, exterminated the Indians, started a town that he named after himself, made a fortune in real estate, and passed on vast holdings to his offspring.

More commonly, northerners could not easily metamorphose from small farmers into country squires. A New England family could not by itself operate a farm on the scale of a Carolina plantation, nor was the climate suitable for cotton, which, in the years between 1800 and 1860, would become the most valuable agricultural commodity in the world. That is in large part why northerners gravitated first to maritime trade and then to manufacturing when new mechanical inventions made it possible. Enriched by these, they could buy country villas in proximity to their seat of business in the city and pretend that they were squires, complete with hobby farms and gardens. Indeed, this became the prototype for the modern suburban house: a pretend manor house.

The Arcadian ideal had barely established itself in the popular imagination when farming entered a swift decline in New England and eastern New York. By the 1840s, eastern farmers were buried by mountains of cheap grain from the Ohio and Mississippi valleys.[2] It was so much easier to grow grain crops in the Middle West. The horse-drawn reaper, invented in 1834, and other new articles of equipment worked wonderfully on flat land—they were nearly useless on hill farms—while the new canals and railroads made even long-range bulk transport cheap. Farmers of ability and ambition headed west. Many of those left behind slid into a bare subsistence, while industry sprang up around them. In Westchester County, for instance, pollution from nearby brickworks bedeviled farmers. On Long Island, hay became the dominant crop, needed to feed the horses of New York City. In all this there seems to have been a general deterioration of the rural landscape of the East. The periodicals of the 1840s are full of references to "slovenly" farms. Into this ragged landscape marched the first true suburbanites, led by their avatar, Andrew Jackson Downing.

Downing (1815–1852) was the son of a Newburgh, New York, nurseryman. He began in life as a gardener and landscapist, developed an interest in country villas, and became the chief popularizer in America of the ideas of John Claudius Loudon, the English garden and villa designer. Loudon would also influence John Ruskin, the Romantic intellectual, who idealized the medieval period as a preindustrial paradise, and promoted its architectural orders as the most appropriate to English culture. All three men—Downing, Loudon, and Ruskin—were revolutionary in directing their ideas to a rising class that had never existed before: common people amassing new fortunes based on commerce and manufacturing.

During the 1700s in England, the aristocracy had practiced a method of private park-making in which property was carefully graded, lakes dug, and trees asymmetrically planted in an elaborate effort to give a "natural" effect. The idea was to produce perfectly composed "wild" landscapes, to outdo the accidental beauty of nature herself. The calculated informality of English landscape design was itself a reaction to the geometrical baroque formalism of French gardens, as epitomized by Versailles with its endless gridlike parterres, just as the Romantic movement in all the arts was a revolt against formality in general.

The American, Downing, passed his childhood in the Hudson Valley, with its superb scenery and splendid views, working in the gardens of wealthy clients who patronized the family's nursery business. The newly invented steamboat had made the mid-Hudson valley a convenient summering ground for New York City merchants seeking to escape the recurrent typhoid epidemics that raged there, and their Grecian temple country houses became a common sight along the shore. Downing married well—Caroline DeWindt, great-granddaughter of President John Adams—and built himself a jewelbox of a house in what came to be called the Gothic style, as a sort of demonstration project, for he strongly disapproved of the Grecian temple mania.

In 1841, Downing published a book on landscape gardening that pared down many of the English ideas into a scale suitable for American consumption. He followed in 1842 with the publication of his best-known volume, *Cottage Residences*, which was reprinted many times during and after his short lifetime. In 1850, he went to England to get a firsthand look at the great English country "parks" (i.e., private estates) and to search for a sympathetic junior partner to help out at the firm—business was brisk and he had just landed a commission to redesign the grounds of the United States Capitol and the White House gardens. The associate that he found, and enticed back to Newburgh, was twenty-five-year-old Calvert Vaux (rhymes with *hawks*), who was steeped in Loudonian theory as Downing had been, and who would go on to design New York's Central Park with Frederick Law Olmsted. Two years later, Downing drowned when a Hudson River steamboat he was on blew up. He was not yet forty. His profound and long-lasting influence on the way Americans built their homes will be discussed in a later chapter.

Vaux stayed on at the Newburgh office, operating it for Downing's widow until 1857. In the meantime, he met Olmsted, two years his senior, who came from a prosperous Connecticut family, and had seen something of the world while sampling various careers. Olmsted had served as a seaman in the China trade, traveled widely in the American South as a newspaper correspondent, publishing articles on slavery, and operated a farm for six years on Staten Island. In 1850, he toured England, where both the industrial debasement of the cities and the first attempts to mitigate it with town planning impressed him deeply. Olmsted published his observations in a book, *Walks and Talks of an American Farmer in England*, the same year that Downing drowned. Olmsted was not a trained landscape architect—then, neither was Downing—but Vaux admired his ideas and persuaded him to join in the 1858 competition for the design of Central Park. Their plan was chosen above thirty-three other entries.

The idea of a large public park designed as a rambling romantic landscape was quite a novelty. Nothing like it existed anywhere in America. In Europe, the closest things to it were formal royal hunting preserves, like the forest at Fontainebleau outside Paris, or the new suburban development of a Birkenhead outside Liverpool, which had a naturalistic park as its centerpiece. But then, nothing like the enormous mechanistic grid of Manhattan existed in European cities either. The explosive and implacable manner of New York City's growth—plus its unique character as an island—had all but completely cut off the population from access to any rural experience. Once Central Park established the value of this sort of landscape as a cultural necessity, it was not a large leap to the idea of residential enclaves in parklike settings.

⁂

Downing's house designs were meant to be carried out in an embellished natural landscape that was definitely not the city, nor *of* the city, nor even the small town. But this new landscape was not quite the countryside either, as it was then understood. The people who lived there would not draw their livelihoods from it, either in farming or business. Rather, it was a place strictly of habitation and pleasure. Suburbs had existed throughout history, of course. City walls could not contain a dynamic, expanding culture even in biblical times, and where proper walls did not enclose a growing town, there were always people settling at the fringes. (Not all towns and cities experienced continual growth; medieval English towns were admired by commentators from Ruskin through Raymond Unwin to Mumford precisely for their resistance to growth and change.) Neither was the wish to escape urban congestion and disease a new thing: the Romans had their country villas, thirteenth-century Florence was ringed for three miles around by estates, and Louis XIV built the immense royal theme park at Versailles twenty miles outside Paris as the ultimate expression of privileged detachment from the toils and stenches of the city.

Until the mid-1800s, the practical distance for commuting was limited to the range of a horse and coach. There were few public coach routes, and private ownership of wheeled vehicles was confined to people of means—contrary to the fantasies of Hollywood, in which horse-drawn rigs are the nineteenth-century equivalent of Chevrolets. Getting ready for a trip—harnessing a team—took time and generally required servants. Roads were bad and many coaches were not weatherproof. And you couldn't just park a horse and coach at the curb all day while you went up to the office. In short, commuting as we think of it was a rarity, and very few businessmen of the city lived outside town. But the railroad shattered any previous constraints of time and travel to lure people away from the city in greater numbers and at greater distances. The prototype of the railroad suburb in America was Llewellyn Park.

Llewellyn Park was the brainchild of a New York City pharmaceutical merchant named Llewellyn S. Haskell, who had grown up in rural Maine and had a certain predilection for rural life. Because the nature of his business brought him into association with doctors, Haskell was keenly aware of the health hazards of city living, so he settled along the Passaic River in New Jersey and commuted to town by coach and ferry boat. But he began to suffer baffling health problems while still in his thirties and became suspicious that the salt marshes near his home were to blame. Pasteur had not yet publicized his germ theory of disease; it was still thought to be caused by "bad air." In 1853, the architect Alexander J. Davis suggested Haskell have a look a few miles west at the heights of Orange, New Jersey, noted for its wild scenery, superior views, and crystalline air. This was the same Alexander J. Davis who had assisted Andrew Jackson Downing with the design of houses for

Cottage Residences in 1842. What made it possible for Haskell to consider moving a full twelve miles away from his business in New York City was a stop at Orange on the new Morris & Essex railroad line. There was one train inbound to the city each morning and a return train in the afternoon. The depot had been built, at private expense, by Matthias Ogden Halsted, another New York City businessman with a country seat there.[3]

Haskell bought forty acres, including an old farmhouse that Davis soon remodeled for him in the picturesque style he and Downing had promoted so tirelessly. Davis added an observation tower equipped with a telescope so that Haskell could enjoy views of distant Manhattan—the heights of Orange were said to offer the best views south of the Catskills. Haskell soon conceived a scheme to surround himself with a community of health-seeking, nature-loving souls, and incidentally to make a fortune in real estate. He bought 350 additional acres, and in 1858, the same year as the Central Park competition, Llewellyn Park was born.

It was an elaborate plan. At the heart of the site stood a 600-foot-high rocky outcropping crowned by looming pines and hemlocks. Picturesque ravines cut by mountain streams threaded the property. Haskell created ten miles of carriage drives circling a central fifty-acre wooded common called "the Ramble," which was deeded to a homeowner's association. He planted the roadsides at great expense with flowering shrubs, and built rustic pavilions with benches for walkers to take their ease on. Lots had to be a minimum of one acre, though most were larger—up to twenty acres. The layout of the homes was about as far removed from a grid scheme as might be imagined. Everything was deformalized: the streets were crooked and winding, gardens rambled, asymmetrical houses sprouted towers like fairy-tale castles to create a fanciful sense of timeless historicity—where, in reality, there would dwell just so many widget manufacturers who depended for their fortunes on the implacable routines of business conducted in the gridded streets of Manhattan. Davis designed all the houses in Llewellyn Park's early phase, including one for himself, and became a vigilant presence on the scene, seeing to it that homes were painted in the drab colors that Downing had promoted to blend with natural scenery, and generally policing the evolving pattern of development to make sure that it remained wild, irregular, playful, and spontaneous.

In time, Haskell acquired another 400 acres so that Llewellyn Park reached almost exactly the same size as New York's Central Park. Except, of course, that Llewellyn Park was entirely private—visitors had to pass through a turreted gatehouse and sign a guestbook; on Sundays in the early years the gates were closed to visitors altogether. By the 1880s it had become such a fashionable address that the super-rich of that era moved in, including Thomas Edison, whose laboratories stood just down from the heights. Many of Davis's original cottages were torn down and replaced by enormous mansions.

It must have been a little bit of heaven in its day, though for all the effort to create a wild and romantic setting, as a community Llewellyn Park couldn't have been more artificial. It lacked almost everything that a real community needs to be organically whole: productive work, markets, cultural institutions, different classes of people. And the houses were so far apart that the residents would lose all awareness of their neighbors. But then, privacy was as much the point of Llewellyn Park as rural scenery and fresh air. Exclusivity was another. America didn't have aristocrats, of course. It had rich people, and soon it would have more of them than England had dukes and earls. Llewellyn Park was the English manor democratized: instead of one mansion in a park, here were *a lot of mansions* in a park. Part of America's cockeyed genius was pretending there were no class differences, that each fellow was as good as the next—at the same time that each individual tirelessly strove to prove that he was actually better than the next fellow. And just as Llewellyn Park became a prototype for many of the American suburbs that followed, including its debased modern variants, so too its shortcomings became embedded in a universal pattern.

⚓

The building of Central Park entailed such a multitude of headaches and hassles that Olmsted quit the job three times. But when it was done and triumphantly behind them, he and Vaux got into the private development act. In 1869, a Chicago real estate developer hired their firm to turn 1600 acres of near-swamp along the Des Plaines River into a railroad suburb they named Riverside. The plan called for a higher density than Llewellyn Park, with many more building lots per acre, but the theme was still romantic landscape. To give all the houses access to road frontage, and at the same time promote the illusion of rural living, Olmsted and Vaux created a plan of irregularly shaped superblocks set in a network of curvilinear streets.

Superficially, Riverside seems a template for all the ghastly automobile suburbs of the postwar era—individual houses on big blobs of land among curvy streets—and in the broader schematic sense it was precisely that. But a closer look at the plan reveals some interesting differences. For one thing, the architects made full use of the site's single geographical strong point, the river, which ran north to south through the center of the development. The extensive park they constructed along both banks, called the Long Common, featured many of the snazzy effects Olmsted and Vaux had pioneered in Central Park: the separation of vehicular and pedestrian paths at different grade levels, and the sequencing of views so that a trip to the park flowed uninterruptedly from open green lawn, to riverbank, to mysterious wooden glade. The public space created was ample, easy to walk to, and of high quality—values absent from practically all suburbs in the late twentieth century.

Another difference from later suburbs lay in Riverside's attention to finely grained detail. Virtually every tree was platted in the blueprints. The lazily curved streets were lined with these trees, planted at formal intervals, and some of the streets terminated in woodsy little squares, while others were divided by a planted median. The formality of the trees connected the sprawled properties at the same time that they provided a sense of shelter on the street. The result was a system of streets that were scaled to the pedestrian, streets that invited walking, offered strong focal points and a sense of destination, and felt good to be in.

Compare this to a modern residential subdivision. Same big blob-shaped superblocks, same curvy streets, only what a difference the absence of *formally* planted trees makes. In today's subdivisions the streets have no other official function except to funnel the cars to and fro. One of the problems with cars is that all drivers are not highly skilled—often they are even drunk—and accidents happen. So to remove some of the danger that drivers pose, highway engineers have developed a standard perfect modern suburban street. It is at least thirty-six feet wide—same as a county highway—with generous turning radii. This makes it easy to drive well in excess of thirty miles an hour, a speed at which fatal accidents begin to happen.[4] The perfect modern suburban street has no trees planted along the edge that might pose a hazard to the motorist incapable of keeping his Buick within the thirty-six-foot-wide street. The street does not terminate in any fixed objective that might be pleasant to look at or offer a visual sense of destination—no statues, fountains, or groves of trees. Such decorative focal points might invite automotive catastrophe, not to mention the inconvenience of driving around them. With no trees arching over the excessively wide streets, and no focal points to direct the eye, and cars whizzing by at potentially lethal speeds, the modern suburban street is a bleak, inhospitable, and hazardous environment for the pedestrian.

Of course, in 1869 there were no automobiles. Riverside's streets were carriage drives. The people who lived at Riverside were connected to downtown Chicago, nine miles away, by a railroad line and the trip took less than half an hour. The tracks ran through the center of the development on an axis with the Long Common, and the station was within a ten-minute walk of any house. The houses, which were very large by today's standards, functioned as institutions, not just dormitories. The many tasks of domestic life, such as cooking, had not been entirely reduced to shopping choices. If you wanted a meal, there was no rushing out to the "convenience" store for a microwavable pizza. Housekeeping required real skills and intelligent management, though servants did most of the labor. Olmsted made it a point to promote the fruit and vegetable gardening opportunities that suburbia offered. The keeping of cows was even encouraged. Otherwise, groceries and household supplies were generally delivered to the house. It was not necessary to make innumerable short trips each day to buy all sorts of things.

The architects first planned a village center featuring stores, churches, and other civilized amenities, but construction of it was scratched with the financial panic of 1873, which put the developer in trouble, and the space reserved for the center was sold off as building lots. (Had it not been for deed covenants, the Long Common might have been sold off as well.) Eventually, a little commercial cluster sprang up around the train station. This too would prove to be a typical feature for the railroad suburbs that followed in the decades before World War II: hardly any of them had formally planned village centers. They made do with a few pokey stores around the depot. Most everything besides groceries and mundane household items was bought in the city, while the network of express agencies made for quick and reliable home delivery.

There was a reason that suburbs like Riverside didn't develop proper civic centers: they were not properly speaking civic places. That is, they were not towns. They were real estate ventures lent an aura of permanence by way of historical architecture and picturesque landscaping. They had not developed organically over time, and they lacked many civic institutions that can *only* develop over time. They were a rapid response to a closely linked chain of industrial innovations: steam power, railroads, and the factory system. More, these suburbs were a refuge from the evil consequences of those innovations—from the smoke, the filth, the noise, the crowding, the human misery—built for those who benefited from industrial activities.

Yet for all their artificiality and impermanence, the early railroad suburbs were lovely places to live: green, tranquil, spacious. The first waves of suburban migrants settled amid large areas of unspoiled rural land. Two generations would pass before an automobile-centered way of life began to destroy the pattern—long enough for people to take for granted that suburbs were the highest expression of civilization. Henry Ford was only three years old when Riverside was built.

In the meantime, a suburb like Riverside offered a fair approximation of country living in convenient reach of the city, while it dispensed with the worst aspects of both. In Riverside, you could wake to the crowing of your own rooster, but you could also enjoy a hot morning bath while someone else—say, an Irish servant girl—gathered your eggs and cooked breakfast. Then it was an easy twenty-minute train ride to business in the city. For children, it must have been paradise. Real countryside, with its wondrous allures, lay close at hand. There were no dangerous highways to hem in the movements of little pedestrians, only farm-to-market roads and country lanes to facilitate them. Teenagers' access to the city was as easy as the adults', and a driver's license was not required to get there.

To protect their plan against future adulteration, Olmsted and Vaux cooked up a set of zoning controls that would become a model for suburban codes up into the next century. These controls made sense from the standpoint of seeking stability in a time of explosive and destructive growth, but they would establish some nasty precedents and lead to unpleasant repercussions once the automobile came along. First, they set a minimum lot size: 100 by 200 feet. Along with this went minimum setbacks of 30 feet from the property lines to ensure that there would always be open space, no matter how grandiose the houses might become. Fences were prohibited so that the overall impression of houses set in a park would not be lost. The houses were required to carry a minimum price tag (at the time, $3000, seemingly insignificant today, but roughly the annual income of a doctor in 1870). Each house had to be owner-occupied, meaning no absentee landlords or careless tenants who might make a mess.[5]

The effect of these regulations was to create a socially one-dimensional community. This was rather a new thing in America. Certainly, there had always been "streets of fashion," better neighborhoods, even whole towns that enjoyed greater prosperity than other towns. But never had the upper class so systematically separated itself from the rest of society. A flood of immigrants provided a supply of domestic servants at bargain rates—maids, cooks, squads of gardeners, handymen, laundresses—some of whom lived in the house, taking the place of formerly independent tradespeople. The house itself became a kind of factory for the production of comfort.

Segregation by income would become a permanent feature of suburbia, long after servants were replaced by household appliances. Factory workers would eventually get suburbs of their own, but only after the rural character of the countryside was destroyed. The vast housing tracts that were laid down for them had all the monotony of the industrial city they were trying to flee and none of the city's benefits, nor any of the countryside's real charms.

The explosion of suburbia in America did not proceed the same way out of every city, nor at the same pace. The geography of New York, for example, was far different than Chicago's. Until the opening of the Brooklyn Bridge, it was necessary to take a ferry boat across the East River to Manhattan, so that Brooklyn developed as a separate city, not as a suburb. When other bridges across the East River followed to open up Queens County, it too rapidly urbanized, and the outlands that did get developed there, well into the twentieth century, were, with some exceptions such as Forest Hills Gardens, appalling grids of cookie-cutter bunkers that were only a little less depressing than the city slums from which their owners had escaped. New Jersey, like Brooklyn, developed a separate urban culture and the pattern of Llewellyn Park was not repeated on a mass scale there until the twentieth century, when the railroads linked up with rapid transit tubes under the river to Manhattan. The Bronx, to the near north, also urbanized rapidly as Manhattan overflowed with immigrants.

Westchester, north of the Bronx, was traversed by several train lines, and there a number of romantic suburbs sprouted, notably Bronxville and Scarsdale. Villas also cropped up around the little villages that dotted two coastlines: New Rochelle, Larchmont, and Mamaroneck on the Long Island Sound shore, and Dobbs Ferry, Irvington, and Tarrytown along that wide stretch of the Hudson River known as the Tappan Zee. Much of the former farmland of Westchester, devalued when the Midwest came into crop production, had been acquired and consolidated into large estates by the Gilded Age rich who were not interested in subdivision, or necessarily even in hobby farming, so that the countryside between settled towns reverted to second-growth forest, giving the county a wild rather than a pastoral character.

On Long Island, beyond the Queens County line, the suburban process was delayed, as industrial millionaires bought up the townships from Hempstead east with a gentleman's agreement between them to keep the area undeveloped except as their own personal playground. J. P. Morgan, Payne Whitney, Henry Phipps (Andrew Carnegie's partner), Willie Vanderbilt (grandson of the Commodore), Claus Spreckles (of the Sugar Trust), Henry Frick (of U.S. Steel) were among those who settled on Long Island's "gold coast." F. W. Woolworth's establishment in Glen Cove had sixty-two rooms and solid gold bathroom fixtures. Louis C. Tiffany's house in Laurel Hollow had eighty-two rooms. Henry Phipp's Westbury spread had only thirty-two rooms but boasted a private golf course and two polo fields. Otto Kahn built himself a private "mountain."

Access to this gold coast was quietly regulated to exclude the wayfaring public. Charles Pratt (one of John D. Rockefeller's partners in Standard Oil) bought up enough stock in the Long Island Railroad to control its policies, and made sure that it ran antiquated and rickety trains to discourage the development of railroad suburbs of the types being built in Westchester.[6] The super-rich had their own private railroad cars. In the early years of the automobile, they controlled town officials, who saw to it that roads remained in a state of rustic disrepair to keep out picnicking day-trippers from the city. However, the mass production and lower prices of cars after World War I started a democratizing trend that even the collective power of the industrial plutocracy could not stop.

Estate owners began selling out. Robert Moses, the master builder of Long Island's highway system, goosed them from behind with his lawyers. And once the first wave of subdivisions were built, with the accompanying commercial "infrastructure," the rural landscape was sufficiently ruined to prompt many more estate owners to sell out.

Chicago, sited on the pancake-flat prairie, suffered few geographical constraints to its expansion. Eleven railroad lines led out of the city by 1861. Chicago's population grew so explosively—from a mere 29,963 in 1850 to 1,698,575 in 1900—that land speculation became something of a sport even among the middle and the working classes. Chicago was also the birthplace of the modern method of wooden house building, the so-called "balloon frame." Its development was spurred by the great fire of 1871, which destroyed much of the central city, including many thousands of wooden homes. After the blaze, a new city fire law prohibited wooden buildings altogether, prompting a rush by speculative builders to put up blocks of cheap wooden houses for working people beyond the city limits. These were *not* houses-in-a-park à la Riverside, but tiny cottages perhaps eighteen by twenty-eight feet jammed on postage-stamp lots. Though the pattern was essentially urban, the density was lower than was common back East. It made for vast monotonous neighborhoods of tiny single-family dwellings lacking both in rural charm and urban variety, and with no civic design features but gridded streets.

Where the rich were concerned, the price of a large airy wooden house surrounded by light and greenery in a peaceful suburb like Riverside was the same as the price of a town house in the noisy, depressing city. But a house in the suburbs was a far safer investment. Before zoning was introduced in 1916, factories could spring up anywhere, and hardly a city neighborhood was not despoiled by some inappropriate business enterprise. In fact, the main purpose of urban use zoning at its inception was to stabilize real estate values in residential neighborhoods. So, in the years between the Civil War and 1916, even a luxurious town house could be subject to instant slumification. This problem was easily avoided in a place like Riverside, which was zoned in effect by deed covenant well before 1916. Around booming Chicago, new suburbs such as Oak Park, Evanston, Winnetka, and Lake Forest sprang up like dandelions on the first sunny day of spring. The only limit to their development was the supply of wealthy customers.

Unlike Chicago, Philadelphia was a city built out of brick, and from the 1700s the row house had been standard for rich and poor alike. The rich just lived in better row houses on better streets. Philadelphia burst out of its old Quaker confines when omnibuses began their runs across the narrow Schuylkill River in the 1830s. Passengers in these overgrown stagecoaches suffered a jolting, crowded ride. The railroads of mid-century made the villages of the "Main Line" an easy and pleasant commute. Out-of-town real estate values rose steadily, but, as in Chicago, the supply of people who could afford suburban villas was limited. The opportunities for tradespeople in such a setting was even more limited. The suburbs were places *without* economies of their own. This was intrinsic to their charm. Economic activity remained behind in the city and workers stayed there with it, near their work.

In 1858 the railroad was augmented by horse-drawn streetcars, known as horsecars. These were enormously successful. Since the cars did not have to haul heavy freight, the rails could be laid among the cobblestones of an ordinary street. Track was cheap to lay and the lines extended outward rapidly. Unlike the jolting omnibuses, the horsecars glided on their rails. The one drawback was that they hogged the center of the street, playing havoc with other wheeled traffic. But the horsecars were a great boon to the masses. They averaged six miles an hour and the fare eventually settled at a few pennies a ride. The horsecars stopped much more frequently than trains, and so promoted a kind of low-density development that stretched out for miles along corridor avenues. This ribbon-shaped town of the mid-1800s was a precursor of today's highway strip, with some important differences.

The grandest villas fronted the main boulevards. Far from being an unpleasant location, a residential lot on the main highway was the most desirable. It made for an effective display of wealth where passersby were most likely to see the big houses and be impressed. The few commercial establishments were physically unobtrusive and vehicular traffic on the whole was light—how unlike our main suburban streets today, clogged with roaring, high-speed motor traffic and lined by gigantic chain stores.

In the early form of ribbon development represented by the horsecar suburbs of Philadelphia, no one wanted to live more than a few minutes' walk from the streetcar stop on either side of the line. Eventually the horsecars were motorized. When the landscape between the highway ribbons finally did develop into a network of side streets, between 1860 and 1900, the infill took the familiar urban form of row houses or single-family cottages jammed nearly shoulder to shoulder, for those who had moved up from the slums. Commerce crowded out villas along the main roads, spacious lots were subdivided, and the quasirural feeling was obliterated. The wealthy, insulated by greater distance in their railroad suburbs, continued to enjoy the fantasy of a rural, preindustrial life.

What this scheme of growth did have in common with today's pattern of development was that it consumed open land like crazy, and included almost nothing in the way of civic features—no town centers, squares, artful groupings of buildings to some social purpose, and little consideration of the public realm, except as a conduit for vehicles.

⚹

By 1915, the romantic suburb of the type pioneered by Llewellyn Park and Riverside was a fixture on the fringe of most American cities and had attained its high-water mark as *the* accepted version of the Good Life. In places like Shaker Heights, Ohio, and Brookline, Massachusetts (where Olmsted lived and kept his main office), the fortunate few could enjoy the dream of an achieved Arcadia completely insulated from the industrial economy that made it possible. It was an artificial way of life in an inorganic community that pretended above all other virtues to be "natural." It drew wealth out of the cities and dedicated that wealth to private pleasure-seeking, returning little in the way of civic amenity. It was nice while it lasted, but it didn't last long in its classic form. Its own popularity killed it.

When successive waves of land developers came along and gobbled up the surrounding countryside, they destroyed the rural setting that had provided all the charm. When the automobile entered the scene it became, in Leo Marx's apt phrase, "the machine in the garden," and made a mockery of the suburban ideal. Afterward, all the elements that had gone into creating an illusion of dreamy timelessness—the rambling wooded streets, the fanciful houses with their storybook turrets and towers, the deep lawns and elaborate gardens—were unmasked as mere stagecraft. They had stopped time for little more than half a century. Pretending to be places of enduring value, the American suburbs had proved to be made of nothing more lasting than parcels of real estate. It was a shame, because the reaction to the disillusion that followed was a far more fraudulent and barbarous movement called Modernism, which dedicated itself to the worship of machines, to sweeping away all architectural history, all romantic impulses, and to jamming all human aspiration into a plain box.

✦

Chapter Five

YESTERDAY'S TOMORROW

When speaking of the faults of our surroundings we are naturally inclined to blame "bad architecture," because buildings are easy to see in the landscape. Architects are, just as naturally, inclined to dismiss this point of view as boobery. It is true that the mess we've made of places where we live and work is not solely the result of bad buildings, though there are plenty of them. But that hardly lets architects off the hook. Rather, with the hubris of religious zealots, they set out on a great purifying mission that damaged the whole physical setting for civilization in our time. The dogmas that guided them went by the name of Modernism. Heretics and skeptics were anathematized as systematically as the opponents of the fifteenth-century Vatican.

Modernism did its immense damage in these ways: by divorcing the practice of building from the history and traditional meanings of building; by promoting a species of urbanism that destroyed age-old social arrangements and, with them, urban life as a general proposition; and by creating a physical setting for man that failed to respect the limits of scale, growth, and the consumption of natural resources, or to respect the lives of other living things. The result of Modernism, especially in America, is a crisis of the human habitat: cities ruined by corporate gigantism and abstract renewal schemes, public buildings and public spaces unworthy of human affection, vast sprawling suburbs that lack any sense of community, housing that the un-rich cannot afford to live in, a slavish obeisance to the needs of automobiles and their dependent industries at the expense of human needs, and a gathering ecological calamity that we have only begun to measure.

Modernism was a response to the rise of industrial manufacturing as man's chief economic activity. By the end of the nineteenth century the factory system had triumphed, growing to enormous scale in the process. Scientific advances spawned by the new industrial order rapidly translated into scores of useful and marvelous devices, promising to improve the lives of ordinary people. One fantastic thing after another was invented—the telephone, electric lighting, the phonograph, the linotype machine, the electric welder, the pneumatic hammer, linoleum, dynamite, oleomargarine, the color photograph, the steam turbine, the zipper, and much more—all within the last half of the nineteenth century. This cavalcade of practical improvements inspired a widespread sense of optimism. Industry and technology would lead to utopia—and utopia seemed to be scheduled to arrive with the twentieth century.

At the same time, the darker social repercussions of the industrial order were obvious to anyone who lived in a major city. The factory system had produced a new class of people, factory workers, mostly deracinated country folk and their descendants, whose lives amounted to little more than a new kind of slavery, and they dwelt in a new kind of habitat, the industrial slum. Among Western intellectuals, the general optimism about industrial progress was dampened by a deep sense of shame and guilt about the plight of these workers. This guilt engendered a good deal of ill feeling toward those who exploited the workers, the proprietors of the industrial system: the company owners, their hired bosses, and their "bourgeois" minions. And it provoked a concomitant revulsion for the goodies that the better-off enjoyed at the workers' expense, especially the fancy buildings where they lived, worked, and were entertained. It was reasoned, therefore, that the coming evolutionary leap into utopia would include the uplift of the workers, resulting in "the new industrial man." Ultimately, reasoned Karl Marx, the new industrial man would attain control of "the means of production" and all class distinctions would be abolished in an ensuing reorganization of life.

Thus exalted and elevated, this new industrial man would require a better place to live than the slums that had been his customary abode.

In fact, he and everybody else would require a new architectural setting for everyday life to replace the structures of the decadent past—else the new industrial man would lose the edge of moral superiority that he had only lately achieved, his evolution having been mostly a moral leap. The solution to this quandary would be an architecture that eschewed all ornamental references to history, a purist architecture of the dawning twentieth century! It would be clean, functional, safe, healthy, and bright, a sort of blank-slate habitat within which the new industrial man might create a new and better culture untainted by the sins of the past.

⁂

To understand Modernism, it is helpful to consider what immediately preceded it. In 1893, Chicago put on a world's fair called the Columbian Exposition, ostensibly to celebrate the 400th anniversary of Columbus's landing but really to showcase America's manufacturing genius. In terms of architecture, the fair was a culmination of all the historical styles that had paraded through the decades of the nineteenth century like a series of marching bands, each in its own striking costume—from the Greek Revival of the 1830s, to the Gothic cottages and Italianate villas of Downing's day, to the Second Empire Mansardic business blocks on every Main Street in America, the Fifth Avenue chateaus of the robber barons, through every other sort of exuberant confection of America's post-Civil War industrial boom. The Columbian Exposition was the climax, the grand summing-up.

The plan for the fair by Daniel H. Burnham comprised a huge layout of man-made lagoons along the shore of Lake Michigan that took five years to build. To that point in his career, Burnham had been best known for designing Chicago's first gigantic office buildings, but by the turn of the century he would be the nation's foremost urban planner. His motto was: "Make no small plans." The enormous exhibition halls, designed by a Who's Who of America's most prominent architects, were done in a high classical manner that went ancient Rome a few steps further—pillars and arches and domes and spires and cupolas and swag-filled entablatures and capitals dripping acanthus leaves, all of it holding to a single unified cornice line. The buildings, the ceremonial arches, and even the lagoons were studded with statuary. Lit up at night by wondrous new incandescent floodlamps, it looked like the climactic scene out of Thomas Cole's "Course of Empire" series. Fair-goers nicknamed it the White City.

Even the usually skeptical Henry Adams gushed: "As a scenic display, Paris had never approached it," he said. "The world had never witnessed so marvelous a phantasm." It was especially amazing, he went on, that such a sublime spectacle arose out of the mercantile banality of Chicago. "One saw here a third-rate town of half-a-million people without history, education, unity, or art, and with little capital— without even the element of natural interest except the river, which it studiously ignored—but doing what London, Paris, or New York would have shrunk from attempting."[1]

This mode of classical architecture would become known as the Beaux Arts style, after the École des Beaux Arts in Paris, largely because at one time or another so many of its American practitioners had studied there. The French Academic tradition promoted the formal vocabularies of antiquity, emphasizing order and continuity, as had the Renaissance masters—indeed, it was a *continuation* of that Renaissance tradition. But in America, where there was little academic tradition, and where artistic continuity was driven only by fads, this renewed interest in the classical orders was really launched by a single person, Charles Follen McKim, just as Andrew Jackson Downing had earlier launched the Gothic revival.

McKim's father, a prominent abolitionist clergyman, was among the first pioneers in the suburban experiment known as Llewelyn Park. The family lived in a house designed by Alexander Jackson Davis, Downing's colleague. Young Charlie McKim studied science at Harvard for one year, then sailed off to the École des Beaux Arts. After three years in Paris, he came home and went to work in the Boston office of architect Henry Hobson Richardson.

Richardson was busy promoting his own special brand of Romanesque-inspired architecture that dominated American public buildings for two decades following the Civil War. Typically, these were heavy, dark masonry buildings with massive arched entranceways and turreted bays or towers. Train stations were Richardson's bread and butter. In fact, sometimes the buildings are disdainfully referred to as Railroad Romanesque. Lewis Mumford called this period the "brown decades" because the buildings were so darkly ponderous.

McKim left Richardson's office in 1874 and joined forces with William Rutherford Mead, whose genius lay more in the area of office management than design. It was a good match. They succeeded quickly together, specializing in country houses for the rich at Newport and the Hamptons, many of them done in the so-called Shingle Style, which they innovated. In 1879, McKim and Mead were joined by Stanford White—who, by coincidence, had taken over McKim's old job in H. H. Richardson's office—and the firm of McKim, Mead, and White was complete.

When the gloomy Richardsonian Romanesque was at its height of popularity, and Frank Furness was doing even weirder mélanges of neo-Egyptian, high Gothic, rustic medieval, and Aztec whatnot in the banks, mansions, and railroad offices of Philadelphia, and Main Street U.S.A. was all caught up in the mansard rage, Charlie McKim was developing a keen interest in eighteenth-century American colonial architecture, which was then very much *outré*. In the summer of 1881, he slipped away from the busy office with his younger partner, White, and made a tour of New England, through Salem, Marblehead, Newburyport, and Portsmouth, for the sole purpose of studying the surviving Georgian buildings—all that Renaissance classicism out of Andrea Palladio as reinterpreted by Inigo Jones, Christopher Wren, and Robert Adam, and then stripped down to its bare essentials for trans-Atlantic shipment, whence it found its way to the houses of American rum merchants and whaling captains. It was the École des Beaux Arts simplified—the grand formal orders of antiquity that America had long consigned to a cobwebby corner of the national attic and forgotten. It was a four-square, rational, and symmetrical architecture. Above all, it was restrained and dignified, an antidote to all the strident emotionalism, to the struggle for picturesque effects, that lay behind the nineteenth century's pageant of romantic revivals.

McKim saw that this classicism was an architecture worthy of the forward-looking, rationalistic culture of big business and big industry that America had become at the end of the nineteenth century. It was calming, orderly, and elegant. It harked back not only to America's glorious past, but to our deeper continuities with European culture. Its restraint expressed supreme self-confidence and intellectual clarity, not the dark superstition and medieval hugger-mugger of the romantic styles. Its decorative motifs—arched and pedimented windows, columns, pilasters, garlands, roofline balustrades, quoins, cartouches—were straightforward in the sense that you didn't have to read the novels of Sir Walter Scott in order to appreciate their meaning.

McKim, Mead, and White's first effort in this new classical manner was the Villard mansion at Fifth Avenue and Fifty-fifth Street in New York City in 1882. (Many years later the mansion became the headquarters of Random House book publishers; the shell of the building is now the entrance to the Helmsley Palace Hotel.) In 1887, McKim, Mead, and White began the Boston Public Library at Copley Square, which set the tone for civic monuments for years to come. Meanwhile, any influence that H. H. Richardson might have had in the debate over architecture's future ended with his premature death in 1886 at age forty-eight.

McKim, Mead, and White led the way in the 1890s, and the rest of American architecture followed them. They specified the best materials. They took advantage of the low prices for quarried stone and the ready supply of cheap, highly skilled immigrant labor to achieve an exceptional quality of workmanship. For example, in building J. Pierpont Morgan's New York mansion, where cost was no object, they employed a nearly lost ancient Greek method of mortarless construction called *anathyrosis* that required thin sheets of lead, one sixty-fourth of an inch thick, to be laid as a seal between impeccably squared hand-ground granite blocks. The firm was renowned for its fussiness, often completely redoing parts of a job marred by nearly imperceptible flaws.

Soon, everything from art museums to public baths were going up in the classical manner. This so-called Beaux Arts style caught on in such a big way that people began to talk about an "American Renaissance." It was as though the whole architectural profession had simultaneously struck a splendid high chord in C major and blinked at each other in self-adoring wonderment.

Except Louis Sullivan of Chicago. Sullivan's Transportation Building at the Columbian Exposition was the only one of the main exhibition halls not designed along classical lines. Rather, it was a massive, filigreed box of vaguely Islamic flavor with a colossal arched, multicolored entranceway that occupied about half the facade, accented with hundreds of incandescent light bulbs. The whole thing looked rather like a gigantic incense burner.

A cranky, visionary, iconoclastic spirit, Sullivan had developed quite an extraordinary vocabulary that presaged much to come in twentieth-century Modernism. By his mid-thirties, Sullivan had achieved startling success—with a partner, Dankmar Adler—designing that new thing called the office building. Here was a structure created explicitly to accommodate the new institution that was American-style big business. It was just the ticket for someone disgusted with America's slavish worship of rank and moldy European traditions—the daily activities of a sixteenth-century Italian duke in his palazzo had little in common with the daily activities of 300 clerks in the Standard Widget Corporation offices; why should they occupy the same sort of building?

The office building was made possible by two technological innovations: structural steel and the elevator. Until that time, buildings were supported by their walls. Large buildings had to be built with heavy masonry walls, and the ratio of weight and mass to strength made it difficult to put up structures higher than 100 feet, because the upper walls would weigh too much for the lower stories to bear. Steel changed all that completely. The weight of the building could now be borne entirely by a light steel skeleton frame. The outside walls, completely relieved from the duty to bear weight, were now a mere "skin," and could be made of anything: tiles, metal panels, glass. And with the elevator, buildings could climb until they scraped the sky.

The tall office building also had a tremendous impact on city real estate values. With added stories, the amount of rentable space occupying a city lot would rise astronomically. This gave big companies incentive to invest in their own building. If done intelligently, such a venture would cover its own costs and yield an impressive revenue stream. Thus, Standard Widget could build the twelve-story Standard Widget Building, take perhaps five floors for themselves, and rent out the rest of the space to other businesses at a tidy profit.

By the early 1890s, big corporations were beating down Louis Sullivan's door. He was one of the first practitioners to appreciate structural steel, and to understand its implications for the future of building. He was well underway with a series of commissions to design tall office buildings when the Columbian Exposition came along.

"Form follows function," was Sullivan's watchword. The outer look of a building out to express its inner structure. This was exactly what the Beaux Arts didn't do, he said, and why it was a fraud. So many of the beloved classical devices—columns, arches, pillars, domes—were forms designed to hold walls and ceilings up. An arch, for example, was a way of distributing loads on masonry blocks. But in the new age of structural steel an arch was no longer necessary. To put a facade featuring arches and pillars on a building that was really held up by a hidden steel skeleton was arrant fakery. Moreover, as a strictly technical matter, the classical orders were not very well suited to buildings over four stories high. There was no precedent for tall buildings in classical architecture. There had been no skyscrapers in ancient Rome. Corinthian columns certainly couldn't rise twelve stories without looking absurd. In fact, the Beaux Arts style worked best when buildings stretched out horizontally—like big-city train stations, museums, and libraries, in which there was no particular need to exceed traditional height. But nobody had really adapted the classical vocabulary to skyscrapers, and Sullivan for one concluded that another approach was needed.

To make matters worse, it happened that all those grandiose classical buildings at the Columbian Exposition were mere plaster and lath facades—for the logical reason that the gleaming White City was temporary construction, meant to be pulled down when the fair was over. This only aggravated things, from Sullivan's point of view, making the buildings seem not just fraudulent but a cheap fraud at that. That people actually admired such meretricious stuff boded ill for the future. Sullivan also didn't like the classical allegory that went along with it—all those statues of Truth, Liberty, and Progress planted all over the exposition grounds. It was pretentious, alien to the American spirit, he said, forced upon a duped public. Sullivan publicly denounced the whole wretched business.

"The damage wrought by the fair," he prophesied, "will last for half a century from its date, if not longer."[2] He was right about how long it lasted. But the worst damage was done by those who reacted to classicism by tossing the whole history of architecture into the garbage can. Anyway, Sullivan apparently missed the most important point of the Columbian Exposition, which was not the style of the buildings, but rather the emphasis on civic art: the way that buildings could be arranged in groups to produce marvelous public spaces on the grand scale. Of course, to appreciate grand public spaces, a culture had to first esteem the idea of the public realm, and this had not been the case in America. Sullivan's blind spot for civic art, then, made him yet more typically American. To him, only the individual buildings mattered.

Despite Sullivan, the idea of civic art really did catch on briefly in America at the turn of the twentieth century. A remarkable series of expositions followed the Chicago fair—the Pan-American Exposition at Buffalo in 1901 (where President McKinley was shot), the Louisiana Purchase Exposition at St. Louis in 1904, the Alaska-Yukon-Pacific Exposition at Seattle in 1910, and the Panama-Pacific Exposition at San Francisco in 1915, among others. They served as demonstration projects for a manner of heroic urban planning that would evolve into the City Beautiful movement in America, a concerted effort to bring focus and unity where chaos, visual squalor, or monotony had reigned, and to do it on a scale not seen since the Baroque period. The City Beautiful movement might be viewed as just another architectural fad. And given its rather short life span of two decades, it probably was, though it left us with some of our most beautiful and enduring public monuments.

World War I effectively swept it away. In a demoralized Western world, classicism, and all the "eternal verities" it supposedly symbolized, stood discredited. Coincidentally, the automobile, with its promise of freedom and adventure, had commenced to transform American space in a new and horrible way, for which no one was prepared.

Around the same time that Henry Adams was being dazzled by the Columbian Exposition, and an American Renaissance was supposedly underway that would usher in the twentieth century with a blaze of neoclassical glory, a different sort of revolution in building was taking place in the industrial backwaters of America. This was the development of another new kind of structure, the daylight factory, made out of reinforced concrete. These hulking behemoths, like the United Shoe Machinery Company factory in Beverly, Massachusetts, the Pacific Coast Borax Company in Bayonne, New Jersey, and Albert Kahn's Packard automobile assembly plant in Detroit, had more influence on twentieth-century architecture than all the acanthus-leaf-bedizened art museums in the Western world. The European avant-garde fell in love with American factory buildings.

The use of steel-reinforced concrete, pioneered by an English-born American named Ernest L. Ransome (born in 1852), solved a number of problems that had plagued industry as the scale of manufacturing grew. One was lighting. An internal skeleton of steel-reinforced concrete pillars and beams meant that the outer walls no longer had to support the weight of the building. Thus, the outer walls could be almost entirely filled with glass panes, flooding the workspace with daylight. Another problem solved by concrete was fireproofing. The earlier brick mills were framed inside with immense wood timbers and each story had a wooden floor—all flammable, of course. Naked steel construction was not any better. Unlike the heavy timbers, which burned slowly enough to evacuate a factory, naked steel beams would begin to twist, distort, and pull a building apart before they melted.[3] A factory made of reinforced concrete, on the other hand, was inherently fireproof, almost indestructible. Concrete could be cast into floor and ceiling panels that laughed at fire. Finally, reinforced concrete could carry immense loads. Its strength permitted huge interior bays—spaces between the pillars—so you could build large things using big, complex machines.

As the twentieth century dawned, the pace of industrial innovation in America had raced ahead of that in Europe, and for the first time Europeans looked west across the ocean for ideas. In 1910, a German entrepreneur named Carl Bensheidt, an admirer of things American, reached agreement with the United Shoe Machinery Corporation of Beverly, Massachusetts, to build a factory at Alfeld-an-der-Leine, Germany, in a joint venture. United's stock-in-trade was wooden shoe lasts, the foot-shaped forms used to make shoes. They were made out of beechwood, *Fagus grandifolia,* so the new German factory was named the Faguswerk in honor of it. Bensheidt had hired a yeoman local architect named Edouard Werner to design the plant, but he apparently found the exterior treatment insufficiently thrilling, so he hired the young Walter Gropius to do a "skin job," hoping to give the Faguswerk a fashionable, up-to-date (that is, American) look.

The result was a building that looks like the prototypical American junior high school: three stories of beige brick, big steel-sash windows, and the soon-to-be canonical flat roof. During this period, Gropius began lecturing on the new American methods of building. To illustrate his lectures—and a seminal article he wrote for the *Jahrbuch des Deutschen Werkbundes*—he used promotional photographs from the Atlas Portland Cement Company. America was the future, he declared, because it was "the motherland of industry."

What dogged Gropius, though, was the plight of the poor wretches who toiled in those factories. It was hard for an educated, compassionate architect to extol the glories of the coming industrial utopia without doing something to improve the workers' miserable lot. "Work must be established in places that give the workman, now a slave to industrial labor, not only light, air, and hygiene, but also an indication of the great common idea that drives everything," Gropius wrote. "Only then can the individual submit to the impersonal without losing the joy of working together for the common good. . . ."

Gropius soon concluded that the American method of factory building pointed the way for all architecture. He doted on those photographs of the massive grain elevators that stood along the shores of the Niagara River at Buffalo, of the colossal railroad coal storage bunkers, and "the newest work halls of the great North American industrial trusts." Here were large, simple forms, "fresh and intact," honestly expressed, as elegant as the megaliths of ancient Egypt. Best of all, they rejected "the romantic residue of past styles" as "cowardly and unreal."

This was a partial restatement of a position taken a few years earlier by the Viennese architect Adolf Loos, who declared that ornament on buildings was "a crime." All those quoins and cartouches, pilasters and balustrades represented a waste of human effort, and of material as well, "and the two things together mean a waste of capital." (Today, substitute *resources*.) Architectural ornament was barbaric, like the tattoos that savage peoples carved into their flesh. Moreover, it expressed "indecent" eroticism. "The man of our time who smears the walls with erotic symbols is a delinquent and a degenerate," Loos wrote.

Yet for someone so disturbed by the fruits of capitalism, Loos hardly lacked for bourgeois clients, and, in fact, he specialized in designing the facades and the sumptuous interiors of Viennese luxury shops—all marble and onyx and gleaming Swedish granite and polished cherrywood paneling. Loos too found much to admire in the massive simple forms of industrial America, the factories and grain elevators. As early as 1904, he was building villas for wealthy clients that featured plain stucco walls and flat roofs. Loos's rationale for the flat roof differed from that of the Bauhäuslers of the twenties—for him, pitched roofs symbolized rural backwardness. So enterprising was Loos that he even managed to execute a few major commissions during the height of the First World War, including a gigantic sugar refinery at Brno, Czechoslovakia.

The war blew up the established European social order. The Austro-Hungarian empire dissolved, and with it the Hapsburg dynasty. In a much reduced and humiliated Germany, the kaiser was dethroned and a shaky democratic-socialist government installed. In Russia the world had turned completely upside down, the czar and all his vassals were gone, and the poor miserable working folk themselves now held the reins of power—or so the Bolsheviks said. For architects, the future had arrived seemingly overnight.

The war had brought ruin to the wealthy classes of Germany, and certainly discredited their cultural establishment—the national academies and institutes—not to mention the less formal relationships that had traditionally tethered talent to wealth. Into this cultural vacuum stepped a youthful avant-garde—artists, writers, musicians, architects—determined to make up new rules and relationships. They allied themselves with the political left, which appeared to be the wave of the future. Socialism now occupied the moral high ground of European politics. It was the panacea for all economic ills, the cure for industrial despotism. In the Weimar Republic and "Red Vienna," a Russian-style revolution was expected any minute. Members of the idealistic avant-garde found it logical and fashionable to subscribe to the socialist program, and to base their aesthetics on it, too. Henceforward, art would be for "the people." Artists even organized themselves into congeries that resembled political parties. They devised doctrines and issued manifestos of correct thinking. Tom Wolfe has described these groups as "compounds," a new kind of institution: the Bauhaus in Germany, de Stijl in Rotterdam, the Constructivists in Soviet Russia, the Futurists in Italy. In the absence of clients—those classes ruined by the war—the compounds occupied themselves with a competition of ideas as to which had the purist vision of the future, the vision least contaminated by the ruinous filth of the past.

With Gropius in charge, the Bauhaus became the leading European compound, a sort of alternative national academy funded by the Weimar regime. With its utopian-revolutionary program, it presumed to represent the interests of the workers; its only client was the state and it soon got into the business of designing public housing projects. In the Bauhaus scheme of things a worker was someone with no aspirations, who had no dream of rising to a "better" position, because in the coming democratic-socialist utopia there would be *no such thing as a better position*. All positions would be equal. A Faguswerk janitor would be as esteemed as an architect, and perhaps equally remunerated. It was an absurd belief, and naturally it put the utopians in a box, which is exactly what Bauhaus architecture looked like: boxes.

The aesthetic-social dogmas of the Bauhaus were wildly reductive. Anything but a flat roof was *verboten*, because towers, cupolas, et cetera, symbolized the crowns worn by monarchs. Anything but an absolutely plain sheer facade was show-offy and, worse, dishonest, because it disguised a building's true structure. Ornament was a voluptuary indulgence only the rich could afford, and in the coming utopia there would be no rich people, or everybody would be equally rich, or equally poor, or something like that, so ornament was out. Color was banned. The postwar avant-garde scaled new heights of puritanism.

The naked brutality of industry was the most difficult thing to reconcile with any new theory of the utopian future. No matter how you rationalized it, factory work was mind-numbing, if not back-breaking. And if the worker was a new kind of slave, then the industrial method of production itself was the new master, whether the system was run by an archduke with a monocle, or a cigar-chomping plutocrat, or a soviet committee. The avant-garde's solution to this dilemma was a bit of intellectual jujitsu, the old *if you can't beat 'em, join 'em* gambit: They romanticized the machine and embraced the growing mechanization of life as a wonderful development. Henceforward, all art would be machine-made, proclaimed the Dutchman Theo Van Doesburg. Not to be outdone, Walter Gropius declared "Art and Technology—a New Unity!" as the Bauhaus's new motto. But the greatest romancer of the machine was Le Corbusier.

A French-speaking Swiss from a watch-making family, Charles-Édouard Jeanneret, who took the hocus-pocus name Le Corbusier, operated as a free-lance guru—a "one-man compound," in Wolfe's apt phrase. Yet he understood all the angles of the new avant-gardism and he functioned in total compliance to its rules—the main rule being that one must have some fresh-baked theories to sell, and the more esoteric the better. Le Corbusier was perhaps the most energetic theorizer of them all and a tireless self-promoter, publishing reams of articles and many books in a febrile, preposterous prose style. Significantly, the things he designed tended not to function very well, whatever they looked like.

In the summer of 1925, the Exposition Internationale des Arts Décoratifs et Industriels Modernes was held in Paris. Essentially it was a show of interior decoration and the purpose was to reestablish Paris as the capital of the decorative arts—a distinction held by Vienna chiefly on account of Adolf Loos's sumptuous prewar interiors. It was in Paris that all the stripped-down, streamlined, jazzified variants of neoclassicism got tagged with the Art Deco label. In a quiet corner of the seventy-five-acre Expo stood a bare little white stucco cube decorated only with the twenty-foot-high monogram EN. One critic said it looked like a "cold storage warehouse." The initials stood for *L'Esprit Nouveau*, a magazine edited by Le Corbusier. The magazine was the prime venue for his "vehement propaganda," as Philip Johnson and Henry-Russell Hitchcock later characterized "Corbu's" writings. His influential book *Towards an Architecture* had lately been published, and, as the co-founder with the painter Fernand Léger of a new two-man movement they called Purism, Corbu was a rising figure among the Parisian avant-garde. The Pavilion de L'Esprit Nouveau was a demonstration project of Corbu's ideas to date, all summarized under the aphorism that "the house is a machine for living."

Perhaps Corbu, the bohemian bachelor who lived in a Latin Quarter garret and took his meals in bistros, just didn't understand much about domestic arrangements. As Witold Rybczynski tells it:

> The effect was distinctly unhomey. . . . There were some
> strange transpositions—the kitchen was the smallest room
> in the house, the size of a bathroom, and the bathroom,

which was intended to double as an exercise room and had one entire wall built out of glass blocks, was almost as big as the living room. . . . The inspiration for the two-story-high living room, overlooked by a gallery and lit by a large window—which he repeated in many houses—was a Parisian trucker's cafe.[4]

The tiny kitchen had little counter space. It was inconveniently placed on the second floor, in poor relation to the dining area. The study had no door to afford quiet and privacy. The stairway railing was made of industrial pipes, the window frames of steel factory sash. Since Corbu disdained the bourgeois habit of collecting furniture, he outfitted the place with common cast-iron Parisian park furniture and the kinds of tables and bentwood chairs commonly found in cafés. He didn't even like the term *furniture*, preferring *equipment* instead. "In an exhibition devoted to the decorative arts, Le Corbusier's pavilion contained neither decoration nor, it seemed to most, artistry," Rybczynski writes. In fact, part of the Corbu doctrine of the Esprit Nouveau, as filtered through Corbu Purism, was a rejection of decorative art per se. Except that for all his rejection of decorative art, his pavilion ended up being about style anyway: the style of *no style*. In a decade preoccupied with glamour, what could be more chic?

The pavilion held another curiosity: an exhibit of Le Corbusier's *Plan Voison*, a fanciful urban renewal scheme to bulldoze the Marais district of Paris—a massive historic chunk of the city a stone's throw from the Louvre that included the Place de Bastille and the old Palais Royale (Place de Vosges)—and replace it with a gargantuan "Radiant City" complex of twenty-four sixty-story high-rises set amid parklike grounds and served by limited-access automobile roads. Sound familiar?

The Esprit Nouveau house was largely ignored, or laughed at, and yet in five years the reductive, industrially inspired manner of building that it illustrated—as promoted also by Gropius, his Bauhaus colleague Ludwig Mies van der Rohe, Bruno and Max Taut, J. J. P. Oud, and their followers—would be christened and enshrined by no less an institution than New York's Museum of Modern Art as the International Style, "a modern style as original, as consistent, as logical, and as widely distributed as any in the past."[5] Of course, the Americans missed something crucial—not because we were dumber than the Europeans but because we lived in a different world, and it was obvious in the way we discussed the subject: To us, it was just another style.

⚐

Though America suffered over 50,000 deaths in the First World War, the battles had been fought far, far away. American property was not damaged. The American social order hardly had been challenged and the cultural establishment remained intact. Socialism found some enthusiasts here, but it lacked the punch it had acquired as a political cure-all in class-bound Europe—here, any ambitious pipefitter or office boy could dream of rising to the top of a great corporation. The American bohemians who flirted with socialism in the years before the Depression often did so in imitation of European artists, because it was part of the bohemian life, like drinking too much. Certainly, it was not part of any respectable architect's intellectual baggage. Frank Lloyd Wright may have operated a fellowship out at Taliesin in Wisconsin, but it was more cult camp than collective, and a man like Wright, who entertained lavishly, enjoyed riding around in a Lincoln Zephyr car, wore elegant capes, and kept mistresses, could hardly have confused himself with a bull-necked welder on the Packard assembly line.

Between 1890 and 1920, Wright was the American working most in a manner resembling the Europeans, but his ideas about building had little in common with theirs, and he was emphatically uninvolved in their debates. However, Wright's work had inspired the Bauhäuslers and their brethren, especially the strong horizontality of his compositions, because for them it "honestly expressed" structure—for instance, the way a floor stretched across the length of the house. Wright himself was less interested in avant-garde metaphysics than he was in the wondrous properties of reinforced concrete and the nifty effects he could achieve by cantilevering long spans of the stuff.

Wright took himself out of the country to Japan in the early 1920s, a time when he might have been considered the leading American in his profession. When he returned home, a housekeeper went berserk at Taliesan, his estate in Wisconsin, stabbed his mistress to death, and burned the place down. The catastrophe threw Wright for a loop. He withdrew from the world at large to brood and rebuild Taliesan.

Out in Los Angeles before World War I, Irving Gill had designed villas and apartment buildings that looked superficially like pure Bauhaus—years before the Bauhaus even existed. Gill's buildings had flat roofs, beige stucco walls, horizontal windows, and zero ornament. But in fact they were inspired by the Spanish architecture of the early Los Angeles pueblo, and rendered in concrete-casting methods as developed by the Army Corps of Engineers.

Otherwise, American architects of the period continued to busily mine the historicist motherload. In 1910, while Adolf Loos was denouncing ornament in Vienna and Walter Gropius was panting over snapshots of American shoe factories, Charlie McKim completed New York's Pennsylvania Station in frank imitation of the Baths of Caracalla, and wealthy Americans were still happily paying for mansions that looked like Marie Antoinette's Petit Trianon. The cutting edge of American architecture concerned itself with the challenge of building skyscrapers and the action had shifted from Chicago to New York, the nation's corporate power center.

The nature of the challenge was to test the limits of the materials, to see just how high a building could go. (Every additional story meant more rents.) The progression was swift, from Daniel Burnham's 20-story Flatiron Building in 1902, to Cass Gilbert's 50-story Woolworth Building in 1913, to William Van Alen's 77-story Chrysler Building in 1930, and finally to the 110-story Empire State Building in 1931. Through the twenties, all skyscrapers were highly ornamented. Ernest Flagg's Singer Building included an elaborate mansardic tower. Gilbert's Gothic Woolworth Building featured gargoyles and flying buttresses. The Chrysler Building also sported gargoyles, while its flamboyant Art Deco tower gave it the look of a Buck Rogers rocket ship.

The Great Depression put an end to this first exuberant phase of skyscraper building. Business was no longer expanding and the last thing people needed was more office space. Some significant buildings were completed in the early thirties—Raymond Hood's McGraw-Hill Building (1931), Howe and Lescaze's Philadelphia Savings Fund Society (1932), and the enormous Rockefeller Center—but these projects were planned well before the stock market crash. Hardly anything in the full-blown Modernist vein got built in America at this time. The Museum of Modern Art's anointing of the International Style with a 1932 exhibition, curated by Philip Johnson and Henry-Russell Hitchcock, also took place with the economy in freefall. It might have just served as an elaborate footnote to an exotic foreign art movement were it not for developments overseas.

In the mid-1930s, Adolf Hitler took charge of the German government and within a few years virtually all of the heavy hitters of German avant-garde architecture had fled to America. Hitler's influence on the future of architecture was more subtle and complicated than that of a mere political maniac scaring the bejesus out of a bunch of four-eyed intellectuals. As a youth, Hitler had done time in art school and tasted the bohemian life. He had a keen sense of the importance of public architecture as a tool for political control, and a rather rabid hatred of all the left-leaning collectivist movements spawned by the First World War, then nurtured by the soft-brained Weimar Republic, including especially the Bauhäuslers and their kindred spirits. Bolsheviks, every one!

Hitler shut down the "degenerate" Bauhaus and with his own court architects, led by Albert Speer, he began erecting large public buildings in a new Nazi style that signaled a streamlined return to the neoclassical style. It was everything the Bauhäuslers had been against, especially ornament. Hitler liked ornament, particularly the Nazi insignia. He used the swastika the way Piranesi had used acanthus leaves. Stalin too, in his crude way, preferred traditional architecture over the wild avant-garde stuff that had sprung from the idealism of the Bolshevik revolution. The neoclassical thus became the official architectural style of despots and maniacs.

Of course, this was a complete vindication of the Bauhäuslers entire metaphysic. Anybody who had declared that ornament was a crime before World War II could afterward point to the bone-heaps of Europe for proof positive. It was more than a crime, it was Evil incarnate. By the time Hitler and his regime were vanquished, in 1945, no decent person in the Western world could speak against Modernism and its practitioners.

They became part of the cultural establishment in America practically overnight, and not in the back galleries either, but in positions of influence. Within a few months of arriving in America, Walter Gropius was appointed chief of the Harvard School of Architecture. Marcel Breuer, who would later design the Whitney Museum, joined Gropius on the faculty. Ludwig Mies van der Rohe, who had directed the Bauhaus after Gropius, was appointed dean of architecture at the Armour Institute in Chicago, which became the Illinois Institute of Technology, and he was given the task of designing a new campus. Lazlo Moholy-Nagy opened the New Bauhaus, which became the Chicago Institute of Design. And, with other refugees, the painter Joseph Albers promulgated the Bauhaus aesthetic at the small but influential Black Mountain College in the North Carolina hills—"a rural Bauhaus," in Tom Wolfe's phrase.

The stage was set for the transformation of American architecture. Americans, with their chronic sense of cultural inferiority, were mesmerized by the refugees with their foreign accents and urbane manners. Gropius at once initiated the Bauhaus method of instruction at Harvard. All the old dogma from the twenties about the "new industrial man," and the class hatred aesthetics about fancy roofs being like crowns, et cetera, which lost much of its meaning in a socially mobile society like ours, was recast in purely formal terms for American consumption: the honest expression of function, the principle of horizontality, the outer walls as the building's "skin," the sanctity of the flat roof, the regularity of fenestration, use of standardized components, no color, no ornament.

In the aftermath of World War II, America was not just the Motherland of Industry, it was the *only* land of industry, for the other advanced nations were bankrupted or bombed to rubble. America's institutions stood intact and our economy would benefit greatly from the lack of worldwide competition—even if we had to lend other nations money to buy things we made. A great building boom lay ahead. And it would all be done in the Modernist style, because it was the morally correct style, the *only* acceptable style, the official architecture of decency, democracy, and freedom. Gropius, Breuer, and Mies, who had come of age mooning over grainy photographs of American cement factories and grain elevators, were about to repay their adopted country in spades. From now on, everything in America would look like versions of the Faguswerk: high schools, hospitals, hotels, office buildings, apartment complexes, college dorms, restaurants, even weekend retreats in Connecticut.

Some successful homegrown American architects, like Albert Kahn, of Detroit, who had designed *both* automobile factories and Beaux Arts university libraries, loathed the new Modernist style. Kahn called Le Corbusier's work "utterly stupid," and asked of Gropius's Bauhaus buildings at Dessau, "Is it architecture at all?"[6] This from the man who built Henry Ford's Highland Park factory—a true son of the Motherland of Industry.

Perhaps more unfortunate than the trend in architecture was the grip that Le Corbusier's particular brand of urbanism came to exert over the planning profession. His Radiant City scheme became the only model for urban development in postwar America. Le Corbusier's reputation had steadily ripened through all the dark years of depression, fascism, and war. As a Swiss national, immune to Nazi persecution, he was never compelled to hightail it out of Europe. When the Bauhäuslers departed en masse, he was the only big gun left on the scene—and he made the most of it. Meanwhile, in America, with thousands of eager students at their feet, Gropius, Mies, and the others vigorously promoted his ideas.

Corbu's Radiant City had all the right ingredients for America's postwar building boom. Its basic component was the high-rise—nobody knew how to build them better than Americans, or believed in them more. (If no high-rise office or apartment building was built in London or Paris before World War II, it was not because they couldn't figure out how to do it.) The Radiant City scheme featured superhighways— Corbu *hated* ordinary streets and messy street life—and America was raring to build more superhighways. Some of the most successful public works projects of the Depression were the early superhighways—creating thousands of jobs, boosting rural real estate values, and promoting the sale of cars and oil, two more items America knew how to produce better than anyone else.

The Radiant City scheme also appealed to Americans because our existing cities were aging badly. Through years of depression and war, routine maintenance had been deferred and nothing new besides a few bomber plants had been built. To put it bluntly, American cities were crummy, and people's affection for them was limited. In a peculiar way, America seemed eager to emulate the postwar devastation of European cities, to envy their chance to clear away the rubble and begin again. Bulldozing the entire downtown of a Worcester, Massachusetts, or a

New Haven, Connecticut, and starting over from scratch, didn't seem like such a bad idea. Americans certainly did not respond to the postwar "urban renewal" schemes with anything like the gape-mouthed horror of Parisians contemplating Corbu's Plan Voison in 1925.

Finally, the Radiant City appealed to all the latent Arcadian yearnings in our culture. It was the old romantic idea—going back to William Penn—of combining the urban with the rural, of living close to nature, of creating a city out of buildings in a park. That it might end up, in practice, as "buildings in a parking lot," as Lewis Mumford put it, was a possibility that planners and architects did not admit.

From the late forties through the eighties, thousands of urban redevelopments in the Radiant City mold went up all over America: housing, office complexes, hospitals, colleges. The defects of the concept quickly became apparent—for instance, that the space between highrises floating in a superblock became instant wastelands, shunned by the public—but this hardly stopped anyone from building them. The construction industry loved them, while politicians pointed at the rising towers and cried "Growth!" Ordinary citizens soon figured out how badly these projects were designed, but they were not guided by any intelligent public discussion of the issues involved. Very few architects or planners challenged the idea that this was the architecture of decency, freedom, and democracy. Nor did they challenge their social assumptions. The government-funded low-income housing projects were built on the old *existenzminimum* principle of a Weimar *siedlung*, which assumed workers to have no higher aspiration for the quality of life than to be stacked like anchovies in a concrete can.

The rise of America's postwar housing projects—the term *project* itself became a derogatory label—coincided with a mass migration of poor southern rural blacks to northern cities, where their presence in such large numbers was not warmly welcomed. The *existenzminimum* housing block was just the place to put them, in large, neat, high-density stacks, out of the way, occupying a minimum of land. It wasn't the final solution, but it might do as long as the buildings lasted—which was not necessarily long. One infamous project, the crime-plagued Pruitt-Igoe apartment complex in St. Louis, was demolished only fourteen years after completion.

Another type of Radiant City, the "big footprint" megastructure embedded in an old bulldozed central business district, such as the Empire State Plaza in Albany, New York, and the Renaissance Center in Detroit, were grimly tolerated by the new postwar legions of bureaucrats and corporate drones. The employee—a step above "worker"— arrived from a green suburb in his car, parked in an underground garage, ate lunch within the complex, and had no need to venture out into the agoraphobic voids between the high-rise office slabs, let alone beyond the voids to the actual city, with its messy street life, crime, and squalor. If his worklife in the place was joyless, he at least had the compensation of a paycheck and dental coverage, and perhaps even a nice view out the window. This sort of office complex was frequently rationalized as a way to "bring vitality" back to rotten old urban cores. It was a lie, of course—why make them so self-sufficient with their own grog shops and lunch counters?—but by the mid-sixties, Americans had all but given up on their cities anyway.

There were some exceptions, notably New York, or at least, Manhattan, still the corporate and financial center of the nation. But its chief symbol, the skyscraper, was also transformed by the architecture of decency, democracy, and freedom. No longer a needle-capped tower sporting gargoyles, it became a box on the purest Bauhaus terms: flat roof, no ornament, glass "skin," gridlike regularity of fenestration, all the old hoo-ha guaranteed to prevent contamination from the ruinous pretensions of the ruling classes. Except that these boxes were the ultimate status symbol of the newest ruling class: the corporate elite.

Mies van der Rohe was the acknowledged master of the form, his position at the Illinois Institute of Technology quite secondary to his booming private Chicago practice. He pioneered the glass box high-rise form with his 1949 Lakeshore Drive apartment plinths in that city, and brought the concept to full flower with his 1958 Seagram Building on Park Avenue in New York. It was the ultimate Faguswerk. "Less is more," was Mies's credo. The Miesian box was knocked off by every commercial architecture firm in America. Up and down the avenues of mid-Manhattan and in the core of every other city that hadn't gone completely to the dogs, the flat-topped glass-walled office buildings rose in monotonous glory, and for one overarching reason, as Mies's chief disciple, Philip Johnson, admitted startlingly in a 1989 *Interview* magazine piece: "The International Style did sweep the world because it came along at the same time developers wanted to make cheap buildings, and this was cheaper than other architectures."

✦

Like any lie, Modernism was eventually found out, but it didn't skulk ashamedly away into the thickets of history. Corporate America still needed large cheap buildings, and the architectural profession still needed corporate America. And intellectually bankrupt or not, Modernism still wore its moral armor: It was still the architecture that had stood up to Hitler, whatever its other failures.

Yet people didn't *like* it very much. Even if they had an inkling why, they were embarrassed to challenge it, to question the Formgivers, as the aging Bauhaüslers now liked to characterize themselves, as though they were dwellers on Olympus. Architects in particular were most reluctant to backtalk these gods, for it was all the huge, out-of-scale, inhuman, corporate glass boxes that put paychecks on their desks every Friday.

One architect who tried to resolve this crisis of values in the profession was Robert Venturi. His 1967 book, *Complexity and Contradiction in Architecture*, ushered in the postmodern era by restating Mies's famous credo, "less is more." Venturi now bravely declared, "less is a bore." The gods up on Olympus, he dared to say, in their puritanical zeal to banish ornament, had simply turned whole buildings into ornaments-unto-themselves. What was Mies's Seagram Building but a gigantic sculpture, a totem, a monument to an ego? And why was this stance any more socially relevant than the attitude that produced the 1893 Columbian Exposition in Chicago, with its fetishistic plaster-of-paris classical facades?

Venturi's interests lay in the creeping crud architecture found sprawling all over the urban fringes and rural hinterlands of America in the form of subdivisions, shopping centers, and commercial strips. Where the Modernists had championed an architecture that was "heroic and original," Venturi now called for one that dared to be "ugly and ordinary." "Main Street is almost all right," was one of the many aphorisms with which Venturi embellished his world view, explicated further in his next book, *Learning from Las Vegas*, written in 1968 with his wife, Denise Scott-Brown, and their colleague, Steven Izenour.

They had fallen under the sway of sociologist Herbert Gans, author of *The Levittowners*, whose theory of "taste cultures" explored contemporary class conflict. It was an update of the old highbrow-middle-brow-lowbrow concept of the 1940s, except it had more categories plus an historical spin. According to Gans, only in the last hundred years or so have the lower classes possessed the leisure and the surplus cash to express their tastes in anything more refined than cockfights and drinking songs. In postwar America, these low-taste cultures came into full flower—thus ending eons of highbrow tyranny—bringing us such important cultural signposts as lawn flamingoes, velvet art, and Liberace.

Venturi and company declared that rather than struggle against this stuff, the correct strategy was to "illuminate the mess . . . by first participating in it." In Las Vegas, they observed, buildings no longer mattered. Whatever their purpose—motel, casino, carpet warehouse, waterbed store, pizza emporium, marriage mill—they were all just cinder-block sheds, and rather "pathetic" amid the sprawl. What mattered were the signs attached to them and how dazzling it all looked at night. American space had ceased to be about forms, they said. It was now about symbols—communication, *advertising!*—and all wonderfully fascinating. Parking lots were fascinating, the vast spaces between the buildings were fascinating, the luridly painted statues ringing Caesar's Palace, the highway, the curbing, even the "zone of rusting beer cans" at the ragged edge of town had something to reward the patient observer. As for the bad urbanism of the strip, the complete lack of relationship between buildings, the obliteration of human scale, the tyranny of the car—no problem. "We might not like cars, but a large part of the population does," Venturi had written earlier. It was a "taste culture" issue. They were like stoned graduate students on a field trip, their critical faculties gone up in smoke.

Venturi proposed an architecture of unpretentious "decorated sheds." Ornament was okay, even historical detail, as long as it was "applied rather than integral," as nearly two-dimensional as possible in the form of "doodads." For example, the firm did a showroom building for the Best Products Company in Oxford Valley, Pennsylvania. The building was to be a typical flat-roofed highway strip shed. They designed a motif of enormous red-and-white cartoon flowers on glazed metallic panels to decorate the facade. It looked like the sort of thing more usually designed by the owner of such a business—at home, at the kitchen table, or by his nine-year-old daughter—to save money. But in this case the flowers were designed by a Yale-trained architect—for a hefty fee, you may be sure. And Venturi was darn proud of them. The flowers were "bold *and pretty*." They "camouflaged the inevitable banality of the architectural form and read as a sign across a vast parking lot and speedy highway." Note the assumption of banality as inevitable. "Many styles relating to many taste cultures is okay with us," he said. Only you could be sure that Venturi himself did not live in a Levittown "colonial" with plywood butterflies screwed to his garage door.

The daisies were an "ironic reference," in Venturi's phrase. Irony was the trick for redeeming such "banality." A little gentle mockery, some good-humored ribbing, mild subversion. As if to say, "Here, you nation of morons, is another inevitably banal, cheap concrete box, of the only type your sordid civilization allows, topped by some cheap and foolish ornament worthy of your TV-addled brains." It must be obvious that there was nothing particularly redeeming about this mind game, really. It was simply parody, which is to say the sophomoric urge to ridicule by means of feeble imitation, in the absence of an urge to create something original of real quality. It was hardly a solution to the problem of banal architecture and bad urbanism in America.

Still, Venturi's "irony" became the cornerstone of the movement called Postmodernism. He eventually moved beyond the vocabulary of kitsch "doodads" to a phase that admitted blatant reference to historical devices—pilasters, Palladian windows, rusticated facades, entablature—and in doing so, started a bandwagon that many architects hopped upon. But the stance was still ironic—which is to say, when you cleared away all the theoretical legerdemain, that they didn't really mean it. To resurrect the architecture of an old-fashioned colonial imperialism would have been quite unthinkable, except as a joke, in the current political climate. And this was a joke. Underneath the tacked-on pilasters was the same old box.

Perhaps the most famous of the Postmodern works inspired by Venturi's lead is Philip Johnson's "daring" AT&T Building in Manhattan: thirty-odd stories of standard-issue corporate box topped by an ultrasimplified broken pediment roof vaguely reminiscent of a Chippendale secretary. That people took it seriously as a step in the right direction was the greatest irony of all.

⚓

In their effort to promote a liberated and classless society, the Modernists and their successors tried to stamp out history and tradition, and the meanings associated with them, as embodied in the places where we live and work. They failed to create a social utopia, but they did tremendous damage to the physical setting for civilization. Worshiping the machine and industrial methods as ends in themselves, they became the servants of an economy that plundered the future in order to power the engines of production and consumption for the present. This is the essence of the hubris that tries to destroy history: Yesterday's tomorrow turns out to be no future at all. And this destructive, futureless economy is precisely the predicament in which America finds itself today.

Chapter Six

JOYRIDE

Imagine a fine morning in May 1929, in Washington, D.C. You are the proud owner of a new yellow Chevrolet AC Sports Coupe, bought with the $650 that you made from selling 100 shares of American Standard Widget—stock that took off like a rocket, just like your brother-in-law said it would. This is one day that you will not be going in to your job at the War Department. Mr. Wilson made the world safe for Democracy, and America's doing just fine now under Mr. Hoover, too.

Like a couple of kids playing hooky, you and Betty steal out to the new Chevy just after 9 A.M. and plant a picnic hamper in the rumble seat. You rev her up and turn onto New Hampshire Avenue, outbound. Dodging the streetcars is a little tricky. And that rag collector with his horse-drawn wagon should be declared a public nuisance. When the last horse is off the streets, you say, there won't be any need for traffic police.

Well before the D.C. line, you leave the row houses and apartment blocks behind. On the city's fringe, between scruffy fields where speculators bought out farmers a few years ago, new streets of bungalows are going up. Each one has a little garage in the back. This is the coming thing, you say to Betty. Soon everyone will have a car and we can get rid of those trolley tracks downtown for good. Along the main road itself is a scattering of new businesses that cater specifically to motorists: gasoline stations, tourist courts, even a lunch counter somebody's gone and built out of an old railroad caboose.

Twenty minutes after setting out from downtown Washington, you have left the last scraps of the city behind and are motoring down a country road, recently improved. The surface is macadam, compressed gravel, and at eighteen feet across, plenty wide enough for two cars to pass, though you haven't seen another motorist since leaving the District. All around, cow pastures and farm fields drowse in the warm May sunshine. At times, the road curls through patches of cool forest. The Chevy's sputtering engine is all that competes with the sounds of nature. Every five miles or so, you come upon a sleepy Maryland farm village, the very picture of rural contentment. A fellow could live all the way out here, you realize, if he was willing to get up a bit earlier and drive to town, especially if the government blacktopped the highway. What an idea!

You stop to picnic along the roadside in a meadow full of buttercups. A cow lows in the distance. It is lovely and yet both of you are so eager to move on that you forgo those slabs of rhubarb pie and climb back into the Chevy to roam wherever you like, wherever the road leads.

"Isn't this swell?" Betty sighs. "I feel like the whole country is ours. It's like a dream, a wonderful never-ending dream!"

There was nothing like it before in history: a machine that promised liberation from the daily bondage of place. And in a free country like the United States, with the unrestricted right to travel, a vast geographical territory to spread out into, and a national tradition of picking up and moving whenever life at home became intolerable, the automobile came as a blessing. In the early years of motoring, hardly anyone understood the automobile's potential for devastation—not just of the landscape, or the air, but of culture in general. It was assumed that cars would merely serve as wonderfully useful accessories in the human habitat as it then was, that they would make the city a better place, and cure all the troubles of rural life, without altering the arrangement of things in either place.

A civilization completely dependent on cars, as ours is now, was not inevitable. The automobile and the electric streetcar were invented and made commercially viable at roughly the same time: the period from 1890 to 1915. However, the automobile, a private mode of transport, was heavily subsidized with tax dollars early on, while the nation's streetcar systems, a public mode of transport, had to operate as private companies, received no public funds, and were saddled with onerous regulations that made their survival economically implausible.

The electric streetcar was the logical successor to the existing system of urban horsecars. The horsecar lines, fixtures in American cities since the 1850s, had obvious limitations in speed and power. The animals tended to be abused and worked to death. They created a noisome public health problem with their manure and when they dropped dead on city streets, a frequent occurrence—15,000 a year in New York at the turn of the century. Feeding and stabling them was expensive and took up a lot of space.

The technical problems that had stood in the way of a practical electric streetcar were solved in the 1880s by Frank Julian Sprague, a former naval engineer who had worked briefly for Thomas Edison. Sprague invented a flexible cable that transmitted electricity from an overhead wire to the streetcar's electric engine, thus eliminating the danger of an electrified third rail at ground level. (The device was called a troller, because it was pulled along by the car much the same way that a fisherman trolls a lure. Hence: *trolley*.) Kenneth Jackson notes, "By the turn of the century, half the streetcar systems in the United States were equipped by Sprague and 90 percent were using his patents."[1]

The streetcar's heyday was brilliant but brief. It operated cleanly and it moved large numbers of people very efficiently at even cheaper rates than the old horsecars. In the United States, streetcar lines tended to charge a flat fare for a ride of any distance and offered free transfers—as opposed to Europe where the fare was based on the length of the trip. There were two reasons for the flat fare. First, it encouraged weekend joyriding. Second, it helped promote the desirability of commuting from new suburbs at the urban fringe. And it became common for streetcar companies to engage in suburban real estate development. Sometimes real estate was their prime objective and the streetcar was merely the tail of the dog.

The streetcar's average speed was ten to fifteen miles per hour (including frequent stops), and its operation was dependable. It opened up the nether reaches of the city to poor working people who previously couldn't afford to travel far from their neighborhoods. Streetcar companies were also heavily involved in the building of amusement parks on the urban fringe, another spur to weekend riding. At the same time that the cities expanded beyond the old walking limits, downtown business districts boomed from the mass influx of shoppers the trolley now brought from all over town.

In the first decade of the twentieth century, automobiles were considered rich men's playthings. They were handmade and expensive. A chauffeur was a practical necessity, doubling as a mechanic and called upon to deal with the incomprehensible workings under the hood when something went wrong, which was often, or to change blown-out tires, so frequent as to be considered routine. (M. F. K. Fisher writes about a childhood journey from Los Angeles to Palmdale: "We had four blowouts, but that was lucky. [Father] expected twice as many on such a long, hard trip."[2])

Roads all over the United States were quite bad at the turn of the century. They had been neglected since the rise of the railroads, which killed off the eastern stage lines, the roads' chief users. By 1900, all long-haul land transport, freight and passenger, went by rail. The train was also the best way to get from one small town to the next—in many places trolley lines ran between country towns. The only roads of consequence outside the cities were farm-to-market roads, unpaved, poorly marked, with no system of numbered routes. Gasoline stations did not exist. In spring, when the surface thawed and became a viscid mousse over the yet frozen ground beneath, the road could be useless. In summer, wagons raised great clouds of choking dust. In winter, deep snow presented obvious problems, though there was a system for flattening snowy roads with enormous horse-drawn rollers, sprinkling them with water, then using sleighs on the compressed icy surface—but all this was terribly laborious and time-consuming. Merely hitching up a team took a quarter of an hour. Farmers, the chief inhabitants of the countryside, who made up nearly a third of the national population, dwelt in relative isolation, having abandoned the European farm village pattern so many generations before.

City streets were not so wonderful, either. Many were paved with cobblestones, which made for a bone-shaking ride. Trolleys hogged the major thoroughfares, which were further clogged by horse-drawn vehicles. Traffic control meant an occasional cop at the busiest intersections.

Henry Ford did not invent the automobile, but with the Model T he developed a very reliable machine that "the great multitude" could afford to buy, and he dreamed up a means of production—the assembly line—that made his machine cheaper every year for two decades, even while wages, and the prices of other things, climbed. Ford offered the first Model T in the fall of 1908 at $825 for the "runabout" and $25 more for the "touring car." This was a time when $1200 was an excellent yearly salary. By the summer of 1916, with his new factory at Highland Park in full swing, Ford offered the same models for $345 and $360. That year he produced 738,811 cars. In 1927, the Model T's final year of production, with 15 million units sold, the coupe was priced at $290.

Europe did not leap so quickly to embrace the motorcar. From the beginning of the auto age, Europeans had to import oil—mainly from America (the Spindletop bonanza of 1906 opened up the Texas oil fields). Shipping it overseas raised the price, while taxes boosted it further. Europeans adjusted by creating stiff horsepower taxes, which spurred the production of small, fuel-efficient cars that were not very useful for family touring. Altogether, motoring was a much more expensive proposition in Europe, where wages were also significantly lower than in America. James Flink writes, "With its vast land area, hinterland of scattered settlements, and relatively low population densities, the United States had a far greater need for individualized automotive transportation than the nations of western Europe."[3]

While Ford and his competitors churned out more than a million new vehicles a year, politicians and planners soon began a massive restructuring of American cities to accommodate the growing ranks of middle-class motorists. City planning boards were often dominated by realtors, car dealers, and others with a keen personal interest in advancing auto use, and little thought for long-term consequences.[4] By the 1920s a claque of special interests from tire makers to the building trades had coalesced to lobby for the auto. There were fortunes to be made, especially in "development." The streetcar lines had promoted suburbs of a limited scope, a sort of corridor out of the city, because nobody wanted to live more than a few minutes' walk from the trolley stop. The auto now promised to fill in the blanks between the streetcar corridors, and then to develop open space far beyond the city limits.

The costs to the public mounted early. A commission under President Hoover concluded that the automobile was the "most potent influence" on the rise of local taxes between 1913 and 1930. The price of building new roads and repaving the old cobbled city streets was staggering. Chicago spent $340 million on street-widening alone between 1910 and 1940. The new low-density auto suburbs required expensive sewer and water lines to be laid *before* the new homes were sold—meaning that the carless urban working class had to pay for the new infrastructure that the car-owning middle class would enjoy. Police forces were motorized and many new officers hired specifically to control increased traffic. Stoplights by the thousands had to be installed. But perhaps the greatest cost to the public was one that can't be quantified in dollars: the degradation of urban life caused by enticing the middle class to make their homes outside of town. It began an insidious process that ultimately cost America its cities.

The federal government got into the act of subsidizing auto use in 1916 with the $75 million Federal Road Act to improve post roads and to encourage the states to organize their own highway departments by giving them money. A second Federal Road Act in 1921 sought to improve 200,000 miles of state highways with the idea of linking them up to form a national network. The programs got many parts of rural America "out of the mud." In 1925, the national system of numbered routes was adopted, and for the first time highway spending topped $1 billion for a single year. Kenneth Jackson makes the shrewd observation that "although the motorcar was the quintessentially private instrument, its owners had to operate it over public spaces."

By contrast, streetcar companies received little government support, and the organized auto interests conspired actively to kill them off. By the eve of the First World War, lines were already hard-pressed to make a profit—and as private companies, with stockholders, they had to make a profit to justify their existence. Many companies were stuck with guaranteed nickel fares under franchises that granted them the right to operate on city streets. These cheap fares were a political gimmick that required private streetcar companies to subsidize transportation for the poor. City governments wouldn't allow them to cease operating unprofitable routes, but neither would they help defray the expense of operation. Inevitably, this led to a spiral of decline: service got worse, ridership declined, profit vanished, upkeep had to be deferred, service got worse, and so on toward bankruptcy. And the streetcar companies were far from blameless in their own demise. Some watered their stock shamelessly. Others rose and fell with the success of their associated real estate ventures.

In 1925, with the acquisition of the Yellow Coach company, the General Motors Corporation undertook a systematic campaign to put streetcar lines out of business all over America. General Motors erected a byzantine network of subsidiaries and holding companies to carry out its mission, using its financial muscle to buy up streetcar lines, scrap the tracks, and convert the routes for buses. General Motors also moved to horn in on regular railways, becoming the largest stockholder in the Greyhound Corporation—which bought all its buses from Yellow Coach. Sniffing opportunities among financially troubled railroads as the Great Depression deepened, GM organized a holding company called the National Highway Transport Corporation—which became Atlantic Greyhound Lines—to provide intercity bus service in the southeast. In 1932, General Motors formed the United Cities Mobile Transit (UCMT) corporation to create a market for its products by taking over streetcar lines in small cities, and converting the lines to buses. UCMT was dissolved in 1935 after the American Transit Association censured it for trying to dismantle Portland, Oregon's, electric trolley lines. But this didn't stop General Motors.[5]

That same year the mammoth company joined with the Omnibus Corporation—whose chairman, John Ritchie, was also head of Yellow Coach—in a scheme to replace New York City's electric trolley system with buses. The switch was loudly endorsed by Mayor Fiorello H. LaGuardia, who viewed streetcars as hopelessly "antiquated." The conversion of Manhattan was largely accomplished in an eighteen-month period, despite a hue and cry among the riders.

In 1936, a combination of General Motors parts suppliers, Standard Oil of California, and Firestone Tire and Rubber formed a company called National City Lines. Two years later, National City Lines spun off an affiliate called Pacific City Lines and proceeded to buy and dismantle streetcar systems in San Jose, Stockton, and Fresno, California. In 1943, another NCL affiliate, American City Lines, converted trolleys to buses in nineteen more cities, including Pacific Electric's "Big Red" trolley line in Los Angeles. A federal grand jury indicted GM for criminal conspiracy in the Los Angeles case in 1949, but the eventual fine of $5000 was about equal to the company's net profit on the sale of five Chevrolets. By 1950, General Motors had converted more than 100 electric streetcar lines to gasoline-powered buses.

This sordid tale of greed was finally aired in a 1974 investigation by the Senate's Subcommittee on Antitrust and Monopoly chaired by Senator Philip A. Hart. But by that time it was ancient history and the damage could not be undone. General Motors defended its actions, saying that all the buses they had sold and their aggressive deployment of capital had given mass transportation a "new lease on life" at a time when "times were hard and transportation systems were collapsing." Anyway, the question of exchanging buses for streetcars tends to obscure the greater issue. General Motors' ultimate goal was to replace public transportation with private transportation, meaning the car, and in this they triumphed. The bus was only an excuse to rip up the trolley tracks, which cluttered up the street and represented a difficult and competing technology. By the time the Hart subcommittee held its hearings, only the lowest orders of society rode city buses. Everybody else was out on the freeway.

↟

The automobile rapidly reshaped the nation's economy in ways that had strange and unforeseen repercussions. Certainly, the car was the main force behind the economic boom of the 1920s. Refitting the human habitat to accommodate the car required vast capital expenditures that translated into jobs with rising wages and business activity with soaring profits. Real estate and construction boomed as the urban outlands were carved into homesites for the new automobile commuters. Small businesses sprouted to serve the new auto culture. Even more important, the techniques of the assembly line pioneered by Henry Ford quickly spread throughout American industry, resulting in a deluge of consumer goods, everything from toasters to radios, which were bought by those workers with their rising wages and businessmen with their soaring profits. But the system was booby-trapped and it would blow up in 1929. The first signs of trouble appeared out on the farms.

The automobile revolutionized farm life, in many ways for the better. But it also destroyed farming as a culture (*agri*culture)—that is, as a body of knowledge and traditional practices—and turned it into another form of industrial production, with ruinous consequences.

Around 1900, fully one third of the U.S. population lived on small family farms. They had grown increasingly isolated from the benefits of industrial civilization. Medical care often lay beyond their reach. One-room schools could be dismally inadequate and hard to get to. A simple trip to the nearest small town might be an ordeal. Henry Ford, himself a Michigan farmboy, had farmers very much in mind when he developed the Model T, and they were among his most avid early customers. They emptied their savings accounts and forsook indoor plumbing to buy cars. The Saturday trip to town became an overnight institution all over rural America. Farmers now had regular access to a society beyond their little hill or hollow, to libraries, to popular culture, to ideas besides those in the family Bible. The car also lightened work by serving as a mobile power plant around the farm. With its driving wheel jacked up, its engine could run other machines, saw firewood, pump water. The improvements in rural life even spawned the expectation that urban working folk, oppressed by dreary factory labor and fractious tenement living, would flock to the bucolic hinterlands. In fact, the opposite happened. The mechanization of the American farm disrupted the rural economy so badly that more farmboys fled to the cities than ever before and the farm population plummeted.

In 1918, Henry Ford sold his first Fordson tractor, superior to all other early makes and models of its day, and, like the Model T, the first tractor mass-produced for "the great multitudes" of farmers. By 1929, the number of tractors in use on American farms leaped to nearly one million. The tractor was soon hitched up to an array of new and expensive accessory machines—reapers, seed drills, threshers, diskers, mowers. At the same time, having given up their horses, farmers suddenly came to depend on artificial fertilizers. What had formerly cost them a great deal of labor, mucking out stalls, collecting manure, now cost them a great deal of cash money.

What followed is a prime illustration of the principle that more is not necessarily better. Mechanized farming allowed farmers to boost their output tremendously in a very short period of time. But the demand for their commodities, the whole market structure, remained much the same as it had been before. Nor did the farmers themselves stop to rethink their economic strategy in terms of, say, product diversification and specialty crops. In fact, mechanized farming lent itself to monoculture, the growing of single crops on an ever-larger scale. Consequently, the supply of staple grains soared while the demand stayed relatively constant, and so prices plummeted. Catastrophically, the bottom fell out of American agriculture.

Meanwhile, the farmer was introduced to another new accessory: the mortgage. He suddenly needed to borrow cash each spring to buy the fertilizer that he formerly got for free, to buy pesticides to protect his monoculture crop (which could be wiped out by one kind of bug), and to purchase new mechanical equipment to increase his production to make up for the falling price of his commodities. The farmer now entered a precarious relationship with banks in which each year he literally bet the farm that he could bring in a profitable crop.

The long-term result was the death of the family farm in America, the replacement of agriculture by agribusiness. By 1940, the percentage of the population on farms fell to 23 percent, and by 1980 it had dwindled to 3 percent. In and of itself, this population shift might not have been a bad thing, but it was accompanied by another terrible cost. A way of life became simply a means of production. Human husbandry gave way to the industrial exploitation of land. Left behind was the knowledge of how to care for land, so plainly evinced in today's problems of soil erosion and in pollution from chemical pesticides and fertilizers.

The cycle of overproduction, debt, and foreclosure in the late 1920s was the first sign that accommodating a new technology like the motor vehicle in an established economy could be wildly disruptive. The farming situation would worsen in the 1930s, when cyclical droughts in the plains combined with new mechanical means of soil cultivation to produce the dust bowl, a disaster of Biblical dimensions.

⚓

The rest of the American economy soon followed the farmers into the Great Depression, and for much the same reason: the overproduction of consumer goods and the disruption of markets. By the early 1920s, it was obvious to a few of the saner individuals in the auto industry, like

Charles Nash, that they were approaching the point of market saturation, where everybody who *could* buy a car, would *have* his or her car.
By 1926, an industry survey estimated that only one third of the nation's auto dealers were making a profit. No sales gimmick could overcome the fact that the industry was now turning out far more vehicles
than it could sell. Overseas markets would not absorb all that excess
capacity. Europe had different needs, different social priorities, and car
manufacturers of its own. The rest of the world might as well have been
living in the twelfth century—no amount of salesmanship was going to
put 300 million Chinese peasants behind the wheel.

The boom of the 1920s was based not simply on the steady sales of
cars and other consumer products, but on a continual expansion of sales.
When these leveled off, the results were disastrous. The building boom
associated with the new automobile suburbs started fizzling in early
1928. There were only so many office managers, regional sales directors, and other business executives to buy those new "colonial" houses
out in Lazy Acres. The bulk of American workers toiled in the very
factories that were overproducing cars and electric waffle irons, and
even before they were laid off in the Depression, few blue-collar workers could have afforded a new house in the suburbs and a car to drive
there. They were the very ones who remained behind in the cities until
after World War II.

The huge public expenditure in paving streets and building new highways had also reached a kind of natural limit in the late twenties; the
basic infrastructure for cars was now in place. The slowdown in car and
home sales and in road-building affected suppliers down the line: steel
makers, tire makers, glassmakers, lumber companies, cement companies. The makers of smaller consumer products like waffle irons, having
adopted the assembly-line methods of Ford, also ran up against the wall
of market saturation. American industry had geared up for rates of
production that could not be justified by flattened demand.

These events led to a fundamental crisis of capital. The boom had
generated a tremendous amount of additional wealth for America's
upper classes. This surplus money sought an outlet in investment,
meaning stocks and bonds, or interest-bearing bank accounts. Through
these avenues, the money would be put to use financing new enterprises
and expanding existing ones. At least that was the accepted theory. But

as sales of everything sagged in the late twenties, corporations quietly scrapped plans for further expansion and new equipment. Political denial, aggressive professional boosterism, and a climate of mendacity in the securities industry combined to float the illusion that the American economy was still expanding. The money that went into the stock market accumulated paper profits and inflated the stocks of companies that could no longer rationally grow. The banks, with no one coming for commercial loans, funneled their depositors' money into the stock market. The result was the runaway bull market of the late 1920s, a fantastic spiral into casino-style unreality that climaxed in the Black Friday crash of October 13th, 1929.

‡

Despite the onset of the Great Depression, the automobile remained an irresistible force in American life. The transformation of the landscape continued. Some Americans were willing to give up their homes before they sold off their cars. Indeed, the car was often the best means for getting away from home and resettling elsewhere—as it was for the Okies who left their dust-blown farms in "rolling junks" and set out for California. To them, the car was more than a symbol of freedom; it embodied the elemental need of living creatures to flee adversity and seek a new home where they might thrive. And many did thrive. After their travails in the pea fields of the Central Valley, the deracinated midwesterners discovered that Southern California had much to recommend it—for instance, two new industries with a future: oil and motion pictures. And since the car was the instrument of their deliverance to this promised land, it is little wonder that these newcomers to Los Angeles and their descendants enshrined it as an object of near-religious worship in the years ahead.

Back East, where most Americans still lived, the car was regarded as a means of "recovery." The 1920s boom had cemented the idea in the American psyche that the best economy was an explosive technocentric economy. The Depression lured a few young intellectuals into the Marxist salons, but on the whole, Americans dreamed of a return to robust private enterprise. Even in the midst of hard times, one piece of the economic equation had not changed for America: Gasoline was still cheap. While production of new cars sagged during the 1930s, many used cars remained in service. So a culture based on driving could be maintained with the equipment on hand, even if an economy based on the sales of cars was temporarily on the rocks.

While all other sectors of the economy were grinding to a halt, highway building went on at nearly full tilt. Between 1933 and 1940, federal relief agencies poured $4 billion into roads and streets. It was a great way to put people to work and get visible results. No one was better at getting highways built than Robert Moses.

He wasn't a national political figure, but the chief of a series of New York state agencies and quasigovernmental "authorities" that he virtually created himself. The projects Robert Moses built set the pattern for imposing the automobile on cities all over America, and for destroying the countryside that surrounded cities. Moses was in power, in one office or another, for over forty years, from the 1920s to the 1960s, crucial years when American life was completely reshaped. Often referred to as the "master builder" of his age, his true genius lay in administration, and it was quite an evil genius. His career is worth a look.[6]

Born in 1888 to a wealthy New York mercantile family, Moses went to Yale and then to Oxford, where he studied the arcana of public administration. He served as democratic Governor Alfred E. Smith's personal boy wonder during the 1920s—though later Moses would run for governor himself as a Republican. Smith appointed Moses Long Island Parks Commissioner in 1924. Long Island then—a year before publication of The Great Gatsby—was rural and lovely, the abode of farmers, fishermen, and also dozens of industrial millionaires, whose estates made a broad patchwork along the island's north shore. Moses saw the political hay to be made by opening up Long Island as a playground to middle-class city dwellers, with their new funds of leisure, and he believed that the car, not the train or the interurban trolley, was the ideal instrument to do this. He had big plans for these cars, but little thought for the long-term consequences of his plans; scant vision of what the landscape would become, only dreams of his marvelous highways arcing across the landscape. Indeed, Long Island would become the prototypical landscape of highways and their accessories, while both the farms and the millionaires' estates were bulldozed into parking lots.

Before the Depression, Moses had built the Southern State Parkway from the city out to Jones Beach. Here he learned how to seize land by eminent domain, to use commission lawyers to confound his opponents in the courts, and to exploit the press to slander opponents—a habit that backfired badly the one time he ran for public office and got drubbed by Herbert Lehman in 1934. Moses also learned the trick of misleading the state legislature to get his projects underway. He called it "stake driving." He would grossly underestimate the cost of a project to get it underway fast. Then he'd blackmail politicians into funding the rest, saying that their ignorance about the real cost of the project made them derelict in their duty and unfit for office.

At the height of the Depression, Moses became head of the Triborough Bridge and Tunnel Authority, where his peculiar gifts came into full flower. An "authority" was a hoary old device out of British law that Moses had discovered as a public administration student at Oxford. To raise funds an authority could issue bonds, just like a government or a widget company. Once a project like the Triborough Bridge was completed, the tolls it produced went solely into the authority's coffers, like corporate profits, making Moses's power base financially independent of the city and the state. And once Moses flim-flamed the state legislature into voting for the Bridge and Tunnel Authority, he was untouchable. He had personally crafted a quasigovernmental body that operated like a private corporation and didn't have to answer to any government. He wrote clauses in its charter exempting his decisions from higher review.

Because Moses hadn't been voted into office, the voters couldn't remove him. Nor could the mayor or governor oust him once he was in office; only his "independent" hand-picked board could do that. It was Soviet-style politics minus the Leninist ideology.

Moses's only ideology was to get highways, bridges, and tunnels built. This happened to jibe nicely with the Roosevelt administration's efforts to battle the Depression with highway construction projects. Never mind the fact that FDR had learned, during his years as New York's governor, to loathe Robert Moses; federal relief money was always available for Moses's projects because they put people to work. These projects, for example, received one seventh of the total U.S. allocation of WPA funds in 1936.

The building of motor highways was a new field of human enterprise in the 1930s, but even as its mysteries were unraveled in practice,

Moses liked to ignore the more unpleasant newly discovered facts. Among the most crucial of these was the principle of traffic generation, the mathematical rule that any highway built to alleviate congestion on an earlier existing road, would only succeed in generating a larger aggregate amount of traffic for all roads. This rule was proven time and again with every one of Robert Moses's bridges and highways.

Throughout his career, Moses showed a strange enmity for railroad trains and mass transit. He didn't seem very fond of buses either, since he took pains, on his earliest highways out on Long Island, to design overpasses only eleven feet above grade, knowing full well that this would prevent buses from using the roads. But it was toward trains that Moses behaved most irrationally and with particular contempt for the public interest. It helps to understand the numbers involved. A basic formula of traffic engineering states that one lane of limited-access highway can accommodate 2500 cars per hour, while one lane of light rail can accommodate 40,000 passengers per hour. Cars on Long Island carry an average of 1.1 persons.

When Moses built the Van Wyck expressway through Queens to Idlewild (now Kennedy) Airport, city engineers begged him to include a mass transit right-of-way either along the center median or along the side of the new highway. They didn't ask him to lay tracks, only to make provision for some future need. Besides the airline patrons who had to get to the airport, thousands of workers had to get out there every day, and the numbers were only bound to increase. Moses said no mass transit, even though the added cost would have been marginal, and that was the end of it. There was no appeal from a Moses decision.

He did it again twenty years later on the Long Island Expressway. Before construction was to start, the state of New York hired an engineering firm, Day and Zimmerman, to study the feasibility of adding a mass transit line along the road's right-of-way. Moses was so alarmed at the prospect of trains cluttering up his highway that he ordered construction to start before the report could be issued, borrowing $20 million from the Triborough Authority's slush fund to do so. By the time Day and Zimmerman issued their report—which, of course, recommended the addition of a rail line—the subject was moot because to incorporate it would now require the demolition of the work already completed.

Lee Koppleman, in his youth a top Moses aide and for many years after, until 1990, the chief planner for Nassau and Suffolk counties, Long Island, advanced an explanation for Moses's behavior. "Moses was a product of the 1920s," Koppleman said. "His entire orientation was anti mass transit because the early twentieth century was the age of the automobile as the nineteenth century was the age of rail. Personalized door-to-door service, that was the idea. The federal government turned its back on the railroads, and they set the tone. For the professionals who worked for Moses, mass transit was always a bottomless pit. Mass transit does not produce a profit. It is a social good, but a financial loser. They didn't want to touch it with a ten-foot pole. And to the extent that they could be autocratic and avoid it, that's exactly what they did. So there was no incorporation of mass transit in the design of [the Long Island Expressway]."[7]

The end of World War II found Moses at his most glorious and most dangerous period. "The postwar highway era is here!" he proclaimed in 1945 with a zeal that seems rather fiendish in hindsight. During the period from 1945 to 1960, agencies controlled by Moses spent $4.5 billion, none of it on mass transit. During the 1950s, Moses had more money to spend on public works than the entire City of New York, and nobody could tell him how to spend it. The tolls on his bridges and tunnels raised huge sums of money; by 1968, his Triborough Bridge and Tunnel Authority was running an annual surplus of $30 million—at the same time that every suburban railroad line was either bankrupt or teetering on the brink. His Cross Bronx Expressway all but destroyed the life of the borough. It is estimated that during his career Moses caused a quarter of a million people to be evicted from their homes to make way for his highways. When he began his career, Long Island was rural. When he retired in 1968, it was a parking lot. His expertise at building—at "getting things done," as he liked to put it—was divorced from a realistic notion of consequences. The *idea* of the automobile intoxicated him and spurred his quest for power. But aside from a few lessons in the early 1920s, the man never drove a car.

↑

The Great Depression shocked the nation the way the First World War had shocked Europe, rattling America's basic assumptions about its economic life—for instance, Say's Law of Markets, a proposition that had ruled American economic thinking for more than a century. This historic dictum stated that the production of goods would automatically stimulate enough demand to buy those goods: that a market was assured for all that was produced. Say's Law clearly failed in the late 1920s, when Henry Ford's assembly-line techniques had altered the terms of production. The system of individual enterprise that made America so optimistic and successful during the nineteenth century had evolved into a corporate industrial juggernaut, prone to fabulous booms and cataclysmic busts—in either case an enterprise destructive of lives, cultural traditions, and the physical setting of life whether city, town, farm, or forest.

And yet, perhaps because they occurred so rapidly, these changes failed to register at a deeper psychological level, that of cultural myth—the ongoing story a people tell themselves to understand who they are. Americans still liked to think of themselves as rugged individualists, as pioneers out on the frontier, no matter how many of them really worked as factory slaves or office drones. The crisis of the Depression did little to alter this. The 1920s joyride was still a fresh memory, and not every fortune had been lost in the crash. Collectivism, of the kind practiced in Russia, would have been out of the question for people of such a character. So, rather than scrap an economic system that had caused so much grief, America strove to get it going again on an even grander scale than before, to base it on that myth of rugged individualism, of every spot welder and assistant regional sales manager bethinking himself a pioneer out on some woolly frontier, and to sell the whole package as the American Dream. The true frontier was still the frontier of personal success in business, and what better business was there in a nation of cheap land and cheap transportation than the land development business?

The Dream, more specifically, was a detached home on a sacred plot of earth in a rural setting, unbesmirched by the industry that made the home possible; a place where one could play at cultivating the soil without having to rely on husbandry for a livelihood; a place that was, most of all, not the city. This would be the new covenant between the people and its government, a reason not to overthrow it. Of all industries during the Depression, the building trades were hardest hit. Helping them out on a more or less permanent basis would lead to a more or less permanent prosperity—or so went the advanced thinking of the day.

In the years immediately following the stock market crash of 1929, home building fell by 95 percent. Repairs on existing homes all but ceased. Bankruptcies and foreclosures shot up until, in the spring of 1933, half the home mortgages in the United States were technically in default.[8] The Roosevelt administration stepped into the crisis with a new creation called the Federal Housing Administration (FHA). The express purpose of the act was to put construction workers back to work by building homes. The corollary gain would be new and better housing for the multitudes.

It worked like this: The banks would still make the mortgage loans, but now the federal treasury, through the FHA, would guarantee them. The government guarantee reduced the risk on the part of lenders, which resulted in lower interest rates for borrowers. Before the Depression, ten years was considered a long-term mortgage, and a 30 to 50 percent down payment was normal. Under the rules of the new FHA, mortgages were extended to twenty, even thirty years so that, in theory, a sober citizen could stretch out house payments over most of his working life. The down payment was also reduced to 10 percent. This radically transformed home ownership in America.

The FHA set standards for the kind of house that could qualify for one of their guaranteed mortgages. Not surprisingly, these turned out to be new houses, the ones being built by those construction workers called back on the payroll. These new houses tended to be located outside the dense cities, because during the Depression vacant land on the periphery was very cheap. The kinds of houses that the FHA frowned upon were those in the cities: old houses with leaky plumbing, jammed into narrow lots on crowded streets, inhabited in some cases by immigrants or, increasingly, African-Americans. Houses like these were losers from the FHA point of view and the agency wouldn't guarantee mortgages on them. Worse, the evaluation policy tended to disqualify whole neighborhoods, in effect to draw a line around them on the map and say, "Don't even think of buying here because this part of town is heading down the tubes, and we don't back losers." The process came to be called *red-lining*. It had self-fulfilling consequences.

The FHA program thus overwhelmingly favored single-family detached homes in the suburbs. In the thirties, these new suburbs were only a few miles out of town, a short drive, and gas was cheap—the price of everything fell during the Depression. A serviceable car could be bought for a few hundred dollars. Commuting might not be an economic obstacle for a citizen fortunate enough to be employed.

If measured by new house construction, the program was a success, though it did not propel the nation into another great boom à la the twenties. Housing starts rose from nearly none at the depth of the Depression to well over half a million on the eve of World War II. But throughout the 1930s grave structural problems remained in the economy. Unemployment stayed stubbornly high. Nobody had solved the problem of excess capacity, of large-scale manufacturing's tendency to crank out more toasters, hair curlers, washing machines, or Ford Model A coupes than people could hope to buy, or the destabilizing effect this tendency would have on the basic organizing principles of capital enterprise. The nation had still not crawled out of Depression's shadow when the Japanese bombed Pearl Harbor.

↥

The war economy was, of course, completely abnormal. The nation's dormant industrial capacity was suddenly cranked up full bore and directed toward the single task of defeating the enemy. Factories quickly retooled to produce war products—jeeps, tanks, airplanes, uniforms, helmets, parachutes, et cetera—for which the government was sole customer. (William S. Knudsen, President of General Motors, became the government's Director of War Production.) The effort might have bankrupted the United States had it not been for our extraordinary insulation from the war's vicissitudes. As in the First World War, the action all took place elsewhere, with no damage to the physical plant back home. Equally important, America produced its own petroleum—then the world's largest developed supply—and our wells and refineries remained intact.

By contrast, at war's end the other industrialized nations, including the victors England, France, and Russia, lay ruined or significantly disabled. With the rest of the world economically crippled, the United States was finally able to solve its problem of excess industrial capacity.

We jump-started the economies of Europe and Japan, and loaned them money to buy our tools and machines, with the reasonable expectation that, once revived, they would buy more stuff from us. At home, America redirected its economic energies to what it barely had begun before war broke out: the Great Enterprise of emptying the old cities and building a substitute of far-flung auto suburbs.

American GIs returned from Europe and the Pacific to a severe housing shortage. The war had put residential construction back into a coma. Sixteen years of depression and war were also hard on city housing. A lot of it was not very nice to begin with, and the FHA didn't want to subsidize its improvement. The years of neglect showed. Black migrants from the rural South, displaced by the new mechanical cotton picker, began to migrate to northern cities at a great rate. They were poor, uneducated, and rustic in culture. And they were hardly in a position to buy city properties and improve them without assistance. Whites who could afford to get out, fled, and before long this included most whites, because the government made their flight affordable via mortgage guarantees. Blacks could not flee even if they could afford a house in the suburbs, because in most places developers wouldn't sell to them.

Beyond race politics, an idea prevailed that since the United States had endured a long, traumatic depression, and had then so decisively won a huge war against manifest evil, its heroic citizens deserved a reward in the way of nice new things. A little house with a picket fence topped the wish list. At the war's end, Congress added another program of easy mortgages under the Veterans Administration (VA) on top of beefed-up FHA appropriations. These now made it possible for many qualified buyers to purchase a suburban house with no down payment. In each of the years between 1947 and 1957 the percentage of houses sold with FHA or VA mortgages ranged from just under 40 percent to over 50 percent. These immense market subsidies spurred a housing industry that had learned the mass-production techniques of Ford and General Motors.

A developer like William Levitt could whack together 150 houses a day in the potato fields of central Long Island, using a production system of specialized work crews and prefab components, until more than 17,000 nearly identical four-room "Cape Cod" boxes stood in Levittown, as the agglomeration was named. Levitt made buying a house so easy that you could sleepwalk into ownership, eliminating even closing costs. Classes of citizens formerly shut out of suburban home ownership could now join the migration, in particular blue-collar workers and young marrieds. The monthly mortgage payment for a new suburban house was commonly less than rent on a city apartment, or the cost of maintaining an older city house. Under the new federal income tax rules, mortgage interest became deductible, another whopping subsidy for prospective homeowners. The American Dream of a cottage on its own sacred plot of earth was finally the *only* economically rational choice.

By the time the merchant builders like Levitt and his kindred spirits got through packaging it, however, it was less a dream than a cruel parody. The place where the dream house stood—a subdivision of many other identical dream houses—was neither the country nor the city. It was noplace. If anything, it combined the worst social elements of the city and country and none of the best elements. As in the real country, everything was spread out and hard to get to without a car. There were no cultural institutions. And yet like the city, the suburb afforded no escape from other people into nature; except for some totemic trees and shrubs, nature had been obliterated by the relentless blocks full of houses.

But whatever its shortcomings as a place to live, the suburban subdivision was unquestionably a successful product. For many, it was a vast improvement over what they were used to. The houses were spacious compared to city dwellings, and they contained modern conveniences. Air, light, and a modicum of greenery came with the package. The main problem with it was that it dispensed with all the traditional connections and continuities of community life, and replaced them with little more than cars and television.

By the early 1950s, the government's strategy of subsidizing the building trades and promoting the auto industry and its dependencies as a way to drive the economy seemed to be paying off. The creation of a suburban culture and all its trappings, along with our fortunate position vis-à-vis other nations, augured an era of boundless prosperity, security, comfort, and ease. It is no wonder that the pop culture artifacts of that day—the movies, early TV shows, and magazines—reflect a smug uncritical optimism about American life that seems rather cretinous now—Mom, Dad (puffing on pipe), Skippy, and Sis driving up the parkway in the new DeSoto to look at the new model homes out in Lazy Acres.

The auto industry boomed like never before. Many people had nursed old junkers all the way through the Depression and the big makers had not turned out any cars for the civilian market during the war years. But at the war's end, easy credit terms released tremendous pent-up demand, car sales soared, and the automobile entered its high Baroque age. I'll pass over the questions of styling and merchandising that adumbrate the American-Love-Affair-with-the-Car myth, except to suggest that if Americans loved their cars, perhaps it was because the machines allowed them to escape from reality—which raises the more interesting question: Why did America build a reality of terrible places from which people longed to escape?

By the mid-fifties, the Great Enterprise of suburban expansion began to run up against apparent limits to its growth. Existing highways could not accept ever-greater volumes of traffic if the build-out continued apace. But if the build-out stopped, the whole economy would nose-dive again, since it now *was* the economy. Using public works as an economic pump-primer was no longer a partisan political issue, as in the days of Franklin Roosevelt, for now both parties understood the stakes. The solution to the looming crisis was the interstate highway system.

The idea was to build a brand-new national network of uniform four-lane limited-access expressways that would eliminate the bottlenecks in the old hodge-podge of state roads, highways, and parkways. An irresistible coalition of lobbying interests—the combined might of the auto, trucking, oil, tire, asphalt, cement, steel, lumber, and construction industries, and their unions—got behind the idea and commenced a lavish campaign to promote it. In 1954, President Dwight Eisenhower appointed a committee to study the matter. It was no surprise when the committee's report enthusiastically endorsed a massive investment in the superhighway scheme—the commission chairman, Lucius D. Clay, happened to be on the board of directors of General Motors. In 1956, Congress approved the Interstate Highway Act. It was passed none too soon, for the fabulous postwar economy was about to slide into recession.

The package called for 41,000 miles of new expressways, with the federal government picking up 90 percent of the tab and the states 10 percent. It proposed to link up most cities with more than 50,000 inhabitants, and included circumferential "beltways" around the largest. The bill also heavily subsidized the improvement (read, widening) of innumerable ordinary local roads to facilitate further suburban sprawl. The chief political justification was that the new expressways would ease the evacuation of cities during a nuclear attack.

The program gave the Great Enterprise of suburban expansion a bright new horizon and the American economy boomed during the 1960s, even though the government was prosecuting a major war in Vietnam. The construction of the interstate highway system was itself an undertaking of unprecedented scope. It kept hundreds of thousands employed at all levels, from laborers to engineers. It devoured as much steel and concrete each year as a hundred cities. It required armadas of colossal earth-moving machines. It was simply the largest public-works project in the history of the world.

The new superhighways created tremendous opportunities for land development in the remote hinterlands of big cities. An unthinkably long commute on old country roads now seemed reasonable on the freeway. So up went more raised ranches and the new split-levels. Each of the thousands of new highway interchanges begged for commercial exploitation. Up went shopping strips and the new "convenience" stores. Businesses of all descriptions fled the decaying urban cores and relocated on the fringe, as close to the on/off ramps as they could get.

The cities, of course, went completely to hell. The superhighways not only drained them of their few remaining taxpaying residents, but in many cases the new beltways became physical barriers, "Chinese walls" sealing off the disintegrating cities from their dynamic outlands. Those left behind inside the wall would develop, in their physical isolation from the suburban economy, a pathological ghetto culture.

The distinction between the booming economy and what that boom yielded can't be stressed enough. The great suburban build-out generated huge volumes of business. The farther apart things spread, the more cars were needed to link up the separate things, the more asphalt and cement were needed for roads, bridges, and parking lots, the more copper for electric cables, et cetera. Each individual suburban house required its own washing machine, lawnmower, water meter, several television sets, telephones, air conditioners, swimming pools, you name it. Certainly, many Americans became wealthy selling these things, while many more enjoyed good steady pay manufacturing them. In a culture with no other values, this could easily be construed as a good thing. Indeed, the relentless expansion of consumer goodies became increasingly identified with our national character as the American Way of Life. Yet not everyone failed to notice that the end product of all this furious commerce-for-its-own-sake was a trashy and preposterous human habitat with no future.

The Aquarian uproar of the late sixties was largely a reaction to this crisis of cultural values and the sense of doom it induced. A generation came of age and realized with a rude shock that there was something very wrong with the creeping-crud economy they had grown up with, with its voracious appetite for natural resources, its tawdry material rewards, its lamebrained notion of the Good Life, and ultimately its dreadful heedlessness of long-term costs. In rejecting it, these aptly named counterculture folk attempted a return to tribalism in order to recapture a sense of human continuities in their everyday surroundings. But the movement found its most vehement expression in the Vietnam War protests—the war being a violent projection overseas of what was most unwholesome and destructive in our national life—and when the war came to its long-delayed conclusion, it proved a practical impossibility to exist in an alternative culture—or alternate economy—within the larger one, so the movement fizzled out.

Meanwhile, the Great Enterprise churned on and on. Work on the interstate highway system progressed despite the costs of the Vietnam War and by the early 1970s the system was all but completed. As expected, the new expressways promoted an ever-farther-flung suburban expansion. A new merchandising gimmick called the shopping mall began to sprout up around the highway interchanges, offering a synthetic privatized substitute for every Main Street in America. A golden age of ever-greater profit seemed to beckon . . . but then the first of the oil shocks struck: the so-called Arab Oil Embargo.

Whether any actual oil shortage existed during those autumn weeks of 1973 is arguable, but the distribution and pricing apparatus certainly went amok at the threat of one. Since World War II, America's oil use had shot up so steeply that by the seventies many old American oil fields were pumped dry, and nearly half of our petroleum was coming from overseas.

The short-term result of the embargo was a sudden near-breakdown of the whole automobile system in America. Erratic deliveries of gasoline caused localized supply shortages. Lines formed at pumps everywhere, people panicked, fistfights broke out, work schedules were disrupted, vacations were canceled, and nobody knew if the country would be able to carry on as before. A longer-term result was the rising cost of practically everything, otherwise known as inflation, since the price of all commodities and goods were linked, through manufacturing or distribution, to the price of oil. The oil shock also temporarily discouraged more migration to the new outer limits of the urban fringe. For instance, the trip from Mira Loma to downtown Los Angeles might take only fifty minutes, but who was crazy enough to move that far when an Arab cartel could shut the oil spigot any time they pleased? In short, the Great Enterprise of continued suburban expansion suddenly lost its plausibility. And the whole economy went to hell—in a strange new way.

Economists scratched their heads as though it was the world's most baffling math problem. Inflation, they reasoned, was generally the result of an overheated economy, not a stagnant one. How could this be? Finally, they pronounced the mess "stagflation." President Nixon was too preoccupied with the scandal that would drive him from office to face effectively the questions raised by the Arab Oil Embargo. Under his successor, Gerald Ford, high oil prices shoved the economy into the worst recession in thirty years, and Ford's accidental administration was shown the door. Along came President Jimmy Carter. The oil cartel inflicted a second oil price hike on the United States during his single term, and it led to another round of inflation and stagnation. Carter told Americans the truth and they hated him for it. He declared the "moral equivalent of war" on our oil addiction, and diagnosed the nation's spiritual condition as a "malaise," suggesting, in his Sunday school manner, that the nation had better gird its loins and start to behave less foolishly concerning petroleum. The nation responded by tossing Mr. Carter out of office and replaced him with a movie actor who promised to restore the Great Enterprise to all its former glory, whatever the costs.

Aside from being nearly killed by an assassin early in his first term, Ronald Reagan was the luckiest President of the century. The oil cartel fell apart while he was in office without America's having to do a thing. Greed, desperation, and a war between Iraq and Iran that spanned both of Reagan's terms, foiled the oil cartel's ability to operate in concert and keep prices jacked up. The poorer oil nations, like Nigeria, tried to undersell the others, while the richest ones, like Saudi Arabia, could not resist the temptation to compete by overproducing, thereby glutting the market. Hence, the price of imported crude oil dropped steadily during Reagan's tenure and he abandoned the alternate-energy research programs that Carter had started.

Reagan professed to believe literally in the fundamentalist Christian doctrine that the end of the world was at hand. At the very least, this should have called into question his concern for the nation's long-term welfare. Unburdened by such mundane cares, he cast aside all restraint in the pursuit of economic "growth," and financed the next phase of suburban expansion by encouraging the greatest accumulation of debt in world history. Why worry about borrowing from the future when you don't believe in the future? His government ran up an unprecedented public debt, his securities regulators allowed corporations to borrow absurd sums by issuing high risk "junk" bonds, and personal credit was extended to any shmo who could sign his name on a retail receipt, until an alarming percentage of ordinary citizens were in hock up to their eyeballs.

Reagan's bank deregulation and tax policies promoted gigantic and unnecessary land development schemes that benefited their backers even when the schemes failed by any normal standards. This is how it worked: a developer and a bank would get together to build a shopping mall outside Denver. The bank would take enormous fees off the top of the total investment, as a reward for its participation. The development company would pay itself a large fee up front for supervising the construction. The money invested in the project would have come from federally insured bank deposits. For any number of reasons the shopping mall might fail to attract enough retail tenants, or customers—too close to other established malls, too far from population centers, whatever—and go out of business. When the tumbleweeds blew through the empty parking lot, the banker could feel perfectly secure knowing that the deposits he had thrown away on a foolish venture would be fully repaid by the U.S. Treasury; while the developer's corporation would seek protection under the bankruptcy laws, and the developer himself would hold onto his personal fortune without liability—minus, perhaps, a few thousand dollars in criminal fines and maybe a term in the slammer. Deals like this happened so many times in the eighties that the whole rotten fabric of bad loans and fraudulent ventures threatened to bankrupt the federal deposit insurance system.

Reagan's energy policy was likewise predicated on the idea that the future didn't matter. By the time he left office, America was importing more than half of its oil, and as long as the price was reasonable, why make a fuss? Meanwhile, try extracting as much petroleum as possible from American fields, wherever they might be: on national park lands, off the California coast, the Alaskan tundra.

Reagan's "voodoo economics" was a strategy to keep the game going at the expense of the future—the game being an economy based on unlimited automobile use and unrestrained land development. By the time Reagan was replaced by George Bush—who had invented the term "voodo economics" only to become its chief practitioner—the future had arrived and was calling in its notes. Major banks collapsed, largely as a result of foolish real estate ventures. Millions of square feet of office and retail space stood vacant across America. Unemployment climbed, especially in the building trades, and because of the gross overbuilding of the eighties, the government could not artificially stimulate more new construction with the same old tricks. Car sales plummeted—and anyway, half of American drivers owned foreign cars by now. In fact, most of the things that Americans bought, period, were manufactured elsewhere. The nation had entered what was being referred to as a postindustrial economy, but so far it was unclear exactly what that meant—perhaps people selling hamburgers and movie tickets at the mall to employees of other malls on their days off. This was a patent absurdity, of course, but without industries of some kind in America, the prospects for maintaining the consumer economy at the accustomed level seemed rather dim.

The known global reserves of petroleum are expected to last roughly another thirty years. This means that in the lifetimes of most Americans living today, the essential fuel that has powered the suburban-consumer way of life will no longer be available. It will not be necessary to run out of petroleum in order to fatally disrupt a petroleum-dependent economy. As the 1970s oil shocks demonstrated, all that it takes to mess things up is some instability of supply and price, and surely we will reach that stage before the wells run dry. Despite a lot of wishful thinking, and a near-religious belief in the "magic of technology," there is no alternative in sight to the internal combustion engine that the masses of motorists could afford.

In any case, by the late 1980s the Great Enterprise of an endless suburban expansion finally crashed up against the ultimate natural limit: Researchers discovered that the burning of fossil fuels was altering the earth's atmosphere so drastically that a projected "global warming" effect could melt the polar ice caps, flood low-lying areas where most of the world's population lived, and destroy world agriculture by disrupting weather patterns, all within the next sixty years.

To Americans, it must seem like a scenario from a 1950s horror movie: *The Day the Earth Caught Fire!* To contemplate it in the comfort of an air-conditioned sedan, cruising up Interstate 87, pleasured by iced drinks and packaged snacks, must add to the unreality. But the joyride is over. What remains is the question of how we can make the transition to a saner way of living. To do so will certainly require a transformation of the physical setting for our civilization, a remaking of the places where we live and work.

Chapter Seven

THE EVIL EMPIRE

Americans have been living car-centered lives for so long that the collective memory of what used to make a landscape or a townscape or even a suburb humanly rewarding has nearly been erased. The culture of good place-making, like the culture of farming, or agriculture, is a body of knowledge and acquired skills. It is not bred in the bone, and if it is not transmitted from one generation to the next, it is lost.

Does the modern profession called urban planning have anything to do with making good places anymore? Planners no longer employ the vocabulary of civic art, nor do they find the opportunity to practice it—the term civic art itself has nearly vanished in common usage. In some universities, urban-planning departments have been booted out of the architecture schools and into the schools of public administration. Not surprisingly, planners are now chiefly preoccupied with administrative procedure: issuing permits, filling out forms, and shuffling papers—in short, bureaucracy. All the true design questions such as *how wide should Elm Street be?* and *what sort of buildings should be on it?* were long ago "solved" by civil engineers and their brethren and written into the municipal zoning codes. These mechanistic "solutions" work only by oversimplifying problems and isolating them from the effect they have on the landscape and on people's behavior.

It has been established, for example, that suburban streets all over America ought to be as wide as two-lane county highways, regardless of whether this promotes driving at excessive speeds where children play, or destroys the spatial relationship between the houses on the street.

Back in the 1950s, when these formulas were devised, the width of residential streets was tied closely to the idea of a probable nuclear war with the Russians. And in the aftermath of a war, it was believed, wide streets would make it easier to clean up the mess with heavy equipment.[1]

Zoning codes devised by engineering firms have been "packaged" and sold to municipalities for decades, eliminating the need for local officials to think about local design issues. This is one reason why a subdivision in Moline, Illinois, has the same dreary look as a subdivision in Burlington, Vermont. All the design matters are supposedly settled, and there has been little intelligent debate about them for years. At the layman's level the principles of good town-making are probably as obscure as the religious ideas of the Toltecs.

America has now squandered its national wealth erecting a human habitat that, in all likelihood, will not be usable very much longer, and there are few unspoiled places left to retreat to in the nation's habitable reaches. Aside from its enormous social costs, which we have largely ignored, the whole system of suburban sprawl is too expensive to operate, too costly to maintain, and a threat to the ecology of living things. To lose it is tragic not because Americans will be deprived of such wonderful conveniences as K Marts and drive-in churches—we can get along happily without them—but because it was a foolish waste of resources in the first place, and it remains to be seen whether its components can be recycled, converted to other uses, or moved, or even whether the land beneath all the asphalt, concrete, and plastic, can be salvaged. In the meantime, Americans are doing almost nothing to prepare for the end of the romantic dream that was the American automobile age.

⚑

This is a good place to consider in some detail why the automobile suburb is such a terrible pattern for human ecology. In almost all communities designed since 1950, it is a practical impossibility to go about the ordinary business of living without a car. This at once disables children under the legal driving age, some elderly people, and those who cannot afford the several thousand dollars a year that it costs to keep a car, including monthly payments, insurance, gas, and repairs. This produces two separate classes of citizens: those who can fully use their everyday environment, and those who cannot.

Children are certainly the biggest losers—though the suburbs have been touted endlessly as wonderful places for them to grow up. The elderly, at least, have seen something of the world, and know that there is more to it than a housing subdivision. Children are stuck in that one-dimensional world. When they venture beyond it in search of richer experience, they do so at some hazard. More usually, they must be driven about, which impairs their developing sense of personal sovereignty, and turns the parent—usually Mom—into a chauffeur.

The one place outside the subdivision where children are compelled to go is school. They take buses there—a public transit system that operates at huge expense, is restricted to children, and runs only twice a day. Even if children happen to live relatively close to school, there is good chance that it would not be safe for them to travel there on foot or by bicycle. This is because the detailing of the streets is so abysmal. By detailing, I mean all the big and little design considerations, including the basic dimensions, that make for good relationships between the things along the street, between the things that streets are supposed to connect, and between people's different uses, as, say, between motorists and pedestrians. For example: what are the building setbacks? Can cars legally park alongside the street? Will there be sidewalks, trees, benches where people can rest or simply enjoy the public realm? Will there be lighting, trash baskets, plantings, et cetera?

The suburban streets of almost all postwar housing developments were designed so that a car can comfortably maneuver at fifty miles per hour—no matter what the legal speed limit is. The width and curb ratios were set in stone by traffic engineers who wanted to create streets *so* ultrasafe (for motorists) that any moron could drive them without wrecking his car. This is a good example of the folly of professional overspecialization. The traffic engineer is not concerned about the pedestrians. His mission is to make sure that wheeled vehicles are happy. What he deems to be ultrasafe for drivers can be dangerous for pedestrians who share the street with cars. Anybody knows that a child of eight walking home from school at three o'clock in the afternoon uses a street differently than a forty-six-year-old carpet cleaner in a panel truck.

Most citizens do not drive as fast as the subdivision streets might physically permit, but some drive faster than the legal limit, say twenty-five miles per hour. It is easy to do. The scale of the street is so immense that, at twenty-five, a motorist hardly feels he is moving. Suburban streets commonly lack sidewalks. Each lot is so large—perhaps 100 feet of frontage—that installing a sidewalk would entail considerable expense for the homebuyer. Besides, it would be a contribution to the public realm, which has little value in our culture; the $3000 would be better spent on a vinyl swimming pool in the back yard, which is to say in the private realm. Moreover, jurisdictional disputes might arise over the future maintenance of the sidewalks: should the community pay for their upkeep? And how do we raise the taxes to do this? Instead of addressing these questions, suburbanites have taken the easy way out and decided that there will be no sidewalks, period. So, children walk or ride their bikes in the same space as an equal number of 4000 pound steel projectiles traveling in excess of twenty-five miles per hour.

Suburban streets invariably debouch into collector roads—that is, two-lane or four-lane highways. Somewhere along the collector road is the place where a school is apt to be located. If the housing developments in the area have been in place for more than ten years, then it is likely that the collector roads will have accumulated a hodge-podge of businesses: little shopping plazas, convenience stores, muffler shops, plus a full complement of fast-food emporiums. The hamburger and pizza chain shops are magnets for children. So the kids are out on the collector road, having skipped the bus home in order to get some pizza.

Here there is no pretense of being in a place for pedestrians. The motorist is in sole possession of the road. No cars are parked along the edge of the road to act as a buffer because they would clutter up a lane that might otherwise be used by moving traffic, and anyway, each business has its own individual parking lagoon. Each lagoon has a curb cut, or two, which behaves in practice like an intersection, with cars entering and leaving at a right angle to the stream of traffic, greatly increasing the possibility of trouble. There are no sidewalks out here along the collector road for many of the same reasons as back in the housing development—too expensive, and who will maintain them?—plus the assumption that nobody in their right mind would ever come here on foot.

Of course, one could scarcely conceive of an environment more hostile to pedestrians. It is a terrible place to be, offering no sensual or spiritual rewards. In fact, the overall ambience is one of assault on the senses. No one who could avoid it would *want* to be on foot on a typical collector road. Any adult between eighteen and sixty-five walking along one would instantly fall under suspicion of being less than a good citizen.

The two elements of the suburban pattern that cause the greatest problems are the extreme separation of uses and the vast distances between things. The idea behind the separation of uses had its origin in the nineteenth century, when industrial activity became an obnoxious nuisance to city dwellers. The first zoning codes explicitly sought to protect the property values of residential neighborhoods against such incursions. So industry was led off and given its own part of town in which to be dirty and noisy. With the advent of the car, shopping became a more or less mechanized activity—motor vehicles generated noise and fumes and cluttered up the street—so there began a trend to separate commerce from places of dwelling too. Today, of course, the idea has been carried to absurd extremes. This is why there are no corner stores in housing subdivisions, though the lack of them is a great inconvenience to anyone who would like to buy a morning newspaper or a quart of milk without driving across town. The separation of uses is also the reason why there are no apartments over the stores in the thousands of big and little shopping centers built since 1945, though our society desperately needs cheap, decent housing for those who are not rich.

The ultimate way to protect property values under this regime is to zone wealthier neighborhoods against the incursion of those with less money who are apt to build less grand houses. So today it is common for zoning codes to dictate that houses in a given neighborhood must be single-family dwellings and no smaller than, say, 3000 square feet. Since such a house cannot be built for less than half a million dollars, the neighborhood will be restricted to only those persons in a high income bracket. Garage apartments, or any similar auxiliary use that would attract other kinds of people, are strictly forbidden. There is not even any place for the gardeners and housekeepers who work there to live—which leads to the sort of obscene spectacle as the daily exodus of Mexican maids and yard workers out of Beverly Hills every day at five o'clock as they trudge down the canyon roads to the bus lines in Hollywood. This segregation by income group extends downward, with each group successively outlawing those in the groups below them, until we arrive at the level of public housing, which no suburban towns want to have within their limits, and which are therefore relegated to the decrepitating inner cities, where property values can't get any lower.

Today, we have achieved the goal of total separation of uses in the man-made landscape. The houses are all in their respective income pods, the shopping is miles away from the houses, and the schools are separate from both the shopping and the dwellings. Work takes place in the office park—the word *park* being a semantic gimmick to persuade zoning boards that a bunch of concrete and glass boxes set among parking lots amounts to a rewarding environment—and manufacturing takes place in the industrial park—ditto. This has some interesting, and rather grave, ramifications.

The amount of driving necessary to exist within this system is stupendous, and fantastically expensive. The time squandered by commuters is time that they cannot spend with their children, or going to the library, or playing the clarinet, or getting exercise, or doing anything else more spiritually nourishing than sitting alone in a steel compartment on Highway 101 with 40,000 other stalled commuters. Anybody who commutes an hour a day in each direction spends seven weeks of the year sitting in his car.

The costs of all this driving in terms of pollution, which includes everything from increased lung diseases all the way up to global warming, are beyond calculation. The cost to society in terms of money spent building and maintaining roads and paying for traffic police, courts, accidents, insurance, is also titanic. The least understood cost—although probably the most keenly felt—has been the sacrifice of a sense of place: the idea that people and things exist in some sort of continuity, that we belong to the world physically and chronologically, and that we know where we are.

The extreme separation and dispersion of components that use to add up to a compact town, where everything was within a ten-minute walk, has left us with a public realm that is composed mainly of roads. And the only way to be in that public realm is to be in a car, often alone. The present arrangement has certainly done away with sacred places, places of casual public assembly, and places of repose. Otherwise, there remain only the shopping plazas, the supermarkets, and the malls. Now, American supermarkets are not designed to function like Parisian cafés. There is no seating, no table service. They do not encourage customers to linger. Yet some shoppers will spend as much time as their dignity affords haunting the supermarket aisles because it is practically the *only* place where they can be in the public realm and engage in some purposeful activity around other live human beings. Here they even stand the chance of running into someone they know. A suburbanite could stand on her front lawn for three hours on a weekday afternoon and never have a chance for a conversation.

This vacuum at the center of American life led to the phenomenon of shopping malls. Of course, the concept of a marketplace was hardly new, and large marketplaces under a roof have existed in history too. But the marketplace had always been a public space, part of the fabric of the town, usually at the heart of it, existing in continuity with the rest of town life. By the 1970s, when malls started to multiply across the land, the public realm had been pretty much eliminated from the American scene. Yet that hunger for public life remained. The mall commercialized the public realm, just as the insurance business commercialized fate. What had existed before in an organic state as Main Street, downtown shopping districts, town squares, hotel lobbies, public gardens, saloons, museums, churches, was now standardized, simplified, sanitized, packaged, and relocated on the suburban fringe in the form of a mall. Well, what was so bad about that?

Quite a number of things, actually. For one, the mall existed in isolation, connected to everything else only via the road, and the road was often the type of multilane highway that a pedestrian or bicycle rider might use only at peril—in short, you needed a car to get there. People without cars were just out of luck. It was ironic too, because one reason that people flock to malls was that, once inside, they didn't have to look at all the goddam cars and be reminded of what a depressing environment they lived in.

For another thing, the mall wasn't really a public space. It was a private space masquerading as a public space. Sure, people were free to come and go (during shopping hours), and they were not charged an admission fee to enter, but in reality, they were the guests of the Acme Development Company, or whoever owned the mall. The developer was also entitled to control all the activities that went on inside the mall. This meant no free speech, no right of assembly. In a nation as politically complacent as the United States in the 1970s and '80s, this might seem trivial. But imagine if America got involved in another war as unpopular as Vietnam, and the political temperature rose. Or if our dependence on cheap oil started to cause political problems. Acme Development might not be so tolerant about political rallies held around their philodendron beds, or protest marchers interfering with sales at the Pet-O-Rama shop. Where, then, are you going to have your public assembly? On the median strip of Interstate 87?

Thirdly, the real Main Streets of America developed organically over time, and included both the new and the old, the high rent and low rent. Out at the mall, all rents were necessarily high because of the high cost of construction, maintenance, heat, and air conditioning. The only merchants who could afford such rents, it turned out, were the large chain-store operations—the Radio Shacks, the Gaps, the Footlockers—who had the financial muscle and the proven sales volume to enter into long-term leases. Invariably, these chain stores destroyed local businesses outside the mall, and in so doing they destroyed local economies. The chain stores' profits were funneled to corporate headquarters far away. The chains gave back nothing to the locality except a handful of low-wage service jobs. Since the people who worked in the mall stores were not the owners of the stores, they did not have a long-term stake in their success or failure, and so they had limited incentives to provide good service.

It remains to be seen how the shopping malls of America might evolve over time. The conditions under which they flourished—cheap energy, cars for everyone, a credit-driven consumer economy, special tax breaks for big real estate ventures—may be viewed as abnormal and transitory, a fragile equation that could fall apart like a house of cards if any of the factors changed—for example, if gasoline prices go up enough to erase the profit margins of mass retailers; or if citizens have to establish credit-worthiness before banks issue them charge cards; or if more banks themselves fail. Only one thing is certain: The malls will not be new forever. And none of them were built for the ages.

✦

The public realm suffered in another way with the rise of the automobile. Because the highways were gold-plated with our national wealth, all other forms of public building were impoverished. This is the reason why every town hall built after 1950 is a concrete-block shed full of cheap paneling and plastic furniture, why public schools look like overgrown gas stations, why courthouses, firehouses, halls of records, libraries, museums, post offices, and other civic monuments are indistinguishable from bottling plants and cold-storage warehouses. The dogmas of Modernism only helped rationalize what the car economy demanded: bare bones buildings that served their basic functions without symbolically expressing any aspirations or civic virtues.

The Greek Revival merchants' exchanges and courthouses of the early 1800s symbolically expressed a hopeful view of democracy, a sense of pride and confidence in the future, and significant public expense went into that expression. Public buildings such as the Philadelphia water works or Jefferson's Virginia state capitol at Richmond were expected to endure for generations, perhaps centuries, as the Greek temples had endured since antiquity. These earlier American building types were set in a different landscape, characterized by respect for the human scale and a desire to embellish nature, not eradicate it. Try to imagine a building of any dignity surrounded by six acres of parked cars. The problems are obvious. Obvious solution: Build buildings without dignity.

This is precisely the outcome in ten thousand highway strips across the land: boulevards so horrible that every trace of human aspiration seems to have been expelled, except the impetus to sell. It has made commerce itself appear to be obscene. Traveling a commercial highway like Route 1 north of Boston, surrounded by other motorists, assaulted by a chaos of gigantic, lurid plastic signs, golden arches, red-and-white-striped revolving chicken buckets, cinder-block carpet warehouses, discount marts, asphalt deserts, and a horizon slashed by utility poles, one can forget that commerce ever took place in dignified surroundings.

There is no shortage of apologists for the ubiquitous highway crud.

The self-interest of its promoters in the highway, auto, and construction lobbies is obvious. Harder to understand are its boosters in academia—for instance, John Brinckerhoff Jackson. At Harvard, J. B. Jackson was credited with founding the field of landscape studies, as distinct from, say, geography or cultural anthropology or other ways of interpreting man's use of land. An eastern patrician by birth, Jackson spent much of his youth motorcycling around the West. Later, he lived for part of each year in New Mexico, where, except for the Indian pueblos, the towns were all brand-new and uninfected by the viruses of history.

Jackson was fascinated by the postwar commercial highway scene as a fabulous new phenomenon in the grand pageant of our national life. He loved the freedom of the strip, the energy and outlaw charm of it. He especially loved the task of trying to *understand* how it all worked, watching the cars cruise up and down, observing how parking lots were turned into flea markets on Sunday mornings, reveling in the vernacular ingenuity of the strip's denizens—for instance, the way they transformed bankrupt roller rinks into evangelical churches. "I find myself reconciled to a great deal of ugliness, a great deal of commonness," he told me, "and I don't object to it at all."[2]

What J. B. Jackson appeared to lack, it turned out, were critical faculties. So caught up was he in the empirical dazzle of his observations that he seemed unable to make judgments about what he was observing. He was not interested in consequences, only manifestations. Jackson, in turn, deeply influenced Robert Venturi, whose explication of Las Vegas strip culture never questioned the strip's economic ramifications, or its consequences for the greater environment. Peirce Lewis of Penn State, another disciple of Jackson, and a shrewd analyst of the postwar landscape, was more frankly cognizant of its imperfections, but took the position that there was not much to be done about it. Lewis wrote:

> It is past time to remind ourselves . . . that whatever is done about the galactic metropolis, it is not going to go away. Planners may groan when they look out airplane windows and reach for the airsick bag, but Americans are not going to abandon those freeways, nor their ranchhouses on those cul-de-sacs in the woods. Nor will the old nucleated city be restored to its former eminence. . . .

What shall be done about the new ubiquitous metropolis?
The answer is simple to phrase but not so simple to execute.
We must learn to live with it.[3]

Incredibly, Lewis wrote this in 1983, only a few years after the two oil shocks of the 1970s gave America a taste of what life will be like when the price and supply of petroleum begin to destabilize. And while he was at great pains to describe and categorize every last particular of the suburban landscape—he and Jackson share a passion for morphology—Lewis seemed unconcerned with whether or not it was a good way for human beings to live on planet Earth. Another failure of critical faculties.

The intellectual position of Jackson, Venturi, and Lewis vis-à-vis the American landscape illustrates how the discontinuities of our everyday surroundings are mirrored by the discontinuities of the university. Viewing a landscape full of totem objects designed to convince us that we live in a thing called *a community*—"colonial" houses, Red Barn hamburger joints—the academics declare that these objects may be minutely observed without considering their value in relation to other things—for instance, to some notion of what makes a community authentic or false, good or bad. Their position is an outgrowth of a technocratic view that believes only in measuring and quantifying. Perhaps those in the arts and humanities take refuge in this position out of a sense of inferiority toward those in the sciences. By turning the arts and humanities into pseudosciences, the ideas they contain assume a false empirical authority. And when the arts and humanities no longer deal with questions of value, of what constitutes a life worth living, they give up altogether the responsibility for making value judgments.

Thus, a Jacksonian student of landscape can observe a Red Barn hamburger joint, he can remark on its architectural resemblance to certain farm structures of the past, measure its dimensions, figure out the materials that went into building it, record the square footage of its parking lot, count the number of cars that come and go, the length of time that each customer lingers inside, the average sum spent on a meal, the temperature of the iceberg lettuce in its bin in the salad bar—all down to the last infinitesimal detail—and never arrive at the conclusion that the Red Barn is an ignoble piece of shit that degrades the community.

⚑

The Auto Age, as we have known it, will shortly come to an end, but the automobile will still be with us. Whatever the fate of the petroleum supply, there will be cars and trucks around in any plausible version of the future. They may be smaller, leaner, slower. They will likely be more costly to operate. They may run on electricity, hydrogen, vodka, cow flops, or something we do not know about yet. We will almost surely have proportionately less of them per capita, so that each and every adult is not oppressed by the expense of maintaining one. Possibly only the rich will be able to own cars, as in the early days of motoring; the rest of us may rent one when we need it, for a day in the country or a vacation. This was how society managed with the horse and carriage for many decades, and this is how many Europeans still manage with cars. If we are lucky, and wise, and can intelligently redesign our towns to eliminate the absolute need to drive everywhere for everything, and give up some of our more idiotic beliefs about what comprises a Good Life—such as the idea of speed for its own sake, which is practically a religion in America—we may possibly be able to adapt to the new realities without a lot of political trouble.

It is quite possible to have streets that accommodate the automobile and are still charming, as long as you observe some elementary rules, respect the presence of humans, and pay attention to details. The Miami-based architect and urbanist, Andres Duany, demonstrates this very nicely in his lecture on principles.[4] Duany shows two slides. The first is an American-style elevated urban megafreeway: twelve lanes jam-packed with cars (presumably moving at a rush-hour crawl) amid a desolate featureless landscape. The second is a Parisian boulevard, which also happens to contain twelve lanes and yet exists within a very gratifying and richly detailed urban environment.

The deficiencies of the American urban freeway are immediately apparent. It is designed solely from the vantage of the traffic engineer. It is monofunctional. Its only purpose is to move cars—and it does not even perform that function very well at certain times of day. No other activity can go on at its margins. It does not respect the presence of humans without automobiles, cyclists and pedestrians, who, in any case, are forbidden by law to be there. The freeway is not part of the urban fabric. Rather, it is superimposed upon it, often physically perched above the city on trestles, as the Southeast Expressway floats above downtown Boston, or else slicing through the city below grade, like the Fisher Freeway in Detroit. When it defines urban spaces, it does so only in a crude and disruptive way, creating "Chinese walls" of noise, danger, and gloom that cut off neighborhoods from each other—as Boston's North End is cut off from the rest of town, and Manhattan is cut off from the East River by the FDR Drive. Being "limited-access" roadways by definition, these freeways connect with the city only at infrequent intervals, and so they embody the discontinuity that afflicts the present urban arrangement.

Observe how the Parisian boulevard behaves. In the center of the boulevard are several express lanes for fast-moving traffic. At each side of the express lane is a median island planted with trees. These medians define an outer slow lane on each side of the boulevard for drivers looking for a local address. There is space for parking along both sides of each median island and along the sidewalk. Finally, the outer edges of the sidewalks are planted with formal, orderly rows of trees. In other words, you have a twelve-lane road in which half the lanes are used for parking and the rest for moving cars at two different speeds, express and local.

Thus, the boulevard is part of the urban fabric of the city. It celebrates the idea of the city as a place with value, a place where a human being would *want* to be, not just a one-dimensional office slum to be fled after the hours of work. It defines space in a way that allows for multiple functions: motoring, strolling, shopping, business, apartment living, repose. The subtleties of its design make all the difference. It can accommodate twenty parked cars for every fifty linear feet of boulevard, eliminating the need for parking lots. The cars parked along these edges serve another crucial function: they act as a buffer—both physically and psychologically—between the human activities on the sidewalk and the hurtling cars in the express lanes. The two rows of trees per side (four in all) provide additional cushioning. This system works so well that Parisian boulevards are typically lined with outdoor cafés, full of people relaxing in comfort and security. Imagine sitting at a little round table in the breakdown lane of the Santa Monica Freeway at 5:30 in the afternoon.

One of the clues that tell us what kind of place people find most desirable is the price of real estate. As Duany points out, it is no accident that a house in Washington's Georgetown neighborhood, or Boston's Beacon Hill, or the old section of Charleston, has a higher dollar value than a much larger jive-plastic colonial on a big lot in a "good" suburb. Many people assume, incorrectly, that the high value is due to the sheer age of the older houses, that they are antiques. This is only part of it. Much more important is that the neighborhoods as a whole contain types of buildings, building patterns, and relationships that are no longer being built, that, in many cases, are not legal to build within the present codes.

The high price of real estate in Georgetown, for instance, has more to do with the charm of the streets than the charm of the individual houses, many of which are quite as banal on their own terms as today's suburban bunkers. Standing shoulder-to-shoulder, the row houses of Georgetown create a pleasant streetwall that affords a sense of secure enclosure so that the street seems like an outdoor room. Mature trees in orderly rows along the sidewalk provide additional enclosure as the boughs spread up to form vaulted roofs over the sidewalks and the street. Cars parked along each side of the street provide cushioning for pedestrians from the moving vehicles. The streets, being old, were not designed by modern traffic engineers to allow cars to move at fifty miles per hour. In some blocks, the ancient cobblestones remain, so cars tend naturally to move even slower, which makes the pedestrians feel more comfortable. The sidewalks, in many blocks, are paved with bricks laid in patterns—a small detail, but something that adds richness to the whole. These details make the streets of Georgetown exceedingly pleasant to walk in. The houses, designed in the styles of many periods, all conform to roughly the same scale—none taller than five stories. Some, of course, are finer examples of their types than others, and not a few are drab, awkward, or cramped, but altogether they comprise the variety in unity that underlies all coherent design.

Streets of these dimensions, with these details, are no longer being built. It would not be legal to build them in just about any part of the United States. (When Mr. Duany's firm designed a development in

Miami with narrow streets and old-fashioned service alleys, his client was denied a building permit. They submitted a new set of blueprints on which the streets were relabeled "parking lots" and the alleys were relabeled "jogging paths"—and then the project won approval.) The average postwar suburban street doesn't even have trees growing at uniform intervals along the sides—probably the one *legal* thing that could be done by the homeowners to make the street more tolerable—as its precursor, Elm Street, once had in towns all across America. Instead, there are the dreary voids we call front lawns and dull exercises in miniature vignette-making known as *landscaping with shrubs*—but nothing to tie together the individual houses in a coherent scheme by embellishing the street itself. Nor are there sidewalks, nor cars parked along the edge of the street, nor do the houses stand shoulder to shoulder, nor, finally, is the street remotely like an outdoor room. It's a gold-plated wasteland. The result is that nobody wants to be on the street in such a neighborhood, except inside a car, and pedestrians there are regarded as freaks.

Neighborhoods like Georgetown or Beacon Hill are walking neighborhoods. It is not necessary to hop in the car to get an ice cream cone or a bottle of aspirin. You walk to a store—enjoying the felicities of the street as you go—and you are able to see other people along the way. You may even have a conversation with a stranger. This is called *meeting people*, the quintessential urban pleasure. (Or else it is called *a mugging*, the quintessential urban calamity.)

The elements that make the streets of Charleston, South Carolina, so pleasurable are anathema to traffic engineers—specifically, narrow streets that end at a T-junction. The marvelous thing about T-junction streets is that they have natural focal points. In the past, the building lots at the junction of the T were reserved for important public structures: a church, a post office, a college. Human beings *love* focal points. The restless human mind loves to have a goal in view, to savor the approach, to enjoy the reward of reaching the destination, and to then get on with the next thing. People love breaking up their journeys into smaller increments. That is why the interstate highways are such terrible bores, and why people who have time often prefer to take the back roads through small towns. In a city street where the houses stand shoulder-to-shoulder, a T-junction adds to the sense of enclosure that makes the street a big outdoor room. And if the buildings do not exceed a scale of five or six stories, the intimate effect is especially pleasing. The T-junction also has the side benefit of slowing down cars, making the neighborhood more comfortable for pedestrians and children.

The arrangement of streets, the human scale of the neighborhood, and a splendid architecture featuring deep porches that connect the private world of the home with the public realm of the street, are the reasons that real estate in Charleston is so expensive. It certainly isn't the climate, which is like a steambath half the year. The T-junction street is an extinct pattern in America. We do not build it anymore because traffic engineers do not like mandatory right-angled turns, precisely because they slow down traffic. And who knows but that someday a drunken driver might miss the turn, plow into a focal point, kill himself, and damage somebody's property—an inadmissible risk in a tort-happy society.

The present solution to creating focal points in suburbia is the curvilinear street. Make a bend in a roadway of only a few degrees and you will close the vista. You can demonstrate this to yourself by looking through a two-foot length of hose and bending it: the view out the other end disappears. Closing the street vista with this gimmick provides a crude sort of psychological comfort, but affords nothing in the way of real visual interest. It merely protects someone from the depressing sight of all the tract houses lined up in a relentless row, leading to a single vanishing point. On a typical curvilinear street the focal point changes as you move forward, but it is always just another house, not a library, a grocery store, or a theater, which are banished to other parts of town by zoning. From the traffic engineer's point of view, the curvilinear street has another side benefit: Cars can still move at speed with no problem—which is exactly what you shouldn't want in a place where children play.

You will not find alleys in postwar suburban developments, yet alleys were one of the great devices of American urban design. Here, residents kept their ash cans, stables, and later garages. Low-income people too made their homes in little houses along the alleyways and in apartments over the stables or garages. They may not have been delightful abodes, but they were surely better in social terms than our present-day vertical slums.

The existence of back-alley dwellings allowed poor people to live throughout the city—not just in ghettos reserved exclusively for them—cheek-by-jowl with those who were better off, who were often their employers and landlords. They were part of the neighborhood and accepted as a presence there. The children of the poor saw how sober and responsible citizens lived. They saw something tangible to aspire to in adult life. And mixed into a neighborhood of law-abiding property owners, who knew them, the poor did not indulge in the kind of tribal violence that plagues them today.

Alleys are now *verboten*. The official reason is that a classic alley is not wide enough to accommodate a fire truck. To make it wide enough for a fire truck, and therefore acceptable under the official codes, would make it the size of a regular street—and then it wouldn't be an alley anymore. The lack of alleys and their ancillary buildings has contributed greatly to the segregation of people by income groups, so that the well-off are all by themselves in their leafy neighborhoods—even their servants must drive to work!—and the poor are off in their own ghettos—meaning the inner cities, because that's where the only cheap rentals are.

Without alleys, garages have moved to the front of the house in America. As a matter of design, the garage in front of the house is a disaster. The gigantic door presents a blank wall to the street. Tarted up with extra moldings or a checkerboard paint job, it can look even worse by drawing more attention to itself. Anyway, it is inescapably the dominant feature of the house's front. And if it takes up a third of the facade, which is often the case, then it disfigures what remains, no matter how elegant. Moreover, when you consider that every house on the street has a similar gaping blank facade, you end up with a degraded street as well as a degraded architecture.

⚓

On the back roads of upstate New York you see, every now and again, a grand old farmhouse—a brick place in the proud, upright federal style, an idealistic Grecian temple made of wood, or a Victorian colossus skirted by deep porches and wearing all manner of carpentered verge-boards, spindles, crestings, brackets, and frets. It is a touching sight, especially when they stand abandoned and decrepit, their columns listing with rot and fuzzy sumacs poking up through the front steps. Where, on the busier county highways, they stand hard by a new double-wide modular house or a convenience store, or between a drive-in bank and a car wash, they can bring you close to tears. These were the homes of people who did well in the world, who put a considerable portion of their wealth into their houses, not just to advertise their status but to honor their little corner of the world.

These houses commonly stand right along the roadside, no more than a hundred feet from the edge of the road. Nowadays, the road seems uncomfortably close. You realize that in the era before the automobile, these houses existed in a completely different relationship with the road. The houses honored the road because the road was worth honoring. Building and road mutually reinforced the sense of place within the landscape, the feeling that you knew where you were in the world, that one's home was recognizable and beloved.

The sparse traffic on the pre-automobile road was almost entirely local. Vehicles moved along at a pace that posed no particular hazard to pedestrians. The road connected each house to the larger world by discrete increments: first to the neighboring houses, then to the nearest town, and from there by a wholly different type of road, rail or river, to the great city. When travel was slow and houses were scattered, with no trivial structures in between, each house stood as a celebration of effort and achievement in the life of its owner. The approach to a house along the road was gradual and, as in the case with focal points in city streets, getting to it induced a feeling of having really arrived somewhere. To leave home even for a short journey was a matter of import, and homecomings were among the momentous events of life.

When I was a newspaper reporter twenty years ago, I interviewed the chief parole officer in the city of Rochester, New York, an esteemed figure in his realm, who was retiring with a bit of fanfare. We got to talking about how crime-busting had changed since he started out, and he said something that made quite an impression on me. "Today, a couple of guys can take off from Scranton, Pennsylvania, drive up here, kill some old lady and rob all her things, and drive back home to Scranton in time for supper," he said. "And we might never find out it was them."

After that, it was not easy to drive down an ordinary highway without wondering if those hypothetical guys from Scranton were in one of the cars I passed. The road is no longer a friendly place. It is not necessarily overflowing with roving serial killers, but it is full of passing strangers, and some are people you would not want to meet. Travel is now incessant and inconsequential. Tens of thousands of motorists die in cars every year, yet Americans have a strangely detached attitude about it. Where I live, fatal car crashes get a few scant paragraphs in the back pages of the daily paper. We get a hypothetical reconstruction of the crash—"Mr. Wiggins' car apparently left the road, entered a ditch, and rolled repeatedly before striking the catalpa tree"—but nothing about where that person was going or why, because the journey meant nothing.

The road is now like television, violent and tawdry. The landscape it runs through is littered with cartoon buildings and commercial messages. We whiz by them at fifty-five miles an hour and forget them, because one convenience store looks like the next. They do not celebrate anything beyond their mechanistic ability to sell merchandise. We don't want to remember them. We did not savor the approach and we were not rewarded upon reaching the destination, and it will be the same next time, and every time. There is little sense of having arrived anywhere, because everyplace looks like noplace in particular.

♠

Chapter Eight

HOW TO MESS UP A TOWN

Saratoga Springs, in upstate New York, where I live, calls itself a city, officially, but possesses the qualities that most visitors would associate with the term *small town*. In many ways it is as near to being as classic an American small town as a town could be—given my predilections, that is why I chose to settle here twenty years ago. Its commercial life is concentrated on a typical main street, called Broadway here. There are many graceful, tree-lined streets of old houses, some of them quite grand. Until recently, the town had a palpable edge at which development ended and true open countryside began.

Saratoga is best known nowadays for its racetrack, but the town has been a resort for two centuries. The mineral springs first brought it renown as a watering hole after the American Revolution. It was especially popular with southern families seeking to escape the heat and summer plagues of their home country. Following the Civil War, it flowered as the East's preeminent high society playground, attracting the new class of northern industrial millionaires who built fantastic "cottages" (mansions), and spent the bright summer days tirelessly parading their wealth, and their marriageable daughters, about town. It boasted two of the largest hotels in the world of that time, the Grand Union and the United States, behemoths with hundreds of rooms and gargantuan porches. Gambling was centered in Richard Canfield's elegant Renaissance Revival casino.

During the 1920s, as a result of prohibition, gambling (and with it drinking) was dispersed to the woodsy hinterlands of town—a move made possible by the rise of the automobile—where organized crime ran a string of posh private nightspots out of sight of the police, who were well-paid not to notice these operations. This wholesale perversion of the law led to the peculiar spectacle of society swells rubbing elbows with some of the nation's most notorious gangsters. Charles "Lucky" Luciano presided, making sure that mobs from the major cities each got a piece of the action.

After World War II, Saratoga had lost much of its luster as a resort. The racetrack remained, but casino gambling moved west to Las Vegas, a town created by gangsters for gangsters. The gigantic old hotels, built during an era when labor was cheap, became maintenance nightmares and were torn down. The railroads embarked on their forty-year decline and service was whittled down to one train a day. Many of the large Greek Revival and Victorian "cottages" went to rack and ruin. By the mid-1960s the whole town was full of decrepitating white elephants. Anything new built during this period—shopping centers, the first fast-food joints—tended to disrupt the existing town pattern. Combined with an aggressive, federally funded "urban renewal" program, the effects were very destructive.

When I arrived in the early 1970s, Saratoga was struggling to get back on its feet. Interstate 87, running between New York City and Montreal, had recently opened, and with it came the hope for redevelopment. But the Oil Embargo of 1973 made people think twice about commuting to the state capital, Albany, and the hoped-for boom was postponed. However, Saratoga was a good place to be a starving writer. Many of those grand decaying nineteenth-century houses contained magnificent apartments, surprisingly cheap to rent. As a result, the town acquired a lively hippie-bohemian community of young arty people who, like myself, preferred the scale and pattern of small-town living.

In the 1980s, practically every old house in town was renovated—including the one I now live in—and out went the magnificent, cheap apartments. Hippies became yuppies. The number of real estate firms in town quadrupled. The oil shortages of the previous decade were forgotten—in fact, the price of gas declined steadily—and commuters flocked in. A great deal of new stuff was built, almost all of it inimical to the town's essential character. Meanwhile, everything possible had been done to accommodate automobiles at the expense of pedestrians, and of civic life in general. The edge of town, that transitional zone where real countryside begins, was erased in a frenzy of condo building. Saratoga is surely not a better place for all these things, though I remain because I have a life here now, and the same disease of townscape and landscape is prevalent everywhere else in the United States. The Saratoga I shall describe in this chapter is a fitting case study of this disease. The bad buildings and the bad relationships between things here are familiar symptoms everywhere.

⁂

In the era before automobiles came on the scene, you took a train to Saratoga Springs. The train ran on tracks up a narrow right-of-way, through farms and forest, and stopped at the Saratoga depot, a block from Broadway. Goods shipped from elsewhere—everything from pineapples to pianos—also arrived at the railroad depot, where they were either picked up by the local merchants, or forwarded by the local express agency.

Imagine what the town would have been like if railroad tracks ran down every single street carrying a constant stream of privately owned locomotives. Imagine further that the sides of every street were lined with idle engines, boxcars, pullmans, tankers, and cabooses, so that all of Saratoga was a gigantic railroad yard that only incidentally contained houses, shops, schools, churches, and businesses. This is roughly the situation today with the automobile. Saratoga, like virtually every other town in America, has become one big automobile storage depot that incidentally contains other things.

Today, you are apt to enter town on South Broadway. A zone of roadside commerce greets the visitor. There are, for instance, two car dealerships. By necessity the lots in front of the dealerships' buildings are filled with inventory. The buildings themselves hardly matter. One-story concrete-block affairs with flat roofs, they were not designed to be beautiful. They are just places where paperwork can be signed out of the weather.

This part of town is not friendly to pedestrians. Not that it's against the law to walk here, only that no one would have much reason to walk here unless his car broke down. It's not between any two places that people would walk to and from on their lunch hour—e.g., homes and offices—or at any other time for that matter. There are no sidewalks out here on South Broadway, just strings of parking lots punctuated by curb cuts.

A little further up the street comes an inexpensive eating place called the Cobbler House (formerly a Lums franchise), and next to it, a Monroe Muffler outlet. Both are plain industrial boxes designed with no other purpose than to expedite sales of the products sold within. Both are painted in garish colors to snag the attention of passing motorists. Both buildings are surrounded by parking lots that are nearly empty all of the time.

That the parking lots are so much bigger than they need to be is a result of several things. First, the zoning laws in this part of town ordain a minimum lot size. Your business has to occupy a lot of *at least* one quarter acre, whether it is a hot dog stand or a car dealership, which makes for a lot of dead space between business establishments. In effect, it mandates the same relationships between buildings as you would find in a suburban subdivision.

The zoning laws also require deep setbacks from the street, from the side property lines, and from the rear lot line, which encourages placing the building in the exact center of the lot with parking all around. The parking area, naturally, is paved with asphalt. Landscaping costs more to install and creates obstructions for motorists, not to mention maintenance headaches. So paving the whole lot is the easiest and least expensive solution, whether you need all the parking or not. Empty parking lots are the most common little dead noplaces of the postwar streetscape. Great big noplaces are made up of many little noplaces.

It's a bad practice done partly out of misguided good intentions. Businesses in this part of town are required by the codes to have a minimum number of parking spaces. There is no on-street parking here on South Broadway and the customers' cars have to go somewhere. So the business is expected to make provision. This is a good intention, though it results in a place that is unfriendly to pedestrians and oppressive to look at.

Building up to the sidewalk line is one of the crucial elements in creating places that are appealing to people on foot. The arrangement affords a feeling of enclosure and of visual interest, especially if the buildings contain retail shops with merchandise in their windows. It might be preferable to build all these businesses out to a sidewalk line and stash the cars in the rear, but the setback law won't allow that. The law here on South Broadway assumes that it would be obnoxious for the building to begin right up at the sidewalk, because it would obstruct the motorists' view of *other* business establishments further up South Broadway—and, anyway, there aren't any sidewalks. The law has to assume that cars are more important than people.

On the other side of Monroe Muffler, heading deeper into town on South Broadway, is a small realtor's office ensconced in what appears to be a miniature New England church, complete with steeple. The whole structure is about the size of a detached garage. It is a holdover from the period between the two World Wars when it was the fashion to put roadside businesses in cartoon-like buildings: gas stations that looked like mosques and log cabins, motels like windmills, lunchrooms shaped like hot dogs, hats, bulldogs, igloos.

The little white church functions as a sign as well as a miniature office building. In symbolic shorthand it says, "We sell traditional real estate here! We sell the coherence and stability, the enduring *community*, of traditional New England town life!" Saratoga is not a traditional New England town and never was. At the present time, Saratoga is the remnant of a Victorian gambling resort overlayed by an urban sprawl-scape, with all the disconnectedness and loss of traditional values that implies.

Why should this matter? Why not just accept the little fake church as a playful, harmless, adorable architectural oddity, as the lovers of kitsch do? Because it's a bad building, cheaply cute, out-of-scale, symbolically false, and stuck in the middle of a parking lot, a little noplace that contributes to the greater noplace. Because if the town had not been degraded by other bad buildings and bad design relationships, there would be no need for its mendacious symbolism, which cheapens the town just a little more.

Next is a Dairy Queen, housed in an industrial box with a gambrel roof so it resembles a barn. The barnyard is paved and is occupied by half dozen head of automobiles. In quick succession we pass a "convenience" store and a dry cleaner, both with plenty of parking. Across the street there is a diner that doubles as the local bus depot. (This is a wonderful idea—to place the bus depot a good half mile from the center of town!) Then, a Chinese restaurant in another industrial box, a drive-in bank, a gas station, a minimall with a deli, video store, and laundromat, and a carwash.

Each business has its sign, of course, many of them plastic and internally lighted. In the 1970s, the town authorities put a limit on the size and height of commercial signs in this part of town, a political sop to those who objected to the stripification of South Broadway. Now instead of being gigantic, the signs are just very large.

In this instance the city fathers told the local property owners what they were *not* allowed to do. What the city fathers consistently fail to do—all over America—is come up with any coherent vision of what South Broadway *ought to* look like. This is due in part to a lack of good models. We have built so many terrible communities since 1945, and destroyed so much that *was* good, that there is very little to refer to. The design of almost anything is now reduced to a mere set of shopping choices for mass-produced components straight out of the builders' catalogs. At the official level, design is regarded as hopelessly effete, not something for real men sitting on zoning boards.

Town planners routinely pawn off design questions onto technical experts who, it turns out, often have selfish professional interests quite at odds with the public good—for instance, traffic engineers who are dedicated to building more and bigger highways, no matter how destructive these things prove to be for a town. Commonly, the experts do not live in the communities they are paid to advise, meaning that they don't have to live with the negative effects of their work.

The unwillingness to think about the public realm of the street in any other terms beside traffic, shows how little value Americans confer on the public realm in general. By any standard, South Broadway looks terrible. No thought has gone into the relationships between things—the buildings to each other, the buildings to the street, the pedestrian to the buildings. The *detailing* of the street is a mess. I have already mentioned the lack of sidewalks. The absence of trees planted along the sides of the street lends it a bleak, sun-blasted look, which the clutter of signs only aggravates. Even experienced from inside a car, the place is depressing. At the intersection of Lincoln Avenue, motels stand on two corners, both of early 1960s vintage. Each one presents a blank brick wall to South Broadway, as though the street were too hideous to bear looking at. The fast-food strip follows, all the little cartoon eateries in a row: McDonald's, Dunkin' Donuts, Long John Silver, Pizza Hut, Kentucky Fried Chicken.

As a sort of crescendo to this long avenue of junk architecture, we arrive at the Holiday Inn. It is a three-story structure in what the construction industry calls "rainbow brick," designed to simulate the mold of antiquity. Here the effect is wasted. The building has all the formal charm of a junior high school. Parking is in front, of course, because cars are so decorative. A free-standing brown anodized aluminum plinth topped by the company's characteristic logo occupies an otherwise useless grassy median between the parking lot and the street—another little noplace. Presumably this is necessary because without the sign, visitors would not know whether the building was the county department of social services, a Jehovah's Witness Kingdom Hall, a minimum security prison, or a place of lodging.

There's a cute touch to the left of the grand entrance: a little fountain up against an enormous blank brick wall. It spurts water perhaps four feet up in the air, no higher, so that a man of average size, if sufficiently enthralled, could walk over from the parking lot and gaze down upon it in awe. It is about as tall as a foundation shrub, one of those clumpy junipers or yews beloved of suburban landscapers. Most sublimely, a blue floodlight plays through it, even at high noon, in case anyone fails to register that he is looking at real live water.

We are now entering the old city core of Saratoga Springs, where South Broadway becomes simply Broadway. On the left stands St. Peter's Catholic Church. The main front entrance was permanently sealed with concrete twenty years ago. This was the church's way of saying that the town's main thoroughfare had become too abominable to connect with. The same attitude is echoed across the street in the Congregation Sherei Tefila synagogue, which presents to the street a huge 30-foot-high and 50-foot-long red brick wall that is absolutely blank except for two dark recessed doorways. There is no ornament, nothing. You could play jai alai against it. The motif of utter blankness extends another amazing 100 feet with the facade of the Saratoga County YMCA, only here the color changes from brick red to cinderblock gray with a decorative horizontal stripe running the whole length.

Just past the YMCA lies what used to be the heart of town. On one side of Broadway is Congress Park, eight acres of pastorale designed by Frederick Law Olmsted. Across the street from the park, a gigantic parking lot occupies the former site of the Grand Union Hotel. When the hotel was razed in 1955, it was replaced by a Grand Union supermarket (no relation). The block-long, one-story flat-roofed plaza is now nearing the end of its "design life." At the time the plaza was built, it was against the zoning law to build apartments over new retail developments. This meant, in effect, that the historic pattern of Broadway could no longer be built, even on Broadway. This pattern was of buildings three to five stories tall, with retail on the first floor and offices, hotel rooms, or apartments above, with the buildings built out to the sidewalk—in short, a typical American small-town business district pattern. It made people feel good. They could mingle with neighbors on the sidewalk. They had something to look at in the shop windows. The multistory buildings with their decorated facades afforded the street a comforting sense of enclosure, as of a big room with pretty walls. The parking lot and plaza that replaced the Grand Union Hotel has none of that. Rather, it is a block-long hole in the pattern of downtown Saratoga, a big noplace. At night, under the pink-green glow of the halogen lamps, the parking lot is even more forbidding.

Why did the city fathers allow it to be built? Because the plaza complied with the building law. The law represented a number of attitudes in the collective mind of the community at that time—and was typical of the United States in general then. One was that an "old-fashioned" downtown had little value, especially compared to the value of easy parking. In the 1950s, when the plaza was built, most of the buildings on Broadway were at least a half-century old. They needed maintenance or rehabilitation. In America of the 1950s there was little interest in fixing up old things. America had just won a big war and its citizens felt entitled to new things.

Driving around for every necessity of life didn't seem like such a bad idea. Gas was cheap. Nobody gave a thought to the possibility that oil wells would run dry some day. That was sci-fi stuff. Driving to the supermarket was certainly easier than tramping downtown, visiting the grocer, the butcher, the baker, the five-and-ten, and then trudging home with twenty pounds of merchandise like a pack mule.

The historic pattern was also harmed by the postwar notion that people shouldn't live in the same place where business was. After World War II, it was deemed inhumane to let people live over a delicatessen, or an insurance agency, or a plant store—or conversely, to sell milk and newspapers in a residential neighborhood. The logical end of such a principle is suburbia. Superimposed over an older town pattern, like Saratoga Springs, the new pattern is a disaster. Dwellings above stores were the historical version of "affordable housing." The fact that we have not built apartments over stores for fifty years is largely responsible for the present crisis in affordable housing.

Along Broadway today there is still a good supply of old buildings, but over the years many others were lost through neglect, fire, or bad planning decisions, and without exception they have been replaced by worse things. A block up Broadway from the Grand Union once stood the United States Hotel, another colossus. (It served as the setting for Edna Ferber's novel *Saratoga Trunk*.) A Red Barn hamburger shop took its place—along with two acres of parking lot.

In terms of use, the United States Hotel was a building of huge complexity. It was, foremost, a public place, a social center as well as a place of lodging and dining. It contained shops and a parklike courtyard open to the public, an enormous piazza, all on one site. The Red Barn building has only one function: the sale of cheap food in volume. It has no lodgings, or ballrooms, or places of repose. Its plate glass windows contain nothing of interest to the pedestrian, and, anyway, they are set back from the sidewalk by a useless strip of grass. The building's only purpose is to maximize the profit of the Red Barn corporation. It was an insult to the community and, at the time it was built, it conformed to the codes.

After World War II, the Dutch Elm blight killed the towering American elm trees that lined Broadway. Their limbs had arched high over the street, and they combined with the large scale of the hotels (whose soaring facades acted as walls) to make a magnificent green-roofed arcade of Broadway in the summertime. After a while, the city undertook to replace the dead elms. But in doing so, they planted a hodgepodge of trees up and down the street—an oak here, a maple there, a red maple there, a columnar maple there. Perhaps they thought it would be boring to plant just one kind of tree. But they missed the point of how the elms had functioned. The new mix of trees grew to different heights, had different shapes, crown spreads, and foliage color in the case of the red maples. The elms had provided dignified formality and a uniformity of structure. They had behaved architecturally, to form columns at uniform intervals along the sidewalks and a leafy roof above as their branches arched over the street. The new trees could never even approximate that effect.

The town installed benches along Broadway during the 1980s as part of an effort to compete with new shopping malls nearby. The cast-iron and wood benches are bolted in place at the outer edge of the sidewalk facing the street so that those who sit are rewarded first with a view of parked cars, and then, if they can see over the parked cars, a view of traffic on Broadway. It would seem obvious that people choose to sit along the sidewalk in order to watch other people, not traffic.

At the northern end of the business district stands the five-year-old Ramada Renaissance Hotel (to be renamed the Sheraton later this year). Back in the early 1970s, the site contained a row of Victorian mansions turned rooming houses, cheap hotels, and fraternal lodges. They were run down, but with their deep porches, turrets, and intricate detail, they related nicely to the street. Had they survived the comatose seventies, they likely would have been rehabilitated, as practically every other Victorian building in town has since been. But an urban renewal program was underway and the old mansions were razed, along with a lot of other older buildings that stood one block east or one block west of Broadway.

For over ten years, this particular parcel lay vacant. Then the Ramada Corporation came along. Their grim, four-story, red brick, flat-roofed building, with its monotonous industrial-looking windows, looks like it might be anything from a pharmaceutical testing lab to a vocational high school. As architecture it evinces nothing that honors the spirit of the town, echoes its history, or even celebrates the notion that people come here to have fun. Happily, it was, at least, built almost out to the sidewalk edge, with parking in the rear. Unhappily, the folks at Ramada decided that the side facing the parking lot would be the main entrance.

The side that faces Broadway, therefore, functions as the rear entrance. It pays tribute to the town's main street by offering four blank brown steel doors that are the fire exits of the hotel's conference rooms, plus a series of delightful laundry ventilation grilles. Because of this, the sidewalk on the Broadway side of the hotel is absolutely absent of human activity morning, noon, and night. There is no reason for anyone to go there. It is a dead place.

Had retail space gone in at the first floor, with shop windows fronting the sidewalk, the building would have been a continuation of the existing downtown pattern, and pedestrians surely would have ventured up there. Ramada could have put rentable retail space where the conference rooms are—perhaps sacrificing a few guest suites or some precious parking slots, in order to relocate the conference rooms elsewhere. But whatever soulless little bottom-line god the Ramada executives pray to told them that Saratoga's main street was of no importance in the corporation's grand scheme to maximize their profits, so they offered four blank brown fire doors and those lovely ventilation grilles.

Meanwhile, the hotel's main entrance on the parking lot side of the building is connected to the life of the town only by cars. Facing this main entrance are blocks and blocks that were designated an urban renewal zone in the 1960s. Here stood little stores with dwellings upstairs (i.e., affordable housing), public amenities like saloons and lunchrooms, and even a sprinkling of small factories or workshops. Here lived the shop clerks, laborers, small artisans, and in some cases the owner of the business below.

All the urban renewal blocks on each side of Broadway were turned into parking lots. In twenty years, not a single new building has gone up on them. As a result the business district has been reduced pretty much to one street: Broadway. Wherever arson has eliminated a building on Broadway in the past fifteen years, the property has been turned into yet another parking lot, which is to say a little dead noplace between the buildings. If just a few more buildings are lost and replaced with parking lots, Saratoga will have accomplished something rather remarkable: it will have transformed itself completely from a classic downtown business district into a commercial highway strip.

↑

A mile or so northeast of downtown Saratoga, at exit 15 of Interstate 87, lies the new wonderland of shopping malls. Technically, the malls stand in the adjoining town of Wilton, beyond the control of Saratoga

Springs. Two decades ago, Wilton was a township of farms. Since then, it has grown explosively, causing problems both for its older neighbor and its own future. The conflict between these two towns is a classic case of the costs incurred when officials promote growth at any cost.

Saratoga Mall, originally called Pyramid Mall, was built in the 1970s by the Pyramid Corporation of Syracuse, New York. Pyramid developed an interesting reputation for deceptiveness during the 1980s. In 1990, they were cited by The New York State Commission on Government Integrity for attempting to buy the city council election in Poughkeepsie, where their scheme to build a very large mall was not wholeheartedly embraced by local incumbents. Pyramid apparently escaped criminal prosecution because they had violated only the spirit of the law, not the letter, by pumping three quarters of a million dollars in campaign contributions to their favored candidates under the names of individual Pyramid employees—rather than under the company's name—and other stratagems to conceal its source.

Pyramid was welcomed with open arms in Wilton. Wilton had a big problem that was fairly typical of suburban sprawl places all over the country: taxes. In the parlance of planning officials, residential developments are "losers." The people who moved into the colonials and contemporaries all had goshdarn kids! And all the goshdarn kids were required to go to school! And all the suburban streets, like Carefree Lane and Ho Hum Drive (real names, by the way) had to be plowed in the winter and repaired in the summer. And the town of Wilton had to come up with the money to pay for all these services.

For the Mall to come along was a great stroke of fortune for Wilton. In terms of revenue, a shopping complex was considered a big "winner," among "the cream of the ratables" in the words of William H. Whyte, along with light industry and research labs—minimally obnoxious enterprises that produced a great deal of tax benefit. Commercial property carried high assessments so they paid a hefty property tax. But the real plus was that the town of Wilton would receive a cut of the sales tax collected by Saratoga County, too. So every smurf, every Michael Jackson poster, every pair of Levi 501 jeans, every Monkey Ward dinette table that flowed out of Pyramid Mall helped to offset the drain of all those split-level losers out in the piney groves.

It worked so beautifully that by the 1980s Wilton was able to eliminate the residential property tax entirely. The town was in hog heaven. Local officials boasted loudly about it at election time. But what was magic for Wilton was a bitter pill for Saratoga Springs. The mall, predictably, almost ruined Saratoga's downtown business district. The town's movie theater closed. The single "department" store downtown became a steakhouse. The Newberry's five-and-dime became a punk-rock bar. The mall would have killed Broadway entirely had not Saratoga been a popular tourist town with a reliable stream of recreational shoppers. Eventually, though, a lot of the stores that had sold mundane necessities like furniture, auto parts, and brassieres were replaced by gift galleries, boutiques, and real estate agencies.

What goes around, comes around. In 1987, the Wilmorite Corporation of Rochester, New York, announced plans to build a newer, bigger, and better mall in Wilton—on property literally adjoining the first mall. The new mall would be nearly a million square feet on 100 acres compared to less than a half million square feet on 40 acres for the old one. Officials of the town of Wilton were ecstatic. They were going to revenue nirvana.

There was no public opposition to the idea of the second mall, nor any discussion about whether it was necessary. The Pyramid company didn't squawk either. By then it had sold off its interest in the first mall to a consortium of investors. This was part of a clever new practice called "unbundling the rights of real estate." Here's how it worked:

The theory was that optimum profit from a given development could be achieved by deconstructing the ownership into "financial tear parts," the aggregate sale price of the "tear parts" exceeding what the mall would sell for as a whole unit, meaning extra gravy for Pyramid, the seller. So, one bunch of guys buys the land. Another bunch of guys buys the actual mall building and pays rent to the bunch who own the land. A third bunch of guys buys the management contract to make sure that the mall operates properly. Finally, the individual store owners lease their space from the second bunch of guys (who own the mall building) under the administrative supervision of the third bunch of guys (who manage the mall).

Meanwhile, the Pyramid Corporation takes its massive profit, puts together a new war machine, and moves onto the next venue—in this case Burlington, Vermont, a city that has been fighting Pyramid in the courts for ten years to decline the honor of having a mall built on the edge of town.

Above and beyond this welter of real estate machinations, one thing was clear: there weren't enough shoppers in Saratoga Springs and its surrounding towns—Wilton included—to keep two malls in business. There was no question that Wilmorite went into this project knowing that in order to succeed they would have to poach customers from elsewhere. Like any business venture, it was a gamble. The rule of thumb in the mall-building game was that you had to look good on day one and make money for the next three years, then sell off the unbundled real estate rights, take your profit, and move on to the next project. *If* the economy chugged along and the price of gas remained stable so that people could drive any distance to buy a pair of Reeboks, the scheme had a good chance to succeed. The sheer novelty of a shiny new mall would probably suffice to bring those customers in for three years.

Except just as the new mall opened, a combination of forces was gathering to flush the U.S. economy down the toilet. As I write, the first mall is gradually being taken over by marginal enterprises selling joke T-shirts, Asian knickknacks, and the like. In its second year, the new mall is operating at 64 percent occupancy. Just after Christmas of 1992, one of its three anchor stores went bankrupt and closed.

MIT economist Lester Thurow summarized the eighties boom nicely: "We borrowed a trillion dollars from the Japanese and threw a party." Now you could add to that heap of debt the $500 billion price tag on the Savings and Loan bailout, and throw in another trillion in yearly federal budget deficits accrued since Thurow made his remark—the Bush administration looked more and more like a case of fiscal delirium tremens. On top of this, you might also figure in the looming costs of global warming, and the long-term consequences it augured for the national lifestyle. And, of course, sooner or later the price of petroleum was apt to destabilize again. Hence, the overall prospect seemed dim that Americans might continue to afford an economy based on people endlessly driving around, buying smurfs and Michael Jackson posters.

♠

Chapter Nine

A PLACE CALLED HOME

At regular intervals, the United States Government reports the number of "housing starts" as a barometric indicator of how the nation's economic weather is blowing, fair or foul. The more housing starts, the better for the economy, the better for our civilization, so the thinking goes. More families will move into "decent" housing, and more paychecks will go into the pockets of building contractors and cement truck drivers. In 1992, there were 1,200,000 housing starts.[1]

It's a figure that ought to send chills up the spine of a reflective person because these housing starts do not represent newly minted towns, or anything describable as real or coherent communities. Rather, they represent monoculture tract developments of cookie-cutter bunkers on half-acre lots in far-flung suburbs, or else houses plopped down in isolation along country roads in what had been cornfields, pastures, or woods. In any case, one can rest assured that they will only add to the problems of our present economy and of American civilization. They will relate poorly to other things around them, they will eat up more countryside, and they will increase the public fiscal burden.

There must have been a time when people looked forward to the erection of a new house in town, or even at the edge of town. By town, I mean something akin to a living organism composed of different parts that work together to make the whole greater than the sum of its parts—that is, a community. A new building would be expected to add value and richness to this community, as a new child is eagerly awaited by members of a family.

All that has changed in the last fifty years. Our towns no longer have boundaries, but sprawl out of their old containers into the countryside, where the functions of the town—markets, restaurants, law offices, hair salons, TV repair shops—tend to destroy open space without adding up to a community. The separate buildings exist in physical discontinuity with each other and their surroundings, and they promote further discontinuities of meaning and context, especially when they are decorated with symbols intended to snag the attention of passing motorists—and this is true for houses as well as carpet stores and used car lots. Today, when the bulldozers show up to clear the homesites, we greet them with a groan of despair—oh no, not another development!—and with a conviction that whatever gets built will be painful to see, bad for the biosphere, and socially pernicious. One looks upon new home construction as the cancer patient must contemplate the spread of malignant cells through his healthy tissue.

It must be emphasized that the crisis of the American home is not one of interior organization or technical innovation—these problems have largely been solved—but of how it relates or fails to relate to a town. It happens that the symptoms of this disease are most apparent in the way houses look on the outside. All the doodads (to borrow a term from architect Robert Venturi) tacked on to liven them up not only fail to conceal the fundamental illness but make it more obvious. The models costing half a million dollars are as bad as those costing $100,000, and for the same reasons, though they may be more spacious and include luxurious equipment for bathing and cooking. This is quite an extraordinary thing. It can only be possible where people feel no connection or allegiance to their locality—and, in fact, Americans move relentlessly, every four years on the average.

Quickest to uproot themselves are the educated classes, generally to advance their corporate careers. In an earlier era, these would have been the people who stayed put long enough to become stewards, official or otherwise, of that complex of values known as pride of place. They would have owned the business blocks downtown, and taken care of them. They would have built the churches, the libraries, the town bandshell, the ballfields. And they would have built houses for their own families that embodied the ideas of endurance and continuity. Today, this class of citizen is in the service of the large corporations whose very survival is predicated on destroying local economies and thus local communities. So it is somehow just that their hirelings should live in places of no character, no history, and no community.

The tragic thing is that there existed in America a fine heritage of regional home-building traditions, rich with values and meanings, and we threw it all away. Vestigial symbols of that tradition remain—the screw-on plastic shutters, fanlights with pop-in mullions, vinyl clapboards, the fakey front portico too narrow to put a chair on—but the building culture from which these details derive is as lost as the music of the Aztecs.

ĭ

In the colonial period, house-building methods were imported directly from Europe. The early colonists did not adapt the native Americans' style of building for their first rude shelters. Rather, they put up European peasant huts at Plymouth, and, as soon as possible afterward, simple wooden houses. These were the products of a long medieval tradition of wooden dwellings that were never meant to last a human lifetime. The log cabin, a design imported from Scandinavia and first seen in the Delaware settlement, eventually spread throughout the Ohio River frontier. It, too, was essentially a disposable house, built as a cheap expedient.

The vast supplies of timber in America promoted wooden buildings at a time when the forests of northern Europe were vanishing. As wood grew scarce in England and France, laws were decreed limiting its use among commoners, while the church concocted complex dogmas to promote stone construction. This period was known as Victory of Stone over Wood in France, and the Great Rebuilding in England.[2] The European ruling classes had long favored stone and brick for permanence in their own buildings. A stone dwelling was both a monument to the family name and the repository of its wealth. Masonry was also the best medium for classical architecture just then reviving from a long medieval slumber.

Some of these attitudes were transmitted to America. In the mid-1600s, the British authorities decreed that Virginians who owned a hundred acres or more must build in brick. As their society evolved, and their wealth increased, the tidewater aristocrats consciously tried to recreate the manor-house life of the English countryside. They had a clear vision of their descendants enduring on the same plot of earth through time, and they wanted their ancestral houses to express power and permanence.

Early New England society, in contrast, had fewer aristocratic aspirations, and the long-term prospect that preoccupied it was not of dynasty-making on earth but of the soul's passage to Kingdom Come. When a true upper class finally emerged from the communalist murk of the Puritan townships in the early 1700s, it was a maritime mercantile aristocracy, and it built its houses as it built its ships: of wood.

The newly wealthy turned to those Italian Renaissance motifs spreading into England through the reigns of the Georges—a revived classicism of Greco-Roman devices whose structural purpose had become largely ornamental. The Georgian method treated the house as a decorated box. This became more obvious when New Englanders imitated in wood architectural details originally meant to be carried out in masonry. Such a box could be fashionably prettified with tacked-on pilasters, pedimented windows and doors, and other appliqués executed by competent carpenters.

The classic Georgian house was as strictly formal and symmetrical in its interior floor plan as it was in its facade: a central hall separated two sets of two rooms on each side. The second floor was the same. Outside, two sets of windows flanked a central doorway. Except for dormers and roof balustrades, Georgian houses featured little in the way of articulated surface or projections beyond the planes of the walls and roof. And except for greatly expanded window areas—due to advances in glassmaking—there was no attempt to connect the interior with the world of nature outside. The inside of the house stopped dead at the walls, and that was that. There were no porches, loggias, verandas, or balconies extending beyond the walls, creating a zone that was partly outside and yet sheltered—except among the Dutch in New York, who enjoyed deep porches. And American summers were blazing hot compared to northern Europe.

This strict division between the *inside* and the *outside* in Georgian architecture was a byproduct of European rationalism, with its mounting sense of man's superiority to nature—an idea underscored in colonial America by the palpable terrors of the wilderness. Vincent Scully sees it also as the lingering effect of Puritanism, a desire for "perfect, precise, fleshless, puristic shapes."[3] Yet, as Witold Rybczynski has observed, the flatness of the Georgian building scheme probably had much to do with the fact that the English architect of that day "was primarily a draftsman who prepared drawings for work carried out by others," whose theoretical knowledge was based on the study of historical precedent, not on actual construction techniques, and who "was interested more in the appearance of buildings than in their functioning."[4]

There are interesting exceptions to this, mostly in the South, where plantation estates operated as self-contained villages and the master's house had to exist in intimate relation to other practical structures, and to the land itself. At Monticello, Jefferson built long projecting wings, bermed into the hilltop, that served as storage for equipment below and a marvelous outdoor walking gallery above, affording views of the great garden that was Jefferson's lifetime passion. At Washington's Mount Vernon estate, the visitor today can see the intimate connection between the main house and the ancillary buildings around it: the woodworker's shop, the smokehouse, the kitchen, the carriage house. Mount Vernon was unusual for its big front veranda, an oddity in its day, which was built not to provide a place of cool repose from the fierce Virginia heat, but to enable the great man to receive an endless stream of uninvited and annoying visitors without letting them inside his house.

The Georgian house of the mid-1700s—now labeled generically "colonial"—became by far the most popular prototype for suburban dwellings in the modern postwar era. It had less to do with Americans' love of history than with the fact that "colonial" houses were simple boxes. Articulation of surface costs extra money. Any time you put a porch or a veranda on a house, or cantilever a balcony, or add a bay window or any other projecting device, it costs more. But here was a style that lent itself to cheap and expedient mass production.

The original Georgian house had few of the amenities that we associate with modern ideas of comfort. It was heated by fireplaces built into massive masonry chimneys designed to retain heat through sheer bulk of material, and they were not very efficient. The common adage held that a person sitting at the fireside would roast on his front and freeze on his back and a few paces away from the hearth both sides would freeze. The Georgian house had no running water. The technology for household plumbing existed, but towns lacked water and sewer systems to deliver water to individual houses and carry away wastes. Light was in short supply after sundown. Only the rich had beeswax candles. Everyone else made do with foul-smelling tallow tapers or even more primitive fat-burning lamps.

The generation of houses that followed the War for Independence remained faithful to English interpretations of the classical motifs, further stripped-down. Sometimes called the Adam style, after the Scottish architect Robert Adam, these too were decorated boxes. The narrow or gable end was often deployed to face the street—a practical solution when dealing with narrow city lots. The exterior decoration was still flat and tended to concentrate on door and window treatments. It was not a revolutionary architecture.

But a curious undercurrent was gathering in the collective national psyche, which broke like a wave in the early 1800s and resulted in a great cultural transformation: over went the old European rationalist world view, and in its place stood a New World democratic romanticism. The revolutions in America and France were the climactic events of the Age of Reason. In them, the political ideas propounded by Rousseau, Locke, Adam Smith, Hume, Montesquieu, and others—respect for individual rights, democratic self-government, due process of law— were put to a test. In America, the result was a splendid triumph, a constitution in which these ideas were succinctly codified into laws and put into general practice. The yearning for a just society was given an institutional framework—a house, so to speak—in which to dwell. France was not so lucky. After ten years of bloody political convulsion, it failed to overcome the inertia of its own history. It botched the job of transforming its dreams of equality and brotherhood into a workable republican government, and succumbed, at last, to the razzle-dazzle nouveau royalism of Napoleon.

France's failure only made Americans feel more specially blessed. The idea of a just society had been the great culminating vision of the eighteenth century, and in the United States it had come true. Here, people really might make whatever they could of their lives, within very broad limits. It was perhaps ironic that this most romantic of dreams had been articulated by the most rationalistic of men: Jefferson,

Adams, Madison, Franklin, Hamilton—men who valued most their ability to make sense of the world's abiding confusions, men who distrusted the snares of emotion and the delusions they engendered. And ironic too that their achievement unleashed a great flood of romantic feeling in America, an uproar that became part of a general revolt against rationalism throughout the Western world. Inevitably, these feelings would be expressed in architecture.

What we now think of as the Greek Revival movement was America's attempt to fashion an architecture of its own and to do so in highly romantic terms: an architecture of soaring idealism. It took a bit of time after the Revolution for the nation to begin separating itself, culturally and psychologically, from England, and to develop confidence that its republican institutions would endure. This is why the houses of the early Federal period seem such half-hearted versions of the Georgian. And also why, when the Greek Revival got underway, it blossomed in the manner of a true craze.

The architectural elements of the Greek Revival were already present in the Georgian style of building: columns, pilasters, temple facades. But they had been used as flat appliqué decorations and were only dim echoes of their classical models. America, in the full flush of its Periclean pride, would look back to the first principles of architecture from antiquity, just as it bethought itself looking back to the first principles of classical democratic politics.

When Thomas Jefferson went to France in the early 1780s, he was urged by the architects he met, especially Clerisseau, to study the architecture of the ancient world directly rather than through books written by later interpreters such as Palladio. Jefferson's close study of a specific building, the Maison Carrée—a Roman version of a Greek temple—formed the basis of the architectural ideas he brought back to America.[5] For him, the temple represented the culture that had first conceived democracy (Greece), and that which had first devised a republican form of government (Rome), and it carried for Jefferson deep associations with his own classical education and his feeling that a democratic republic could only flourish if its citizens were educated.

He quickly incorporated these ideas into a design he had been working up for a Virginia state capitol at Richmond—the simple massive gable form, the columned portico, the pilasters between the side windows. Afterward, Jefferson continued to favor Romanized treatments of the Greek temple form in all his major projects: the renovation of Monticello with its columned portico fronts, and the University of Virginia campus with its porticoed library and colonnades connecting students' living quarters.

In 1798, Boston architect Charles Bulfinch hung a trabeated portico with elaborate freestanding columns off the front of his Massachusetts State House. Benjamin Latrobe soon emulated Jefferson's Virginia Capitol in his design for the Bank of Pennsylvania in 1801. Latrobe's Philadelphia Waterworks (with Robert Mills), begun in 1811, was a veritable fantasy of Greek temple motifs. In 1818, one of Latrobe's best pupils, William Strickland, designed the Second Bank of the United States at Philadelphia to look like the front of the Parthenon. By 1825, hardly a public building went up that was not in some aspect a Greek temple, or a Roman variation on the theme. It was as ubiquitous in the early 1800s as the factory aesthetic would be in our era.

The War of 1812, in which the English sacked the new national capital at Washington and burned the President's mansion, reawakened the desire of Americans to anathematize things British. And the Greek War of Independence against the Turks, which cost the Romantic poet Lord Byron his life, further stimulated the romantic passion for the ancient Grecian ideal. In the meantime, our troubles with Britain left France as our major partner in trade, and France, from the days of its revolution through the Napoleonic era, had been seized by a craze for classical motifs, especially in women's costume and furniture (Bonaparte had merely imperialized the fashion, preferring Rome to Greece). In any case, a great many of the finished goods that America received from France during the early 1800s were classically inspired. With lyre-ended fainting couches and wallpaper that pictured classical landscapes in the manner of Claude Lorrain making their way into American homes, it was logical that the house itself would soon assume the same full-blown classical look that was becoming ubiquitous in banks, government buildings, colleges, and waterworks.

The first private homes built in the Greek temple style were designed in 1828 by the architect Ithiel Town in Connecticut and Massachusetts. But most of Greek temple style houses that followed were designed and built by housewrights and carpenters. The simple masses and planes of the Greek style were relatively easy to execute in wooden boards and moldings, especially after the convention was broadly adopted of substituting squared columns for round ones. Now any moderately skilled carpenter could build a Greek temple, aided by handbooks like Asher Benjamin's *American Builder's Companion*. Customarily, these houses were painted white, to emphasize their aura of purity.

The style spread like wildfire. When the Erie Canal opened up western New York to settlement in the 1830s, any new house of consequence was a Greek temple, and farmers tried to approximate the look in the plainest dwellings by running pilasters up the corners and treating the gable end as a decorated pediment. It was neither expensive nor difficult to execute, and was a way for ordinary people to express their connection with exalted national ideals—every house a temple in its sacred democratic grove! They named their new towns after the cities of antiquity: Syracuse, Macedon, Ithaca.

Wherever the population boomed in the years before the Civil War, wherever new towns sprang up—in Ohio, clear through the old Northwest Territories into Wisconsin—the new arrivals built Greek temple houses. The craze spread into the deep South as well, to the new states of Alabama and Mississippi, where it became the preferred model for plantation mansions. The deep porticoes afforded a perfect place of refuge from the suffocating southern heat, where one could pass the steamy evening hours out where the cooling breezes blew.

The sight of a Greek temple on a hillside became one of the great romantic clichés of the era. Eventually, the Grecian look was applied to absolutely any and every sort of building—city row houses and business blocks, municipal baths, mausoleums, fish markets—becoming so universal a part of the landscape that it was dubbed the National Style. Nothing like this happened in Europe during the same period—except, curiously, in Russia, where the highly Frenchified upper class also elaborated a Greek temple villa architecture out of French fashions; but the Russian aristocracy was proportionately tiny, while the great mass of peasants and serfs remained mired in log huts. Elsewhere, in deforested England, France, and Italy, cheap lumber did not exist, and to build Greek temple houses in masonry would have been prohibitive for the bourgeoisie, not to mention the peasantry. Besides, what did they have to celebrate in the way of democratic institutions?

The Greek Revival had some great virtues as a building style, conferring a look of dignity and monumentality on even small houses at low cost. Vincent Scully makes the point that the Greek Revival evinced an "anti-urban" bias since a temple house looked best standing free in a rural landscape "pure and unfettered."[6] But houses of this type also went up in the town setting with striking salutary effects. The addition of projecting porticoes, where buildings previously had presented flat facades to the street, afforded a physical connection to the public realm for the first time in American urban life. The main street of Saratoga Springs, New York, for instance, first developed during this period, and its entire length was quickly lined with great verandas, which became the focus of the town's public life—visitors flocked here chiefly for the pleasure of sitting on hotel porches, gabbing the hours away. With the portico, civilized public life really stepped outdoors.

As a scheme for detached single-family houses, however, the Greek Revival had salient shortcomings. The characteristic low-pitched roof was not suited to the heavy snow-loads of a North American winter. Since chimneys interrupted the purity of the temple roofline, they were played down, but reducing their mass made the houses harder to heat in the days before furnaces. The rectangular temple form made for an inflexible interior plan. The old center-hall arrangement of the Georgian days did not work with the front entrance located on the narrower gable end of a temple house, unless the house was enormous. The commonest solution was to run a hall and stairway along one side of the house or line the rooms up end-to-end, in the manner of a railroad train, which had disadvantages in terms of privacy and light. Building wings onto the side, or any other attempt to break out of the rectangular envelope with bays, dormers, and other projections, was expensive and spoiled the temple look. Finally, the style was too puritanical, too symbolically restrictive. It failed to allow enough variety of expression in a culture that extolled each individual's freedom to do things his own way.

By the 1840s, America was again looking to the English for ideas about how to live—their loutish sacking of Washington back in 1812 now relegated to the footnotes of history. All the while that America had been seized with the Grecian mania, glorying in the wonderfulness of its new government, the English had veered down a different Romantic path of its own, into the misty vale of the Gothic. They, too, had gotten tired of the Georgian style, with its predictable formality and stodgy flatness. The English way of returning to first principles was to glory in things medieval, to the period when all the disparate Anglo-Saxon, Celtic, and Norman elements began to fuse into a distinctly English culture. The Gothic had remained a living presence in England down through the centuries, existing comfortably alongside all the neo-classical innovations of Inigo Jones, Christopher Wren, Robert Adam, and John Soane. Ancient castles and ruined abbeys were as much a part of the English landscape as hedgerows and thatched roofs.

When this Romantic impulse began to vie with the dominant Rationalism in the 1700s, some of the first signs appeared in English landscape design. The carefully composed but naturalistic country garden "parks" of the English aristocracy were felt to be incomplete without a "folly," a decorative building to serve as a picturesque foil for the artfully planted glades and man-made lakes. Follies were not meant to be inhabited, or used as anything more than toolsheds or trysting places. The first ones were classical—little temples to Diana and Apollo. But as the century turned, it became all the rage to construct fake Gothic ruins more in accord with the mood of fey melancholy prevailing in the poetry of the day—of Keats, Byron, and Shelley, swept off to premature deaths by the reckless transports of emotion. Wordsworth, who happened to live longer than the others, celebrated the Gothic ruin in his poem "Tintern Abby."

Prose artists also extolled the Gothic. Horace Walpole built the first Gothic-inspired private home in England, "Strawberry Hill," completed in 1777. It featured crenelated towers, lancet windows, pointed arches, and a hodgepodge of other medieval devices. Sir Walter Scott, wildly popular in America—being a Scot made him not quite English—invented a whole body of chivalric literature to flesh out the sentiments of the age. Perhaps to keep himself in a productive frame of mind, Scott built a fabulous neo-Gothic manor that he dubbed "Abbotsford."

Where Scott dreamed up a sunny medieval fantasy world of jousting knights and damsels in distress, American writers of the early 1800s carried on in the vein of Mary Shelley (author of *Frankenstein*), producing a literature of woe, gloom, guilt, greed, torture, insanity, and murder—tinged with shades of the supernatural. In Edgar Allan Poe, one can see a clear connection between his feckless personal life—heartbreak, failure, alcoholism, and penury—and the masterpieces of doom he wrote. In Nathaniel Hawthorne, blissfully married and domestically secure compared to Poe, the objective was to conjure up a romantic history for a culture in which there was little sense of the past and everything seemed depressingly new. Yet, both Poe and Hawthorne managed to express the dark psychic undercurrents that swirled beneath the surface of life in the pre-Civil War era.

The confidence and optimism about America's political future, as symbolized by the Greek Revival, suddenly yielded to anxiety around the question of slavery. What to do about it? The problem seemed unresolvable, and moving inexorably toward an unspecifiable cataclysm. Slavery was at odds with every ideal celebrated in the rhetoric of republicanism. It made a mockery of them. And as the issue heated up, with the rise of an organized abolition movement and rancorous political debates over the admission of new states, the white-painted Greek temple houses that stood so pristinely on rural hillsides came to appear as sham monuments to a society afflicted with moral rot.

Along came Alexander Jackson Davis and Andrew Jackson Downing, introduced in earlier chapters. (It is easy to confuse the two.) Davis, who had been the junior partner of Ithiel Town, arguably designed the first American Gothic house at Baltimore in 1832 and offered more Gothic-inspired ideas in his 1837 book, *Rural Residences*, when the Greek mania was at its height. This was the first comprehensive book of house plans published in America, but it did not find much of an audience. One of the few who read it, however, was Downing, who saw in Davis a potential partner/mentor. Downing loathed the Greek style. He went as far as to declare that a stark white Greek temple house poised on a hillside stood out like a grin on the face of an imbecile.

Downing had been profoundly influenced by the writings of the English landscapist John Claudius Loudon (born in 1783), who advocated gardens that gave both pleasure and instruction. Loudon pioneered the idea of the arboretum, a park where many different specimens of trees are cultivated for observation and study. Loudon was also concerned with designing houses that might fit into the "gardenesque" landscape he was helping to create. A rising class of newly rich commoners, made wealthy by the factories springing up all over England, wanted to build country villas. There was no precedent for this (nor for industrial manufacturing). The English countryside, once populated by immensely rich lords and landed squires on one hand and a nearly serflike class of yeomen farmers, on the other, now felt the influx of a leisured haute bourgeoisie unconnected with agriculture. What this new class required in a dwelling was something a good deal less grand than, say, Blenheim Palace, but more substantial than a crofter's shanty. Loudon came up with a design scheme based on English vernacular farmhouses, which made use of many building devices dating from the medieval period. The result was the so-called cottage orné, a farmhouse elaborated into a villa. (Marie Antoinette had a similar idea fifty years earlier when she constructed a fancy faux farmhouse at Versailles where she and her chums could play at being milkmaids.)

Loudon published a book of his houses, the *Encyclopedia of Cottage, Farm, and Villa Architecture*, in 1833. It struck a deep chord in Downing, who saw in Loudon's ideas a natural and organic approach that might, with aggressive promotion, and with some *reeducating* of the benighted public, displace the Greek temple houses he despised. To this end Downing bent the prodigious energy of his short life, and—though he didn't live to see the result—succeeded rather splendidly.

Downing recognized in Alexander Jackson Davis not only a kindred spirit, but the owner of architectural training that he lacked, and got him to collaborate on a new house plan book. Davis would furnish the drawings, based on his *and* Downing's ideas, and Downing would write the text. The product of this partnership, *Cottage Residences*, was published in 1842. Unlike Davis's earlier tome, this one found a wide audience and went through many printings. It made Downing's reputation and greatly boosted Davis's. The plans offered by Davis and Downing formed a schematic basis for the orgy of styles that followed, which came to be bundled under the rubric "Victorian."

Though Downing spouted torrents of moralistic balderdash to rationalize the designs he and Davis advocated—and the new suburban lifestyle made possible by the railroads—the houses were self-evidently more practical, sensible, suitable dwellings than what had been possible under the Greek craze, and they strove for beauty by reaching out into nature rather than holding it at arm's length. They achieved this by bursting out of the constraining four-wall envelope of the rectangular box. Articulation of surface was suddenly everything. The porches, balconies, bays, dormers, umbras, and towers thrust the life of the house outward into sky and foliage, and created openings to connect directly with them. Nothing could have been more crucial for establishing a sense of continuity between the house and its setting. And it was a welcome innovation in an age when the new disorders and debasements of industrialism made people anxious to reestablish connections with the natural world. For the flight from the cities—for those who could afford it—was very much a quest for sunlight, fresh air, greenery, and open space.

The designs offered in *Cottage Residences* were flexible and various in terms of interior plan. Gone was the peremptory temple facade with its single logical entry place. Now the entrances could go wherever they were most pleasing, and included generous vestibules. Downing and Davis understood that a house must reveal itself by degrees, from the least private spaces to the most intimate, and they designed accordingly. This was quite a new thing. The great Palladio had never concerned himself with the interior rooms of the villas he designed. The Georgians had relied on the standardized, unimaginative center hall scheme, and the Greek temple houses posed severe restrictions on layout. Here suddenly were houses in which the inside was given as much thought as the outside.

In terms of amenities, Downing and Davis were miles ahead of contemporary practice. They designed "water closets," flush toilets gravity-fed by attic cisterns, when nearly everybody was still trudging outdoors to the privy or sliding a chamber pot under the bed. They advocated "bathing rooms," heretofore nearly unknown in occidental society. (In England, the aristocracy still clung to the absurd custom of having a portable tub lugged into the bedchamber.)

Downing believed that "in a country like ours, where the population is comparatively sparse, civil rights equal, and wages high, good servants and domestics are rare, and not likely to retain their places a long time."[7] He was quite wrong about this—a wave of Irish refugees from the potato famine would shortly flood the country with housemaids and ditch-diggers—and of course he implicitly overlooked the domestic role of southern slaves. But the upshot of his belief was a penchant for maximum efficiency and a keen interest in labor-saving gadgets. He and Davis designed dumbwaiters for moving food up from basement kitchens, speaking tubes to save trips up and down stairs, basement coal furnaces for central heating, rotary pumps to bring fresh water within a few steps of every bed chamber without the aid of a servant, and closets, a remarkable indulgence when even well-off American families owned relatively few things.

Downing advocated building in stone or brick (preferably stucco) wherever feasible. He argued that the national proclivity for building with wood was a colossal cultural error: Americans were erecting a new world of temporary structures, wooden towns of wooden houses that would be expensive to maintain, prone to fire, and that even under the very best circumstances could only last for a few hundred years. The bad effects of this practice were hardly evident in the 1840s, when so many wooden towns were spanking new. But it was obvious that weather and rot would destroy them eventually, and Downing said that European visitors, "accustomed to solidity and permanence," were appalled by the prospect. Anyway, this was one battle Downing and Davis were not destined to win, and perhaps sensing what they were up against, they hedged their bets and included plans for several inexpensive wooden houses in *Cottage Residences*.

And it was a good thing they did, since a revolution in wooden building was about to get underway that would make wood houses much simpler and cheaper to build than ever before, and hence available to a much broader mass of the American people.

This revolution started with what was at first mockingly called the "balloon frame." Prior to this time, all wooden houses—whether Georgian, Greek, Federal, Gothic, or vernacular farmhouse—were supported by post-and-beam frames. Massive timbers were connected by joints, such as the mortise-and-tenon, and secured with wooden pegs called "trunnels" (from tree nails). Hand-wrought iron nails existed, but they were used mainly for finish work, and were so terribly expensive that families leaving New England to settle western New York and Ohio knocked apart the insides of their old farmhouses in order to salvage precious nails for the next homestead. Post-and-beam framing required skilled joiners and a great deal of labor, so that building a house was a momentous undertaking.

By the 1840s this began to change. The vast virgin white pine forests of upper Michigan were opened up to exploitation. The wood was milled to standard dimensions in enormous volumes. It could be shipped easily across the Great Lakes and the new network of eastern canals. Consequently, America's preferred building material became cheaper than ever. By this time, too, inexpensive, factory-made steel-wire nails had appeared on the scene, making it possible to connect presawn lengths of wood without fancy joinery. Now a house could be whacked together out of two-by-four inch "studs" nailed at sixteen-inch intervals. A couple of "framers" could do what used to take a dozen carpenters under skilled supervision in the old post-and-beam days. Early doubts about the soundness of the method were soon allayed. Balloon-frame structures proved to be surprisingly strong, at least over the short-term of, say, a single lifetime. Beyond that, as any American who owns a nineteenth-century wooden house knows, gravity and rot inevitably deform the structure. But America was bustling so tirelessly that few cared about the long-term consequences of anything.

Houses built using the balloon frame first appeared in Chicago at this time, and the method spread eastward from there. This was the beginning of that city's great population boom. When the Erie Canal opened in 1825, Chicago was a tiny military garrison called Fort Dearborn. The town was platted in 1830 and incorporated into a village of a few thousand in 1833. By 1850, the population had reached about 30,000. By 1871, it had swollen to 300,000. The "invention" of the balloon frame has been attributed variously to one George W. Snow, a lumberyard owner, and to Augustine D. Taylor, a carpenter-architect. In any case, the need for new buildings in Chicago was so insatiable and the supply of cheap Michigan lumber was so bottomless that the technique seemed historically inevitable.

As Chicago's phenomenal growth was made possible by the balloon frame, so was the calamity that befell the city in 1871: the Great Fire. Built entirely of wood, Chicago was a great sprawling tinderbox. Even the sidewalks were laid with resinous pine. The fire started on an October night after a summer of withering drought. It took only twenty-four hours to level an area of three and a half square miles. Over 17,000 buildings burned to the ground, 100,000 people were left homeless, and 300 lost their lives.

The fire changed the way things were done in Chicago and in other central cities. Downtown was reconstructed in brick and masonry under a new building code. But the wooden balloon frame continued to thrive on the suburban fringe, beyond the code's reach. In the suburban borderlands now developing all over America, as factories boomed and the horsecar lines extended, it became the dominant building method for private homes.

The balloon frame had two profound repercussions on home building. First, it resulted in ever greater and more fantastic elaboration of houses for the well-off: the bursting outward from the four-walled box of the house in picturesque elements. The light and versatile wooden frame made possible all those turrets, balconies, bays, cupolas, and porte cocheres of the Victorian styles. Porches got deeper and ever more elaborate. At the same time, factories mass-produced wooden millwork—brackets, spindles, balusters, shutters, moldings, and all manner of decorative items—while the country was flooded with cheap immigrant labor who could nail this stuff together. These houses became such exercises in wretched excess that the next generation ran shrieking back into neoclassicism. Being made of wood, they rapidly deteriorated. And as they fell apart, their cache and standing fell until by the mid-twentieth century they had become the classic spook houses of the Charles Addams cartoons.

A far more enduring legacy of the balloon frame was that it transformed the craft of house building into an industry. In so doing it turned houses into commodities, things made above all to be sold at a profit, so that those who ended up living in them were not the same ones who built them, meaning that they were houses built without affection—merely products whacked together for a mass market. These became the first speculative subdivisions of identical houses, built for a growing industrial middle class.

A clear evolutionary line led from the mass publication of house plans to the mass production of houses. Many followed in Downing's and Davis's footsteps, offering manuals of design, mail-order house plans, and even whole prefabricated buildings. Standardized lumber made house kits possible. Thousands of precut components and hardware, down to the last doorknob, could be shipped by railroad from factory to any building site, to be assembled by workers of modest skills. Set on a good foundation, these were as sturdy as any other balloon frame houses. Many were sold by Sears and Roebuck. Other technical innovations followed in the early 1900s. Mass-produced components replaced hand work. Sheetrock put an end to the plasterers' profession. Plywood sheathing, which came in four-by-eight-foot sheets, led, in turn, to the full standardization of all building methods to take advantage of four-by-eight-foot components. Among other things, this would spell the end of high ceilings, or any eccentrically shaped rooms.

The Craftsman movement of the early 1900s was the next evolutionary step in American house design. It was a response to many things: to the lingering distaste for Victorian frippery; to the formality of the Beaux Arts movement that followed the Victorian orgy of styles; to the industrial system and its mass-produced junk; to household improvements brought about by electricity; and to a growing young, mobile managerial class who wished to live in smaller houses. Small Craftsman bungalows were especially popular on the West Coast. Young couples flocked there from the heartland, leaving behind their own parents, and ending the tradition of multigenerational households. The Craftsman movement had started in furniture design and the decorative arts— things that really could be made by hand. But when it culminated in whole integral houses, such as the prototypical California bungalow, the movement came to an ironic full circle, for bungalows were by far the most popular mass-produced kit houses sold by Sears and Roebuck.

Frank Lloyd Wright's quixotic genius leaped off the timeline during the same period. Much influenced by Japanese design after seeing their pavilion at the 1893 Chicago World's Fair, Wright shucked off the entire shopworn stock-in-trade of European conventions and began to build eccentric mansions that looked like nothing seen in America before: elongated slabs of concrete with high casement windows like clerestories, barely pitched hipped roofs, and forbidding facades of multiple blank walls that concealed the entranceway. These became known as "Prairie houses," and their chief effect on the accepted notion of what a house should be in America was to emphasize the horizontal, to keep everything low, spread out, close to the earth, and to open up the interior plan. Technically, Wright's Prairie mansions were made possible by the invention of reinforced concrete and structural steel. Spiritually, they expressed not merely the flatness of the Middle West, but the ability, in America, to forever spread out into available open space.

After the stock market crash of 1929, when building came to a stop for a while, Wright occupied himself with reimagining the human habitat on the larger scale, and he came up with a scheme called Broadacre City. In part, it harked back almost exactly to William Penn's screwy original idea for Philadelphia: a spread-out city of houses on one-acre lots, a supernaturally tidy and idealistic version of what would become classic suburban sprawl in our time, as uncomprehending of the destructive potential of cars as Corbu's Radiant City. There was no sense in the Broadacre City scheme of what citizens in such a motorized Shangri-la would have to give up in the way of community connections or urban variety. Wright was chiefly concerned with industrial capitalism's inability to observe organic limits of growth. He was sincere in believing that Broadacre City was the antidote, but he lived long enough to see that it couldn't work in practice. Most architects and planners of the 1930s dismissed it as "impractical," but it proved to be eerily prophetic.

As the basic unit of Broadacre City, Wright conceived his "Usonian house," intended to be Everyman's dwelling, a less expensive version of his prairie mansions. The Usonian house turned a blank face to the street. It was connected to other parts of the "city" only by the automobile. Yet it still used Wright's powerful grammar of heavy, "organic" building materials. After World War II the Usonian house would be bastardized and stripped of its art into the ubiquitous ranch house of the suburbs.

The most influential model for the new postwar suburbia remained Downing's ideal of the villa in the country, which had no pretenses of being part of a "city" of any kind. As Americans in the twentieth century thought less in terms of building towns—in the sense of creating coherent communities—they thought more and more about acquiring a product called a "home."

Here was a neat little semantic trick introduced by realtors as they became professionalized: The prospective buyer was encouraged to think of his purchase as a *home*, with all the powerful associations the word dredges up from the psyche's nether regions; the seller was encouraged to think of it as a *house*, just a thing made of wood where the family happened to sleep and eat, nothing to be attached to. It was most emphatically not *home*. Home was where one was born and raised, a place in time called the past, gone forever. You can't go home again.

By the 1920s, with the car on the scene, all the elements were in place for the mass selling of mass-produced houses to the masses of corporate toilers, except easy financing, and that problem, as discussed in Chapter 6, would be solved as a matter of federal policy between the Great Depression and the end of World War II.

⁂

Across the rural northeast, where I live, the countryside is littered with new houses. It was good farmland until recently. On every county road, every unpaved lane, every former cowpath, stand new houses, and each one is somebody's version of the American Dream. Most are simple raised ranches based on tried-and-true formulas—plans conceived originally in the 1950s, not rethought since then, and sold ten thousand times over.

These housing "products" represent a triumph of mass merchandising over regional building traditions, of salesmanship over civilization. You can be sure the same houses have been built along a highway strip outside Fresno, California, at the edge of a swamp in Pahokee, Florida, and on the blizzard-blown fringes of St. Cloud, Minnesota. They might be anywhere. The places they stand are just different versions of nowhere, because these houses exist in no specific relation to anything except the road and the power cable. Electric lighting has reduced the windows to lame gestures. Tradition comes prepackaged as screw-on aluminum shutters, vinyl clapboards, perhaps a phony cupola on the roof ridge, or a plastic pediment over the door—tribute, in sad vestiges, to a lost past from which nearly all connections have been severed. There they sit on their one- or two- or half-acre parcels of land—the scruffy lawns littered with the jetsam of a consumerist religion (broken tricycles, junk cars, torn plastic wading pools)—these dwellings of a proud and sovereign people. If the ordinary house of our time seems like a joke, remember that it expresses the spirit of our age. The question, then, is: what kind of joke represents the spirit of our age? And the answer is: a joke on ourselves.

Lately among these houses a new fashion has arisen of sticking humorous painted plywood cutouts on the front lawn. Four-by-eight-foot plywood sheets lend themselves nicely to this sort of sculptural treatment. The prototype was a life-sized cutout of a fat woman bending over, as though weeding the flower beds, so that her bloomers are exposed to all passersby—presumably motorists. Soon she was joined by a male companion, also weeding and bent over so as to expose the crack at the top of his butt over low-slung pants. A year or so later, a new character appeared: a mischievous child of about two with his diapers dangling around his knees in the act of peeing. Commonly this impish figure was displayed against the foundation shrubs, with the implication that the house itself was being peed on. Probably unconsciously, the homeowner had surpassed his own humorous intentions. This is what comes of living in houses without dignity.

These plywood cutouts are common lawn decorations in our part of the country, as birdbaths were thirty years ago. One can't pass these cartoon-like displays without thinking of television—indeed, of how much television has to do with the way houses look in the present landscape. The American house has been TV-centered for three generations. It is the focus of family life, and the life of the house correspondingly turns inward, away from whatever occurs beyond its four walls. (TV rooms are called "family rooms" in builders' lingo. A friend who is an architect explained to me: "People don't want to admit that what the family *does* together is watch TV.") At the same time, the television is the family's chief connection with that outside world. The physical envelope of the house itself no longer connects their lives to the outside in any active way; rather, it seals them off from it. The outside world has become an abstraction filtered through television, just as the weather is an abstraction filtered through air conditioning.

The car, of course, is the other connection to the outside world, but to be precise it connects the inhabitants to the inside of their car, not to the outside world per se. The outside world is only an element for moving through, as submarines move through water.

As the outside world became more of an abstraction, and the outside of the house lost its detail, it began to broadcast information about itself and its owners in the abstracted language of television, specifically of television advertising, which is to say a form of communication based on simplifications and lies. As in television advertising, the lies have to be broad and simple because the intended audience is a passing motorist who will glance at the house for a few seconds. So, one dwelling has a fake little cupola to denote vaguely an image of rusticity; another has a fake portico à la *Gone With the Wind*, with skinny two-story white columns out of proportion with the mass of the house, and a cement slab too narrow to put a rocking chair on, hinting at wealth and gentility; a third has the plastic pediment over the door and brass carriage lamps on either side, invoking "tradition." The intent is to create associations that will make the house appear as something other than the raised ranch it actually is, something *better*, older, more enduring, resonant with history and taste.

It must be obvious that there are honest ways to design a dwelling that confer meaning and sensual appeal. But they involve more complicated procedures than the two-second visual pitch to a passing motorist using cartoonish symbolism. And the task is made inordinately more difficult when each house is disposed on its own acre, with only a schematic connection to the land in the form of "landscaping" with shrubs, and no relation whatever to other buildings—even if there are some nearby. It is also difficult when the street is degraded by a lot of automobile traffic.

Americans wonder why their houses lack charm. The word *charm* may seem fussy, trivial, vague. I use it to mean explicitly *that which makes our physical surroundings worth caring about*. It is not a trivial matter, for we are presently suffering on a massive scale the social consequences of living in places that are not worth caring about. Charm is dependent on connectedness, on continuities, on the relation of one thing to another, often expressed as tension, like the tension between private space and public space, or the sacred and the workaday, or the interplay of a space that is easily comprehensible, such as a street, with the mystery of openings that beckon, such as a doorway set deeply in a building. Of course, if the public space is degraded by cars and their special needs—as it always is in America, whether you live in Beverly Hills or Levittown—the equation is spoiled. If nothing is sacred, then everything is profane.

The equation is also spoiled when buildings cease to use the basic physical vocabulary of architecture—extrusions and recesses—and instead resort to tacked-on symbols and signs. One is a real connection with the real world; the other is an appeal to second-hand mental associations. (I saw a wonderful example of this in Vermont: a two-story building on a rural highway that had a gigantic sign on it, with letters four-feet high. The sign said COUNTRY STORE, as though passing strangers had to be informed in written words that they were in the country. The woods and meadows on each side of the road were not enough to get across the point.)

This habit of resorting to signs and symbols to create the illusion of charm in our everyday surroundings is symptomatic of a growing American character disorder: the belief that it is possible to get something for nothing. The germ of this disorder probably has been with us a very long time, because this was such a bountiful land. But our economic luck in the aftermath of World War II accelerated the syndrome. Life was so easy here for so many for such a long time that Americans somehow got the idea that you merely had to wish something was so in order to make it so. The culture of advertising—which bombarded Americans daily, hourly—eroded our capacity to distinguish between the truths and the lies. And not even in moral terms, but on the practical level. You could label a house "traditional" and someone would accept it, even if all the traditional relationships between the house and its surroundings were obliterated. You could name a housing development Forest Knoll Acres even if there was no forest and no knoll, and the customers would line up with their checkbooks open. Americans were as addicted to illusion as they were to cheap petroleum. They had more meaningful relationships with movie stars and characters on daytime television shows than they did with members of their own families. They didn't care if things were real or not, if ideas were truthful. In fact, they preferred fantasy. They preferred lies. And the biggest lie of all was that the place they lived was *home*.

↟

Beyond the spiritual deformities of a people narcotized by fantasy, other forces conspire to degrade housing in our time. Building codes and zoning regulations have made it difficult, often illegal, to build houses that are worth caring about. Where I live, the building codes prohibit new houses in the old residential neighborhoods from exceeding thirty feet in height. Under that rule, my own 100-year-old house could not be legally built today. In effect, it is a law against houses more than two stories high. There are a great many fine examples of "Victorian" houses in Saratoga. These are the houses that wear the little brass plaques from the town historical society. These are the houses that tourists still come to see and enjoy, the houses that the community treasures, that give the town its character, its charm, that make the place worth caring about. None of them could be built legally under the present codes.

Under these codes, new buildings in my neighborhood must be set back from the sidewalk twenty-five feet, no matter what the setback is for the older houses on the street. I know a man who bought a small lot on a street that was lined with houses dating roughly from the 1850s. He wanted to build a similar row house, one that would have fit into context. All the houses on this street were built out to the sidewalk. But the codes compelled him to set his new house back twenty-five feet from the sidewalk. To do this harmed the continuity of the existing street-edge. In effect the code requires him to have a useless front yard while depriving him of backyard space that, in this urban setting, he might have actually used better.

The meaning of the law is clear. It intends to enforce a suburban mode of building even where that mode is inappropriate. Here the result of the law is to actively degrade established urban relationships.

In the countryside, zoning creates another set of problems. Where development threatens farmland, the authorities enact "large lot" zoning regulations that require a minimum lot size of, say, five or more acres per house. The idea is to "preserve open space." In practice, the law does nothing to preserve farms, but rather promotes sprawl of the most lavish, land-devouring sort, and positively prevents the formation of coherent new towns where buildings would necessarily have to stand much closer together.

The tax laws also end up expressing themselves perversely in new houses. One of the criteria applied by the property tax assessors is how many doors a dwelling has. The more doors, the higher the assessed valuation and hence the higher a fellow's taxes. It is a common sight in upstate New York to see houses with no steps leading to the front door. What the homeowner does, acting in rational self-interest, is to render that door nonoperational. The family comes and goes through the back door. The years go by and the two-tone split-level house stands there with its front door hanging incongruously five feet above the lawn. It will remain that way indefinitely, as long as the tax law encourages it.

It will also be just one more joke on ourselves, one more little thing to make us look like a civilization of morons.

⚓

Walk down any residential street in an American small town and you will see the ghastly effects of the home improvement industry. The object of the industry is not really to improve houses but to sell vast quantities of merchandise. It accomplishes this by persuading homeowners that they can "beautify" and "add value to" their houses *and save money by doing the work themselves.* This is appealing in theory, but in practice it is a joke, because most homeowners are not competent building contractors. They may be good fathers and mothers, able optometrists, winning Little League coaches, and loyal friends, but they are apt to be bungling carpenters.

Carpentry is an exacting set of skills. Even at the professional level it has been debased as a consequence of mass production, and the number of incompetent building contractors is disturbing. At the amateur level, it is worse. In fact, the home improvement industry actively promotes the idea that skill is not important. All that matters is buying the right tools and building materials. The tools will do the work, and the materials—such as factory-made drop-ceiling kits—will eliminate thinking. All the homeowner need do is lay out some money at the building-supply store, and then take the stuff home Saturday morning. The job itself is "a snap." All this is based on two contemporary myths: (1) the idea that shopping is a substitute for design, and (2) the idea that it's possible to get something for nothing, in this case skillful work without skill.

The result, of course, is a lot of botched jobs. Worse, when one clod on Elm Street rebuilds his front steps ineptly, his neighbors have to suffer the consequences too, for they have to see his bad work every time they walk out of the house. Some bad work would not look so bad if it was done in traditional materials like brick, stone, or wood. But many cheap, new ersatz materials have come along in recent decades and they happen to age very badly. For example, the turquoise corrugated fiberglass panels, so popular with home-handymen, that are used to roof entrance porches. After a few years of exposure to ultraviolet light and weather, the fibers start to fray at the edges, the color leaches out to a sickly yellow-grayish-green, and fallout from automobile exhaust collects in the grooves.

Aluminum and vinyl siding suffer similarly. The homeowner who slaps these materials over his 100-year-old house does so in the belief that he will never have to take care of the outside of his house again. He is not really paying for the care of his property; rather, he is making an investment in the promise of perpetual leisure, something quite different. In fact, aluminum and vinyl siding are *not* maintenance-free. They just decay differently than painted wood. A few years after installation, aluminum develops a patina of yellow-gray dinge, largely from auto emissions. The color in vinyl siding fades from exposure to ultraviolet light while collecting gray auto exhaust grime. The grime could be washed off, but, judging from the evidence, this is rarely done—it would challenge the idea that the stuff is "maintenance-free." With both aluminum and vinyl the trimwork tends to fall off sooner or later because it is tacked on to unstable old wood underneath. Vinyl siding is particularly susceptible to cracking and warping. Over time, sunlight weakens it, while the weather makes it expand and contract. Aluminum siding is apt to dent. Commonly, you will see dents all around a house at about knee level where the lawnmower has thrown stones up against the siding. The previous generation of homeowners, say 1945 to 1970, favored asphalt or asbestos siding. After nearly half a century, these have developed a special scrofulous appearance that makes rotten wood look elegant in comparison. The vinyl and aluminum will look just as bad in twenty years, but in a way wholly their own.

Pressure-treated lumber has become an exceedingly popular building material in the past ten years. It is pine impregnated with chemicals that kill insects and microorganisms, making it supposedly immune to rot. Its durability is largely theoretical at this point, however, since none of the structures built with it are old yet. There are already some problems associated with it. Many professional carpenters are afraid of working with the stuff, especially of inhaling the poison-laced dust produced by saws and drills. It warps much more drastically than ordinary lumber, and in unpredictable ways over time.

Pressure-treated lumber also has some peculiar aesthetic liabilities. For one thing, it is not available in dimensions used for trimwork—one-by-four, one-by-six, et cetera—and so things built with it end up having a rough, unfinished look. For another thing, it is so saturated with chemicals that the surface will not absorb paint. Buyers are advised to wait at least a year until the outer surfaces dry before they even attempt a paint job. Now, it happens that pressure-treated lumber is popular for building decks, which are exposed to weather and come in contact with the ground—things known to rot wood. It is also used a lot in exterior repairs, for steps and foundation lattice, for the same reason. What happens is that a year goes by and the deck doesn't get painted. The homeowner develops amnesia. He stops noticing that his deck, now mellowed to a yellowish-gray, doesn't harmonize with his red house. It has become familiar and forgettable. Another year goes by. The deck still doesn't get painted. There are too many ballgames to watch on TV. . . .

ℷ

The mobility that Americans prize so highly is the final ingredient in the debasement of housing. The freedom to pick up and move is a premise of the national experience. It is the physical expression of the freedom to move upward socially, absent in other societies. The automobile allowed this expression to be carried to absurd extremes. Our obsession with mobility, the urge to move on every few years, stands at odds with the wish to endure in a beloved place, and no place can be worthy of that kind of deep love if we are willing to abandon it on short notice for a few extra dollars. Rather, we choose to live in Noplace, and our dwellings show it. In every corner of the nation we have built places unworthy of love and move on from them without regret. But move on to what? Where is the ultimate destination when every place is Noplace?

⭫

Chapter Ten

THE LOSS OF COMMUNITY

For two years in the late 1980s I lived in a small town on the Hudson River, ten miles east of Saratoga. It was named Schuylerville after the old Dutch patroon family, whose most illustrious scion was the Revolutionary War general Philip Schuyler. The village lies nestled along the western side of the river valley, which rises steeply to a sort of hilly plateau. The gridded blocks are bisected by service alleys lined by barns and carriage houses. The nineteenth-century houses were cobbled over with 1960s redos, and the materials they used—aluminum and asbestos siding, fake brick—have entered a secondary stage of decay.

Many blue and yellow New York State historical markers stand scattered around the town today. Each tells a little piece of the story of the Battle of Saratoga, which took place in woods and farm fields nearby in 1777. "Here the British Army parked their artillery," says one marker near the driveway of the High School. "Site of the Continental barracks where General Stark tried and condemned the Tory Lovelass as a Spy," says another at the north end of town. A marker in the parking lot of the supermarket commemorates the surrender of the British commander "Gentleman Johnny" Burgoyne. The British grounded their arms on what is now the town ballfield beside the river. Looming over the town on top of the hill that rises out of the valley stands a 100-foot-high granite obelisk that was erected a century after the great battle. It is a fine structure, decorated with statues of the generals who fought there so valiantly, and with other fine touches of carved stonework. Inside the monument an iron staircase spirals up to an observation tower. The view must be superb, but, alas, the interior has been locked for years because teenagers got into the habit of having wild parties inside.

Civilian deeds are also commemorated: "Site of the first flax mill in the United States," declares a marker at the edge of the woods beside Fish Creek, which empties into the Hudson at the south end of town. There is nothing left of the flax mill itself, which was demolished before the turn of the twentieth century, but Schuylerville's economic history is otherwise highly visible in the landscape.

The years I spent there, in a little brick cottage near the river, were the years when President Reagan proclaimed that it was "morning in America." For Schuylerville, it was more like 4 P.M. on the first day of winter. Its economy lay in tatters. In this respect it was not unlike many other old towns that dot the banks of the Hudson and Mohawk river valleys in upstate New York.

Six of the seven factories that once produced paper products in and around town had closed by 1970, and the remaining plant employed fewer than 100 people. Men and women long used to steady jobs at good wages during the best postwar years now had to spend their final working years cobbling together a living from part-time work at lower pay, often a long drive from town. Their children and their children's children, who had no hopes for steady work at good pay, fell into the abyss of welfare, drugs, petty crime, and teen pregnancy—behavior that Americans more usually associate with inner-city ghettos. To understand what the town has lost it might be useful to consider what it had.

⁕

First, Schuylerville was a canal and river town. The Champlain Canal was dug through the Schuyler family's settlement in 1819 to bypass a series of unnavigable rapids in the Hudson River, and a substantial village quickly sprang up along it. The canal completed a direct water route between New York City and Montreal, and for decades it was the only route. It was a great feat of engineering. At the time, American canals were wonders of the world, for they ran much greater distances than the canals of Europe.

In the canal's heyday before the Civil War, Canal Street was lined by warehouses, cold-storage facilities (cooled by block ice), mule barns, boat yards, and hotels for boatmen and teamsters. It was colorful and rough, as any district full of transient laborers is apt to be. Today, all but one of those buildings are gone. On one side of the canal is a two-acre patch of weeds and trees too unkempt to be called a park. It is never used by anyone. At the far end of it the village road crew keeps a mound of sand piled up for their wintertime street-grooming operations. On the other bank of the canal stands a neighborhood of small, motley, run-down trailers—affordable housing.

A block over from Canal Street runs the town's main thoroughfare, Broad Street. Its rows of commercial buildings extend two long blocks. In the canal days, the "downtown" business buildings were full of the offices of freight forwarders, commercial insurers, bookkeepers, and others concerned with the *business* of shipping. There were about twenty-five stores in operation at any given time, three hotels, and three theaters. The people who owned and operated these businesses took pride in their buildings and they took care of them. Many owned dwellings in the village as well. The value that their businesses accrued remained in town.

The chief products shipped through Schuylerville during the canal years were lumber from the Adirondack forests, burnt lime (used for plaster) from the hills across the river in Washington County, and potatoes grown locally for a bottomless market in New York City, 175 miles south. Two hundred farms operated in the vicinity of Schuylerville. These were diversified farms, growing local market produce as well as potatoes, and also hay for the mules that worked the canal. Today, only a handful of dairying operations remain. The town had an additional role as an agricultural trading center; here the farmers came to buy seed and tools. Local merchants profited. The population of the village proper was roughly 2500.

The town's semipastoral canal years ended with a sudden, stark shift to a new economy. Seemingly overnight, Schuylerville became a factory town. An abundance of water power lay close at hand. Fish Creek offered two waterfalls within the village limits. The aforementioned flax mill went up first. A much larger factory was built a quarter mile upstream in 1860. It produced high quality cotton cambric cloth. (In the twentieth century it was converted to make cardboard.) On the other side of the Hudson and less than a mile to the north, another stream, called the Battenkill, empties into the river with even greater force and volume than Fish Creek. Through the second half of the nineteenth century six factories went up in and around the place where the Battenkill joins the Hudson: a box mill (its specialty: cardboard cartons), a sash and blind works (windows, et cetera), two paper mills, a pulp mill that ground up logs into the raw material for the paper mills, and a wallpaper factory. At their peak, around 1900, the plants provided about 1000 jobs in the area. By the standards of the day, the workers were well paid. The money they earned was spent mostly in town. The factories were owned locally. Their owners built impressive houses and lived locally. The money they spent, in turn, supported local tradesmen and local merchants. Part of the wealth that these mills generated was invested in public buildings. No state grants were involved and hence decisions made about public works were made locally, rather than by distant bureaucrats.

The Fitchburg Railroad laid a branch line through Schuylerville in the 1800s (it was rather late in coming) that made the town a link between Albany, New York, and Rutland, Vermont, with its connecting routes to Canada and northern New England. Later, the Boston & Maine took it over. The train tracks ran right up the center of town on Green Street to a depot at Spring Street and then out of town past the cluster of six factories just mentioned. A decade later, a group of private investors backed an interurban light rail service—a trolley system—that ran from Troy, thirty miles down the river, up through Schuylerville, and onward to Fort Edward, Hudson Falls, Glens Falls, and finally to Warrensburg in the southern Adirondacks. That line linked up to another trolley out of Saratoga Springs, and the cars ran every thirty minutes. A spur of the trolley veered east across the Hudson River to the factories on the eastern shore of the Hudson.

Barely any sign remains that the trolley system existed. Occasionally a patch of blacktop at a street intersection wears away to reveal a glimpse of shiny tracks set among fat cobblestones. And a file of twelve massive stone bridge piers stand mutely in the Hudson River stripped of their iron girders near the derelict United Board and Carton factory.

In 1913 the Champlain Canal system had a major overhaul, mainly to accommodate larger boats and oil barges. A channel in the Hudson was dredged and bigger locks installed below the rapids. The stretch that ran through Schuylerville was no longer necessary, and it was simply abandoned. But it wasn't filled in. It still exists as a feature in the town's landscape, a narrow, peaceful backwater full of bullfrogs, carp, and snapping turtles, overhung with trees and largely hidden from the active life of the town—though some houses have yards that back onto it. The water is quiet but not stagnant. It flows in imperceptibly from the abandoned lock at the north of town end and flushes out below Fish Creek. Every year or so a troop of Boy Scouts goes up the old towpath—a turf road once trod by the mules that towed the canal boats—and clears out sumac saplings with a brush hog so townspeople can enjoy walking the mile length of it, all the way up to the modern Lock Number 5.

There was a time just before the First World War when a person could get around this part of the world by train, trolley, boat, automobile, horse, or on foot, and in fact each mode of transportation had its place. This rich variety of possibilities is hard to imagine in our age, when the failure to own a car is tantamount to a failure in citizenship, and our present transportation system is as much of a monoculture as our way of housing or farming. Factory workers walked or took the trolley across the Hudson. Shoppers walked to market. Stores delivered orders too big to carry. Freight moved long distance by rail or boat, and by truck or wagon only locally. Anybody who had urgent business with the greater world at large could hop on a train and get to Albany in an hour or New York City inside of five.

The yearly percentage of town revenue devoted to street and highway maintenance was much smaller in proportion to the lavish amounts that our overblown system requires today. Because of our outlandish expenditure, there is nothing left over to purchase public amenity. For example, in the 1920s, the village of Schuylerville supported an elaborate public bathing beach at the riverside. The setup was complete with bathhouse, picnic tables, lifeguards, white sand brought in from elsewhere, and an impressive battery of floats with diving platforms and slides. The beach has been closed now for many years, the white sand invaded by cattails and pickerel weed, and the changing rooms bashed apart by bored teenagers. Incidentally, the village couldn't even afford its two-man police force, and got rid of it, too, in the early 1980s.

New York Route 4 runs up Broad Street. From the 1920s on, it was a major highway to Montreal. For decades this meant that a great deal of regular truck traffic plied up Route 4 through Schuylerville. The noise must have been a terrible nuisance, but the truckers stopped and spent money in the restaurants and hotels. The interurban light rail system, the trolley, went out of business right after the First World War, having lost too great a percentage of its riders to private cars and buses. Regular train service on the Boston & Maine continued. A special kind of fine sand used in the process of molding cast iron was shipped in gondola cars out of Schuylerville in vast quantities. Drifts of it lay scattered across local farms by retreating glaciers. In the ensuing millennia a layer of rich topsoil formed over it. Extracting the molding sand was easy. It did little damage to farmland, while it put quite a bit of extra money in the farmers' pockets.

In the 1940s there were three major hotels in town, five barbershops, several grocery stores, clothing shops for men and women, three drug stores, four lunch counters, a newsroom, a bicycle shop, a movie theater, and a local newspaper—the Schuylerville *Standard.* Saturdays, shoppers filled the sidewalks. On summer nights, there were street dances for the teenagers. With seven factories humming, the town enjoyed a strong industrial base.

What happened to Schuylerville since then typifies the fate of farm and factory towns throughout upstate New York, parts of New England, and the Midwest: as our national economy became more gigantic, local economies ceased to matter. And with that, they ceased to be communities in the most meaningful sense, though people and buildings remained.

The Boston & Maine terminated rail service through Schuylerville in 1957. The track was too expensive to maintain. It crossed Fish Creek on trestles in several places, and the trestles, subject to spring floods and other stresses, required constant repair. Anyway, it was a period when the entire American railroad industry was stumbling into insolvency. A little trunk line like the B & M spur into Schuylerville was not worth maintaining. They tore up the tracks along Green Street, disassembled the railroad bridge that had crossed the Hudson, and knocked down all the trestles across Fish Creek. And so the tracks are now gone. Even if we wanted to return to a mixed transportation arrangement—and we should not doubt that it will be necessary in the future—it would be fearfully expensive to replace them.

Interstate 87, the four-lane, limited-access superhighway that opened in 1967, was now the main route between New York City and Montreal. It was routed to go through Saratoga Springs, ten miles to the west of Schuylerville, because Saratoga with its famous racetrack is a popular tourist destination. Overnight, long-haul truck traffic vanished from Route 4 and with it vanished part of Schuylerville's economy, because truckers no longer stopped for hash and eggs or a night's rest. With the railroad gone, and canal traffic limited to an occasional heating-oil barge, and no long-haul truck traffic, Schuylerville's restaurants and hotels began to fold. The shopping mall at Saratoga, built in 1972, put the last clothing stores in Schuylerville out of business.

For all practical purposes, Schuylerville became a colonial outpost of another America. Its impoverishment is one of the untallied costs of the policy of limitless "growth." The leading business establishments in Schuylerville these days are the two convenience stores, each operated by large chains—call them X and Y. The main east-west road through town, Route 29, has become a major "feeder" for Interstate 87, and the convenience stores were built to take advantage of that traffic. They sell gasoline, milk, beer, cigarettes, soda, and snacks. Plenty of local dollars are spent at the X and Y stores too—at times, the whole population of town seems to subsist on Pepsi Cola and Cheez Doodles. Perhaps in the future people will look back at convenience stores with fond nostalgia, because they are the late twentieth-century successors to the old general store that sold a little bit of everything. But there is one big difference—the X and Y stores are not owned by local merchants.

The X and Y Corporations pay property taxes to operate their stores in Schuylerville, and a percentage of the county sales tax they pay is returned to the village via a rather abstruse political formula. The stores also furnish a handful of minimum-wage jobs. But what they contribute to the town is far less significant than what they take away: the chance for a local merchant to make a profit, to keep that profit in town, where it might be put to work locally, for instance, in the upkeep of a hundred-year-old shopfront building downtown, or a Greek Revival house on Pearl Street, or in the decent support of a family. But that profit does not stay in town. Instead, it is funneled directly into distant corporate coffers. The officers of the X and Y Corporations, who do not live in Schuylerville, have no vested interest in the upkeep of the 100-hundred-year-old shopfront buildings or the Greek Revival houses there. (They may not even know what the town looks like, or a single fact of its history.) Their success is measured strictly by the tonnage of Cheez Doodles and Pepsi Cola they manage to move off the shelves. The income they derive from their jobs is spent supporting and maintaining distant suburbs—and the cost of that is fantastic. The presence of convenience stores has eliminated many other local operations—the newsroom, several lunch counters, mom and pop groceries—which couldn't compete in volume of sales. The volume of sales is the *sole* measure of what makes Schuylerville a worthy community from the point of view of the X and Y Corporations. So no local businesses thrive and the old buildings fall increasingly into disrepair.

The buildings that the X and Y Corporations put up express the companies' attitudes perfectly. They are cinder-block sheds that have no relation to the local architecture. They do not respect the sidewalk edge of building fronts that line Broad Street, but are set back behind parking lagoons. Their garish internally lighted plastic signs tower above the town's rooflines, and the mercury-vapor lamps in their parking lots cast an unearthly pinkish-green glow far beyond the edge of their properties. What they contribute to the village visually is ugliness and discord. The people who design them and build them do not have to live with the consequences of their shabby and disruptive work.

Today, many of the old shopfronts along Broad Street stand vacant, or have been rented by marginal businesses—a tattoo parlor, a room full of video games, a store that sells dented cans and damaged boxes of food at cut-rate prices. Quite a few shopfronts were converted into cheap apartments—dingy curtains hang across the old display windows—because the Saratoga County Department of Social Services uses Schuylerville as a welfare dump. There is a system in which landlords get grants from the federal Department of Housing and Urban Development to fix up their property on the condition that they rent to people on public assistance. The people on public assistance often wreck the apartments, for which new grants are then obtained, and so on in a downward-spiraling cycle, until the buildings are finally trashed beyond repair. For the landlords it is a sort of extractive process, like mining buildings for profit, with the same kind of destructive consequences as strip mining coal.

The people who live here are losing ground steadily and drastically. Their institutions have failed them. Two generations ago, they were hardworking mill hands who earned decent wages and looked after their families. Now people don't work, or only sporadically, at lower pay, and in any case, no longer in town. They commute to Saratoga, Glens Falls, Albany—an expense that only puts a further drain on their finances. The $4500 it costs to own and operate a car each year could cover a year's payments on a $30,000 mortgage. Often, it is absolutely necessary to keep two cars operating in a family so that two adults can drive long distances to work low-wage jobs. The cost of driving everywhere, to work, or to obtain the necessary goods and services of life, impoverishes families. It makes it impossible for them to own their own home.

Families crack under the pressure. Fathers unable to cope take off for good. Mothers slip into public assistance, depression, obesity, alcoholism. Yet they keep having babies. There are parasitical boyfriends and a heightened incidence of child abuse—county-wide reports of abuse more than doubled between 1983 and 1992.

One night around Halloween I interviewed eleven children between the ages of eight and fifteen at the village youth center, a prefab aluminum structure next to the town ballfield that was put up with a state grant and some money from private charity. Filled with Ping-Pong and pool tables, video games, a computer, a stereo, some battered sofas and card tables, it was clearly a refuge for the kids, and more than once they expressed their gratitude for its existence. It was better than being home. Ten of the eleven kids came from families where the natural father was not present. A few had stepfathers. Four had never even met their real fathers. Most had half-brothers and half-sisters. Only four out of eleven ate breakfast on a regular basis, and all four—including an eight-year-old—said they made their own breakfasts because there was no parent present in the house when they got up in the morning. The majority said that a television was turned on in their house at all hours, whether someone was watching it or not. Later in the session, I asked how many of them knew a teenager who was, or had been, pregnant. All hands went up.

🜋

The signs of decay are visible everywhere in the village. The decay of property is the physical expression of everything the town has lost spiritually while the American economy "grew" and the nation devised a national lifestyle based on cars, cheap oil, and recreational shopping. The movie theater where families came to watch Jimmy Stewart and Donna Reed in the 1940s is a burned-out hulk, the roof caved in, the entrance on Broad Street blocked off with a chicken-wire fence. For a few years before it burned, it was converted into a drinking establishment for bikers. The customers were known to ride their Harley "hogs" through the front door right up to the bar. One afternoon the bartender put a bullet hole through a patron's forehead. Not long after, the place caught fire.

The sidewalks downtown are all broken up, the concrete squares sunken or heaved at angles that make it hard to ride a bicycle over them. The facade of almost every building has been cobbled over with some kind of cheap and preposterous material in motifs that have no relation to the original: fake brick asbestos shingles, fake fieldstone, fake slate, enameled metal in alarming colors, aluminum and vinyl siding. The American Hotel at the south end of Broad Street, with soaring four-story pilasters and pedimented gables, was stripped of its once-magnificent porch and the ground floor was given a "rustic" exterior redo with gray barn board—it is now a welfare apartment building.

The former Grand Union supermarket stands abandoned in the center of Schuylerville's business district with burdocks and spiky mulleins poking up through the heaving asphalt of the parking lot. Strictly on its own terms it was a bad building from the moment it was completed. It ruined whatever charm Broad Street possessed by making it, in effect, a one-sided street. The Grand Union closed up shop, by the way, because central management far away decided as a matter of general policy not to keep open stores that had less than certain square footage of space. The decision had nothing to do with local economic conditions per se; it was imposed on the village like weather. As in the case of the convenience stores, the Grand Union was designed solely to maximize company profits. Not a damn thing about it provided anything in the way of civic ornament. The people who designed it didn't have to live with it. It is arguable whether it looks worse now that nobody takes care of it.

♟

When Americans, depressed by the scary places where they work and dwell, contemplate some antidote, they often conjure up the image of the American small town. However muddled and generalized the image is, it exerts a powerful allure. For the idea of a small town represents a whole menu of human values that the gigantism of corporate enterprise has either obliterated or mocked: an agreeable scale of human enterprise, tranquility, public safety, proximity of neighbors and markets, nearness to authentic countryside, and permanence.

Despite the nearly universal imposition of the straight grid, with all its weaknesses, America's small town streets at their best had some powerful saving graces. The houses were scaled generously—families were larger then, and multigenerational. No matter how fanciful, nineteenth-century homes were built of natural materials that aged gracefully. The procession of porches along the street created a lovely mediating zone between the private world of the home and the public world of the street, further connected and softened by the towering elm trees and the lush foliage.

The organic wholeness of the small town street was a result of common, everyday attention to details, of intimate care for things intimately used. The discipline of its physical order was based not on uniformity for its own sake, but on a consciousness of, and respect for, what was going on next door. Such awareness and respect were not viewed as a threat to individual identity but as necessary for the production of amenity, charm, and beauty. These concepts are now absent from our civilization. We have become accustomed to living in places where nothing relates to anything else, where disorder, unconsciousness, and the absence of respect reign unchecked.

The small town life that Americans long for when they are depressed by their city apartments or their suburban bunkers is really a conceptual substitute for the idea of community. But a community is not something you *have*, like a pizza. Nor is it something you can buy, as visitors to Disneyland and Williamsburg discover. It is a living organism based on a web of interdependencies—which is to say, a local economy. It expresses itself physically as *connectedness*, as buildings actively relating to one another, and to whatever public space exists, be it the street, or the courthouse square, or the village green. "Most important," Wendell Berry writes, "it must be generally loved and competently cared for by its people, who, individually, identify their own interest with the interest of their neighbors. . . ."[1] That notion of community began to vanish in America after World War II. We have paid a lot of lip service to the idea, and indulged in a lot of easy nostalgia about it, but our small towns have never been worse off than they are now.

☆

Many schemes have been advanced in recent years for promoting the economy of Schuylerville. The worst schemes, it seems to me, are pegged to tourism, playing up the Revolutionary War angle. Such schemes suppose endless supplies of leisure and gasoline in America's future. In this scenario, the townspeople will sell hamburgers and souvenir musket balls to tourists. Perhaps these tourists will be folks who make a living selling hamburgers where they come from—America as one big theme park, an endless circle of hamburgers.

Others continue to view the town's future as a bedroom community for Saratoga, and even Albany, over an hour away by car. I think these schemes are improbable. Neither has anything to do with building a true local economy, in the sense of practical skills, or the profitable manufacture of any useful product, or trade that benefits local merchants. They seek to inject prosperity from some outside source.

I believe that we are entering an era when small towns will be valued again, and that out of necessity we will reinvent truly local economies using local assets and resources. An old small town like Schuylerville has one particular hidden asset placing it at an advantage over the present power places of America: It isn't a suburb. When the suburban economic equation fails in America, the physical arrangement of life will fail with it, and many Americans will be stuck in places that no longer function. Schuylerville does not have to be retrofitted to function as a coherent town in the future; it already is one, neglected and tattered as it may be.

Schuylerville's most obvious resource is the Hudson River, the ultimate source of the town's past wealth. Today, the life of the town could not be more disconnected from the river. But one thing we know for certain: the era of cheap gas is drawing to a close, and necessity will make the river valuable again. Schuylerville has water power to run machinery to make useful products in a way that does not have to be harmful and wasteful. It has direct water links to New York and Montreal. In any other civilized country, resources like these would make such a town and its people useful. It would have an economy and be a community.

Chapter Eleven

THREE CITIES

The crisis of place in America is illustrated most vividly by the condition of our cities. Their squalor and impoverishment is the worst symptom of the crisis. Historically, cities contain the essence of a civilization. They are the marketplaces for ideas and cultural values as well as material goods. They are the repositories of cultural memory. The city, above all, is the public realm monumentalized.

I don't believe that automobile suburbs are an adequate replacement for cities, since the motive force behind suburbia has been the exaltation of privacy and the elimination of the public realm. Where city life optimizes the possibility of contact between people, and especially different kinds of people, the suburb strives to eliminate precisely that kind of human contact. And so my argument throughout this book has been that the city in some form, and at some scale, is necessary.

In this chapter I have selected three cities that are strikingly different from one another, and yet all, I believe, represent a type. I have picked Detroit because it is the worst case of an old industrial metropolis gone to hell. Portland, Oregon, in contrast, embodies the most hopeful and progressive trends in American city life and especially in urban planning. Los Angeles, the quintessential city of the twentieth century, wholeheartedly dedicated to cars, is the most problematic place to interpret. The form it has assumed may not allow it to function in the century to come, and so this most modern of places has, paradoxically, the most dubious future.

Detroit ➤➤

The city that spawned the auto age is the place where everything that could go wrong with a city, did go wrong, in large part because of the car. Until a decade ago, Detroit was the sixth largest city in America and one of the wealthiest industrial cities on the planet. In the last ten years alone, its population shrank by 20 percent. Since other nations learned to make better cars more cheaply, the city's auto industry verges on extinction. Anyway, the era of the car-based economy is drawing to a close because we can no longer endure its costs. Detroit, in its present necrotic state, illustrates these costs clearly.

Motoring around Detroit in a rented car, one is not psychologically prepared for the scope of desolation. Beyond the decomposing downtown core of skyscrapers—about the size of ten Manhattan blocks—Detroit is a city of single-family houses that go on and on, seemingly forever, into a drab gloaming of auto emissions and K Mart signs. The innermost ring of houses is now almost completely destroyed. Bear in mind that Detroit was a thriving and highly diversified industrial city decades before the carmakers came along in the 1900s. The men who earlier made fortunes in, among other things, tobacco processing, metalworking, pharmaceuticals, grain milling, meat packing, and brewing, built fancy brick mansions in the gridded blocks off Woodward Avenue, Detroit's grandest boulevard. They were built to endure, yet most of them did not last a hundred years.

These scores of blocks around Woodward were at the heart of the 1967 riot, a disturbance so fierce that Detroit's own police and the Michigan militia failed to contain it, and the U.S. Army had to be sent in. The neighborhood had become a vast slum after the town's wealthiest citizens departed on a tide of automobiles for Grosse Point and other posh outlands. Since the riot, the old mansions have been randomly burned down in an ongoing orgy of arson that climaxes each year on the night before Halloween, known to Detroiters as Devil's Night, when even firemen get shot.

What remains of this enormous neighborhood is something worse than a slum. A scattering of once-beautiful, now hopelessly decayed mansions stand in these blocks like inscrutable megaliths in a wilderness of rubble. Ailanthus trees corkscrew through broken porches and bay windows. Some houses are all but hidden behind rank growths of mid-western weeds. The slumlord/tenant arrangement hardly even pertains here. Remaining denizens come and go on an informal basis, in a fog of drugs, crime, and hopelessness. So desolate is this neighborhood that you can stop at an intersection on Woodward looking straight down-town past the boarded-up storefronts toward the towers of the new Renaissance Center, and not see a single other automobile ahead of you, or behind you, for miles.

Detroit's problems are commonly interpreted in terms of race, blacks versus whites, and a racial analysis conveys much truth about the city's predicament, but it is hardly the whole story. The city's troubles were greatly aggravated by changes in the physical patterns of life wrought by the car culture.

The auto industry exploded in scale after Henry Ford devised the assembly line in 1909, and the city's physical boundaries exploded with it. From 1900 to 1930, Detroit's population ballooned from 285,000 to nearly two million, a sixfold increase. Ford alone expanded from 31 employees in 1904 to 56,000 in 1920. These workers needed homes.

In the early years of the auto age, worker housing was mass-produced on a scale almost as great as the production of cars. Vast, monotonous neighborhoods of one-story workingman's bungalows sprang up near the auto plants and on the fringes of town. In fact, the fringe pushed out so rapidly that each successive boundary road was named to give people a proximate idea of their distance from downtown: Six Mile Road, Seven Mile Road, Eight Mile Road, and so on. At the same time, a class of better-paid executives and sales agents also mushroomed, and with it, neighborhoods of new and larger houses.

The amount of wealth generated by the car business was stupend-ous. It flowed to Detroit from all corners of America. And it showed in the broad boulevards of big, impressive Tudor-style houses, or Mediterranean-style villas with three-car garages, where the growing ranks of the corporate elite settled.

The new neighborhoods spread out relentlessly, unrelieved by parks. Streetcars linked the neighborhoods. The automakers at first supported the streetcar system, at least until the Great Depression, because the scale of their operations required armies of workers, and, above all, the assembly-line method of production demanded that workers show up on time. Of course, Henry Ford wanted his employees to buy Ford cars, but no more than 30 percent commuted to work by auto in the late 1920s, and by then the streets were so clogged with cars that a trip to work in a private vehicle might take two hours.

Whether or not streetcars were vital to the healthy functioning of the city and its factories, they came to be viewed as impediments to cars. There was optimism at all levels of society that the automobile would transform life for the better, and that it was somehow Detroit's obligation, as the industry's hometown, to show America the way to refit a city for motoring.

In 1922, Detroit's mayor appointed a commission chaired by Sidney D. Waldon to figure out a transportation scheme for the future. Waldon had made a personal fortune getting the Packard and Cadillac operations started, retiring at forty-three to do good civic works. He was devoted to maximizing the use of the automobile, which he called "the magic carpet of transportation for all mankind."[1] His commission's report was issued in 1925. It urged clearing the existing streets of streetcars, the construction of subways for five miles out from the city's center, and the building of twenty new 204-foot-wide "superhighways" stretching over 240 miles into three counties.

The subway was never built, and for good reasons. Detroit had become such a spread-out, low-density metropolis of single-family houses that a system huge enough to serve it was mathematically unlikely to attract enough riders to pay for itself. (This would become the basic dilemma of public transit for all of American suburbia later on.) After much quarreling and delay, a proposal to issue bonds for a shorter demonstration line was roundly rejected by 72 percent of the voters. That was April 1929. Six months later, the stock market crashed and the Great Depression was on. Ironically, Detroit did lead the nation in another trend of the times: its corrupt banks were the first to be forcibly shut down for insolvency. The closings set off a chain reaction that collapsed the whole banking structure of the United States.

With the subway idea quashed, and car production way down as a result of the Depression, General Motors embarked on its crusade to destroy streetcar lines and replace them with General Motors buses.

The company's hometown was not spared. The Detroit tax base was low for such a big city. The innumerable single-family homes did not generate revenue the way apartment buildings did in other cities. Detroit could not afford to maintain a large street-railway during hard times. Besides, the big carmakers had a vested interest in promoting highway construction, which jibed nicely with the federal government's evolving program for permanently curing economic depression by building a suburban substitute for cities.

During World War II, the government built expressways from the heart of Detroit, where all the workers lived, to its new Willow Run bomber plant, and to the Chrysler tank factory that was hastily constructed in Warren, beyond Twelve Mile Road. These were prototypes of things to come. When the war was over, Detroit's old grid of coherent city blocks was webbed with limited-access superhighways, built below street grade so they acted like great concrete moats that could only be crossed by infrequent overpasses. They were like stakes driven through the hearts of old neighborhoods, killing whatever life they touched, and erasing thousands of houses and small businesses from the tax rolls. The interchanges became gigantic wastelands of on-ramps and off-ramps. Wherever a street ran alongside a new expressway, the remaining houses naturally became horrible places to live, subject to the pitiless roar of motors and the unearthly glare of mercury-vapor lamps. As everywhere else in America, expressways leading out of Detroit stimulated real estate development in the once-distant hinterlands. A great ring of suburbs blossomed. Here the politics of place coincides with the politics of race.

⚐

Before the turn of the twentieth century, Detroit's small black population dwelt in a neighborhood called Black Bottom, near the Detroit River. Southern blacks began moving to Detroit in great numbers during World War II, when the city became "the arsenal of democracy." Allowed to play only a minor role in the armed services, black men were welcomed in the converted war factories to make up for the shortage of white male workers. Wages in Detroit were fabulous compared to the pitiful rewards of sharecropping in Alabama. A vicious race riot in 1943, instigated by whites, did not stem the migration, and after the war, southern blacks continued to flood into Detroit. By then, the mechanical cotton picker was putting an end to the whole cheap-labor sharecropping system down south.

Meanwhile, car production boomed in the Motor City: "Mo'town." The fifties were like the twenties again, except better, since World War II had eliminated the industrial competition abroad. This was America's golden hour, a time of tailfins and the hoopla of annual model changes. The city could absorb tremendous amounts of labor. But not forever. Because they were poor, the new arrivals moved into the worst housing, as has always been the case in the history of immigration in America. By the mid-sixties, the new emigrants had far exceeded the number of jobs available even during a boom. The fabulous paychecks never materialized. Rural heritage had not prepared these newcomers for city life, particularly one of chronic unemployment. The paternalism of sharecropping, itself a revised form of slavery, translated easily into the paternalistic slavery of welfare. The 1967 riot was an angry expression of these maladaptations and the hopelessness that attended them.

The riot scared the hell out of the other Detroit, the white working class and middle class. It must be emphasized that this was Detroit's second major race riot in twenty-five years—the two worst in American history to that date—and to whites it augured doomfully for the city. In 1967, auto workers with a few years on the assembly line made more money than college professors. Those who could leave their old neighborhoods for the suburbs now fled en masse. Many had little to lose. Their old mortgages were paid off. They were willing to sell their houses at panic prices, or rent them out. Middle-class whites from the big managerial enclaves did lose equity in the rush to leave their spacious houses. But then, houses in the suburbs were still relatively cheap, and white flight was subsidized by FHA mortgages and federal highway grants. Blacks soon moved into the newly evacuated neighborhoods, since the old primary ghettos around Woodward Avenue and on the city's east side had burned down in the riots.

Of course, there was a black middle class: those whose families had been up north long before the great migration, those who had made it in the earlier days of the auto industry, those who succeeded in spite of racial, cultural, or economic disadvantages. There is no doubt that they were made to feel unwelcome in the white suburbs by way of overt racism and discrimination. The white exodus made it possible for the black middle class to suddenly obtain excellent housing within the city at bargain-basement prices—wonderful 1900s-to-1920s houses far more solid, commodious, and elegant than the ticky-tacky boxes that whites were snapping up in the suburbs. These were the heady days of the late sixties, with great stirrings of black pride, black self-determination, and black community. Here was the nation's sixth largest city fast becoming an all-Afro-American metropolis. The most visible black-owned business was Berry Gordy's Motown record company. It was sexy and charismatic and there was serious money to be made in the music industry. It seemed to promise a vital, new, *highly profitable* black urban renaissance rising out of the ashes of the riot, perhaps even a black utopia. . . .

It was a mirage. Detroit's real economy was not Four Tops records but cars, and in the early seventies the bottom began to drop out of the car business. The Japanese entered the American market with small, reliable, inexpensive cars just as the first Arab Oil Embargo struck. The big three automakers failed to adjust to changing times for reasons that boiled down to corporate giantism. Their big, stupid, gas-guzzling cars became obsolete overnight, and people in charge lacked the will or the sense or long-term vision to retool their plants to make smaller ones. So Detroit lost its worldwide preeminence in the industry never to regain it.

As one consequence, the United Autoworkers Union virtually eliminated entry-level jobs for young people, filling the diminishing pool of jobs with recycled experienced workers—"last hired, first fired." This hit young, unskilled black men hard. Hard times thundered down through the hundreds of smaller suppliers in town—everything from car upholstery wholesalers to tool-and-die shops—and the city hemorrhaged high-paying industrial jobs. Motown records eventually moved to Los Angeles, taking with it the illusion of a separate black urban cultural utopia. The bottom line was this: When the car industry commenced its long, slow death—still in progress—and the economy of Detroit failed, the community failed with it. For the situation in a big city is the same as in a small town: the economy *is* the community. Without one, you cannot have the other.

Until the 1967 riot, suburbanites still ventured downtown to enjoy the city's glittering attractions. They saw Broadway-bound musicals at the Fisher Theater, dined at the London Chop House on Congress Street, danced at the Book-Cadillac Hotel, and at Christmas time they dutifully flocked to Hudson's, a department store so colossal and posh it made Bloomingdale's look like a five-and-dime. Today, Detroit suburbanites pride themselves on never having to cross Eight Mile Road, the city's boundary. You can stand in Cadillac Square at high noon on a business day and see fewer live bodies than you would at dawn any Sunday on Wall Street. At night, downtown Detroit looks like a set for some movie about the last hours of the Planet Earth.

This sad condition was supposed to be cured by the Renaissance Center, a "big footprint" development of four thirty-nine-story office towers surrounding a seventy-three-story cylindrical glass hotel, all bestriding a giant shopping mall on fifty acres of riverfront at the base of Detroit's old business district. Henry Ford II, or "Hank the Deuce," as he was fondly known around town, relentlessly pushed the project. It opened for business in 1977 at a cost of $357 million. From the very start it was a financial catastrophe and, as an exercise in civic design, an epic flop.

When it became apparent that few businesses wanted to rent office space there, Ford ordered 1700 of his own employees to evacuate their suites in suburban Dearborn and set a good example by moving into the bright new complex downtown. They occupied one entire office tower. Ford, the RenCen's biggest financial backer, now became its biggest tenant—during a period of time when Ford Motors Inc. was losing hundreds of millions of dollars. In its first five years, the RenCen showed operating losses of $130 million.[2]

From a design point of view, the RenCen was asinine. For starters, the buildings, which occupied thirty acres of the fifty-acre site, had less than half a dozen entrances, and most of them were not at street level, but on a kind of terraced mezzanine that you could only get to via the main entrance. Moreover, the big landscaped podium that the buildings were set on was surrounded by driveways. All of the retail action was deep inside, hidden from the streets around it by windowless stone walls. In short, it was a gigantic fortress. It had no physical connection to its surroundings. It was a big, scary presence looming balefully in the sky. A pedestrian outside the complex, gazing up at the five towers cloaked in dark glass, felt like a bug about to be squashed by a gang of prison guards.

Here was the essence of the dilemma: total security and easy public access contradicted each other. Without easy public access the project would fail to interact with, and thereby enliven, the rest of the business district—which was the whole point of it in the first place. Yet the designers opted for security. They made it easy to get into the RenCen by car (parking for 6000 vehicles!), and they made it an ordeal to get inside from the street on foot. The whole attitude of the place was summed up in a little sign beside one entrance: "Private property. Under 17 must be escorted by guardian." Notice: it said *"escorted by guardian"* not "accompanied by adult." This meant that a group of sixteen-year-olds could not enter in the company of a seventeen-year-old friend. You had to come with Mom or Dad or Uncle Otto. So much for the public realm.

The inside was as misconceived as the outside. Everything was designed in circles. The central hotel was a gigantic tube. The cavernous atrium court at the bottom of the hotel was circular. The shopping corridors surrounding it were circular. Circular subcourts of shops and restaurants radiated from the main atrium. It was completely disorienting. It was especially idiotic in a facility designed for visiting strangers who, by definition, do not know their way around. Because of this, the RenCen's management were forced to set up information desks at every compass point on two different levels—and not out of the goodness of their hearts, either, but because so many people were wandering around lost that it had become a public relations problem.

The final ingredient in the revival of downtown Detroit was supposed to be the People Mover. It is essentially a high-tech elevated streetcar. Its two-car trains zip around a three-mile downtown loop every fifteen minutes, stopping at thirteen mini-stations. It is clean, quiet, efficient, cute, and, as theme park rides go, a bargain at fifty cents.

As a serious element of civic design the People Mover is a joke. The diameter of the loop it toodles around—that is, the distance across from any one point to the opposite side—is precisely the optimum distance for pedestrian movement in a city, meaning you might as well walk, which is exactly what the few remaining daytime denizens of downtown do. Otherwise, the People Mover is unconnected with the rest of the city. It does nothing to bring people from residential neighborhoods to their offices.

I rode the People Mover at high noon on a Thursday morning—that is, on a business day—when reasonably one might have expected some business people to be shuttling to and fro around the business district, at least going from their offices to restaurants. I stayed on for two complete circuits and only one other passenger boarded it—the stations were otherwise deserted. He was a young accountant who had to travel eight blocks from his headquarters at the RenCen to another office on Clifford Street to do an audit. His duties required him to lug around a twenty-five-pound portable computer. "When the boss finally breaks down and buys me a laptop," he said, "I'll probably walk it."

Henry Ford I (1863–1947) had a pet project that occupied much of his energy in later years. Out in Dearborn, just beyond the Detroit city limits, on a parcel of eighty-one acres adjacent to the company's proving grounds and its research center, and not far from its behemoth main factory complex at River Rouge, stands this public attraction that Ford named Greenfield Village.

It was an idea rather like the one that inspired Colonial Williamsburg: to recreate a scene of ordinary American life at an earlier time, in this case the 1880s—coincidentally the years of Henry Ford's youth—with all the visual, aural, tactile, and even olfactory sensations thereof. But unlike Williamsburg, which had always been a real town, there was no original Greenfield Village to restore. Rather, it was artificially assembled, as it were, out of bits and pieces, and given an artificial name that neatly evoked the two primary elements of a bygone American landscape: green fields and villages.

Henry I made a kind of fetish of collecting historical buildings—especially the boyhood homes and workshops of his fellow genius-inventor-entrepreneur-industrialists. Beginning in the 1920s, he acquired the Wright Brothers' boyhood home and the old bike shop in Dayton, Ohio, where they first tinkered with gliders; Thomas Edison's Menlo Park, New Jersey, research lab; the Ohio birthplace of pickle king H.J. Heinz; the Michigan boyhood farmstead of tire mogul Harvey Firestone; and much more, including Ford's own modest birthplace. All were moved to the Dearborn site—along with other miscellaneous period buildings: a gristmill, a covered bridge, a stagecoach inn, a one-room schoolhouse, barns—and reassembled into a sort of village. Today, Greenfield Village is a major tourist attraction run by a foundation that has disentangled itself from the Ford Motor Company. Admission is $10.50 a head.

I had taken perhaps thirty steps beyond the ticket gate when a great pang of rue corkscrewed through me, realizing that here Henry Ford had built a monument to everything that his life's work had obliterated in the American townscape. In keeping with the period scene, there were no cars in sight. How strange it was to amble down car-free streets—even if you could always hear the distant roar of the Southfield Freeway. I was curious what my fellow visitors thought, and so, brandishing a pocket tape recorder, I asked them.

They liked a lot of things about the place. The pottery demonstration, the tintype studio, the "old-fashioned" lunch they got at the Eagle Tavern stagecoach inn, the little watchmaker's shop off "Main Street," the costumed "schoolmarm" ringing her bell on the village green, the sheep grazing in the Firestone farm pasture, and so on. In short, they liked individual bits of this and that. Curiously, I realized, none of them mentioned the absence of cars. It made me wonder if I was putting the question to them correctly.

By and by, I found a young mother relaxing on a bench in a shady spot with her kid dozing in a stroller. She was well-groomed, thirty-something, and said she lived in Birmingham, which is an upper-middle-class suburb. As a "member" of Greenfield Village, she paid annual dues and was entitled to come out any old time and hang around, which she said she did often—it was her "favorite place in the area." Why did she like it so much? "It's so peaceful, and the gardens are beautiful," she said. What was there about the quality of that peace that she liked? "I can hear the birds singing, people seem relaxed here, the pace is slower." Why is it different from Birmingham? "I dunno—I guess it's more old-fashioned," she said. We went on in this vein a while longer. I tried and tried, but I could not drag out of her any admission that, perhaps, the place was peaceful because there were no cars around. She did not strike me as a stupid person. Her manner of speech, her clothes, her situation in the world, suggested that she was, if anything, a bit above average. She might have been a whiz at crossword puzzles, a collector of folk art, a Garrison Keillor fan. But as far as Greenfield Village was concerned, she didn't get it.

I left her sitting in her pool of shade and continued on, stopping folks to chat into my tape recorder here and there. None of them mentioned cars. In exasperation, I just came out and started saying, "Have you noticed there aren't any cars around here?" They replied by saying, "Well, sure, you have to park outside," or "They got some Model T's in that building over there," or "Gee, you're right—weird, isn't it?" I might as well have asked if they noticed that there were no swarms of locusts around.

Eventually I came to the far end of the village and entered a fenced vegetable garden. A middle-aged woman sat there in period clothes, shelling beans, one of many such costumed employees posted around the village.

"What do you think of our place?" she asked cheerfully, yet in the manner of someone obviously habituated to playing a role.

I didn't want to upset her, but couldn't help blurting out my true feelings: "It makes me ashamed of my civilization," I said.

Portland, Oregon ➤➤

Could this be America? A vibrant downtown, the sidewalks full of purposeful-looking citizens, clean, well-cared-for buildings, electric trolleys, shopfronts with nice things on display, water fountains that work, cops on bikes, greenery everywhere?

Portland, a city of 429,000, a little bigger than Pittsburgh and a bit smaller than Atlanta, seems to defy the forces that elsewhere drag American urban life into squalor and chaos. It has accomplished this with a lot of conscious, intelligent planning, plus a little geographical luck.

Metropolitan Portland straddles two banks of the Willamette River valley, which runs between the shining Cascade Mountains to the east and the Coast Range to the west. The mild climate accounts for its nickname: "City of Roses." Maybe twice a year it gets a dusting of snow or an ice storm, but generally winter tends to be "misty," as one native put it. The annual precipitation is actually less than that of New York City, and it hardly lives up to the rain-drenched image that outsiders have of, say, Seattle, its larger neighbor 175 miles to the north. Summer days the mercury rarely kisses eighty degrees.

Because of the weather, the Willamette valley is a kind of agricultural paradise. Blackberries here grow the size of plovers' eggs. Nut and fruit orchards abound. Market crops flourish. The common roadside weed is foxglove, that stately habitué of English country gardens. This is a real land of milk and honey, and pioneers willingly suffered great ordeals of overland travel to reach it beginning in the 1840s. Its earthly riches have had a lot to do with molding Oregonians' mentality toward land development.

The main business district, and most of the important civic institutions in Portland, reside on the west bank of the Willamette, hemmed in by steep, wooded foothills. The rugged geography has kept the downtown area necessarily compact. Blocks are laid out in a coherent grid of numbered avenues. Office towers rise alongside apartment buildings. Museums, theaters, and commercial emporiums nestle in between. High-priced boutiques mix with grocery, hardware, and stationery stores. Powell's bookshop, one of the largest independent bookstores in the nation, occupies an entire downtown block. Portland is alive day and night. Because people live there at a high density, the city can support a variety of eating places, bars, cafés, clubs. The rich, up in their sky-high condos, live around the corner from the middle class, who live up the street from the not-doing-so-well. The important thing is that they all live together in proximity, not as though their worlds were separate, dirty secrets. The texture of life is mixed, complex, and dense, as a city ought to be, the way all cities used to be before the automobile and curse of Modernist planning.

Civic-minded Portlanders, eschewing "big footprint" schemes like Detroit's RenCen, paid attention to the details of what was already there, and particularly to the way the elements of the city fit together. They understood that the city was only as good as its connections, that urban ingredients treated in isolation had no meaning. For example, they realized that a building with no shop windows at street level would result in a dead street—no matter how gorgeous the building was as a sculpture viewed from sixteen blocks away. So they passed a zoning code that *requires* buildings to have display windows at street level. Buildings also must be built out to the sidewalk. There are height and bulk restrictions for high-rises, so that downtown would not become a maze of sunless canyons.

Similarly, planning officials rethought the residential zoning codes. Downtown, they created a vigorous program of incentives, such as ten-year tax abatements, so developers would put up apartment buildings of the kind that New Yorkers refer to as "prewar"—that is, buildings under twenty stories with lobbies. City planners were very specific about the desired scale. They wanted population density, but not colossal dehumanizing towers that would overload the infrastructure. So they did what planners have been unable to do elsewhere in America: they showed respect for limits. And they ended up with attractive, profitable, well-made buildings where middle-class people could afford to rent.

In the neighborhoods just beyond downtown, codes were changed to allow row housing and multi-unit dwellings where previously only single-family homes were permitted. Predictably, this led to a lot of public acrimony on the part of high-income people who did not want their neighborhoods invaded by anyone with less income. But the Portland planning department takes the long view that urban life will have to become more concentrated and more mixed in the years ahead.

"We want to commit further urbanization to those areas already urbanized," said Michael Harrison, a veteran of the city's planning battles.

Portland revived the idea of the streetcar. They call it "light rail." It runs above the ground and is electrically powered. The first line went from the heart of downtown east across the Willamette, and clear out to the suburb of Gresham, a distance of about fifteen miles. The "excuse" to build it was to take pressure off the Banfield Freeway, which had become a horrible commuter bottleneck. The line ran halfway out along the same right-of-way occupied by the freeway, and the rest of the way down the center of a wide commercial highway, Burnside Avenue, so building it did not require the destruction of homes. It has been successful enough for voters to approve a bond issue to build a second, western leg of the line.

At the same time that the light rail started operating, the city put a "parking lid" on the total number of parking spaces downtown. The point was not simply to limit the number of cars pouring in, but to stifle the incentive to replace existing old buildings with easy-profit parking lots. To mitigate the inconvenience of limited parking, the city offers free bus service in a 300-block area downtown. The buses run at frequent intervals and each stop has a shelter.

A half-dozen parks full of statues, fountains, and greenery provide breathing space in the business district. Broad tree-filled medians extend more than a half-mile along Park Avenue, and a riverside park runs two miles along the Willamette, complete with paved esplanades at the water's edge. Here was one of the best examples of Oregonians marching to a different drummer than the rest of America. They tore down an old four-lane expressway and reconnected the city with its waterfront. This was accomplished in the 1970s, when other American cities were gleefully taking federal subsidies to build *new* freeways along their rivers and harbors.

The part of Portland east of the Willamette is larger in area than the west bank, flatter, and made up mostly of single-family houses. Most of it is gridded in oblong blocks, with a few eccentric blobs of curved streets, or parcheesi-board diagonals where 1920s developers tried to fancy up the original pattern. Here, broad commercial boulevards like Burnside—as overblown and hideous as any strips in America—roll out remorselessly into the suburban mists. Here, too, lies Portland's low-income section, Albina, a racially-mixed nineteen-square-mile wedge of bungalows between the airport and the industrial buzzard flats on Swan Island. The city intends to build a spur off of the Gresham streetcar line that will make Albina an easy carless commute to downtown. They'll offer tax breaks for people willing to rehab old houses, and incentives to urban "homesteaders." Albina may never be gentrified, in the sense of a lot of rich yuppies taking over the neighborhood—the housing stock isn't grand enough—but the city is making sure that it becomes, at least, a decent, safe, attractive place for working people. This is almost a revolutionary concept in America today: that anyone but the very rich should be able to live in decent, safe, and attractive neighborhoods.

꩜

Much of what is good about Portland came to pass because Oregon was the unofficial capital of the "environmental" movement in the late sixties and early seventies. The state was large, sparsely populated, had a beautiful coast, and lots of mountains, farmland, and high desert. People who liked unspoiled places flocked to Oregon, and once there they became active about protecting what they had found. And since nearly half of Oregon's entire population lives in and around the greater metropolitan Portland area, a lot of these people naturally extended their environmental concerns to include urban matters. During this period they elected a visionary governor, Tom McCall. ("Come visit us, but please don't stay," was a slogan attributed to him.) The city of Portland had an equally visionary mayor, Neil Goldschmidt—later Secretary of Transportation in the Carter administration—who understood that cars were wrecking America and aimed to do something about it.

Under the leadership of McCall and Goldschmidt, Oregon underwent a revolution in land-use policy. Few states had faced the problem of runaway development, and the ones that tried, like Vermont and Florida, had accomplished little. Vermont, for instance, got rid of billboards in 1968, but managed to pass only a squishy law, called Act 250, which did little more than control development on mountainsides above the 2500 feet in elevation. Floridians were making too much money off "growth" to stop and listen to their own land-use experts.

The cornerstone of the Oregon policy was the Urban Growth Boundary (UGB), a law which stated, in essence, that "beyond this line you cannot develop commercial projects, housing, retail or otherwise." Along with the new regulations came an agency to enforce it, with teeth: the Metropolitan Service District, known locally as Metro. The whole package was sold to the public as a measure aimed at protecting Oregon's valuable farmlands—which happened to occupy the same corridor, the Willamette valley, where 80 percent of the state's people lived. But the UGB was as much antisprawl as profarm. Everyone knew it. The act had powerful foes in those who fed off sprawl—the construction industry, the realtors, the steel and cement suppliers—but it was passed over their protests in 1973, a tribute to the leadership of Governor McCall.

That was the year of the first oil crisis, and the whole American economy shuddered. Suddenly, everything that went on in America, the production and transport of all goods, cost twice as much. The "stagflation" recession of the mid-seventies was on. Oregon was hit hard. Its giant lumber industry suffered badly as housing starts plummeted nationwide. So, here the state had gone to all the trouble of setting up an elaborate system to control growth, and suddenly they had no growth.

"It was like we were all dressed up with no place to go," said Ethan Seltzer, a Metro planner. "It was really devastating. We actually lost population."

In the eighties the economy surged. A bunch of computer software companies started up in the Portland area. The Nike running shoe company, headquartered there, took off with the national fitness movement. The lumber industry awoke from its slumber as construction boomed. The population of suburban Gresham swelled from 12,000 to 50,000. Beaverton, to the west, ballooned from 8000 to 50,000. Planners predicted a wave of growth that altogether might bring half a million new residents to the Metro district by the year 2010. Hard-core environmentalists worried that the boundary line had been drawn too broadly. Metro had even created large "exception areas" out in the protected zones—blobs of land deemed useless for agriculture, where building would be allowed—and spec houses sprang up on the hillsides like mushrooms after a spring rain.

Individual towns began to complain that Metro and its UGB had usurped their zoning prerogatives. Not able to lure industry or shopping malls into their district with favorable zoning, they lost the ability to jack up their tax revenues. Unfair, they cried. Metro was actually telling people over a three-county region exactly how their land was going to be used. It was Lewis Mumford's dream come true: authentic regional planning. It was un-American. *You can't tell me what to do with my land!*

Realtors complained that the UGB had perverted the market for developable land. There was a shortage of ten-acre parcels suitable for shopping centers. And taking farmland off the market suddenly made it difficult for speculative builders. One spokesman for the realtors explained it very nicely at a 1990 conference on growth:

> I had a call the other day from an out-of-state developer who has been very successful around the country developing what would be called high-end golf course residential tracts. . . . He operates with a minimum of 1000 acres and would prefer to have 2000. One of the requirements is to be able to buy some of that property at farm values because you are dealing with a twenty-year absorption program. If you have got to pay the current asking price for residential land, you can't afford to carry. The project just doesn't pencil and the developer would then go to a different community to do his project. Maybe I missed something, but I believe that, within the Portland metropolitan urban growth boundary, I could not meet that prospect's needs.[3]

Well, wasn't that the whole idea? The unstated bottom line was that Oregonians were going to have to find new ways of doing things: of making a living without destroying land, building real towns and city neighborhoods instead of tract housing pods and commercial strip smarm, eliminating unnecessary car trips and commutes, and, most of all, thinking about long-term consequences instead of mere short-term gain. This was asking a lot in a culture that esteemed moneygrubbing above all else, but they seemed up to the challenge. Let the developers of "high-end golf course residential tracts" go to hell.

It remains to be seen how well the Urban Growth Boundary will work. The world is apt to change radically by the year 2010. In retrospect, our assumptions about the future often seem laughably naive. What planners call "growth" today might be against the law tomorrow, when the greenhouse effect starts to play its nasty tricks on us. In the meantime, Oregonians are acting intelligently and setting an example in regional land-use policy that the rest of the nation would do well to heed. In Portland they have a city, notwithstanding the abysmal standards of American civic art, of which they deserve to feel proud.

Los Angeles ▶▶

Los Angeles the Damned, H. L. Mencken used to call it back in the 1920s, recognizing even then its pervasive aura of doom.

I was in Los Angeles (the City of Our Lady of the Angels of Porciuncula) in the days just after Mr. Saddam Hussein invaded Kuwait in his attempt to control the lion's share of the Middle East's oil reserves. Plying the renowned freeways hour after hour in a rented Chevy, I kept twiddling the radio dial in search of news and opinion about the momentous events unfolding. There were a great many chat shows on the airwaves, full of callers-in vituperating about sports, abortion, personal problems, the homeless, and every other topic under the sun, *except* the invasion of Kuwait. It might have taken place on another planet.

The equation appeared simple enough to me: instability in the price or supply of gas = chaos for Los Angeles. Now, I took the radio chatters to be average Angelenos, and their complete obliviousness to a world situation that threatened their way of life seemed to exemplify what is wrong with their city and their vaunted culture. Or maybe it was just a whopping case of mass denial, as a psychiatrist friend proposed. For in LA they have built a metropolitan system so physically enormous and so enormously susceptible to sudden ruin that anyone who took a long-term view of the city's problems would have to go crazy.

This was ironic, because driving around the far-flung compass points of the Angelene metropolis, it was the long views that uplifted the spirit: the Hollywood Hills from Wilshire Boulevard; the Pacific Ocean from high up on the Santa Monica Mountains; the spreading grid of twinkling lights viewed at night from a terrace in upper Bel Air; downtown's black glass office towers soaring sculpturally from six miles away up the Harbor Freeway; the San Gabriel Range looming to the distant east on those rare days when the air is not a soup of toxic effluents. These are the distant sights that set your pulse racing.

It's the short views in LA that bring on melancholia: the stupid, boxy, cheap, flimsy commercial architecture, whatever its fantasy veneer, that degrades every inch of streetscape; the bleak, monotonous, decaying bungalow neighborhoods on the endless numbered blocks in the LA flatlands (eighteen months later the scene of the Rodney King riots); the desolation of downtown when you give up the security of your car to wander the androidal corporate "plazas" on foot; the dead-end streets ending in freeway embankments; the ubiquity of other people's taillights and bumpers always in your face; the view around any parking lot where you have just left your car. These are the sights that bring on nausea and depression.

✦

The standard rap about LA is that the car created it. This is not so. Rather, the pattern was established by the railroads and their little brothers, the electric trolleys. Today's freeways run along routes that echo the five original railways out of the old pueblo. From the outset, the settlement pattern was a dispersed one. The first wave of American settlers were transplanted midwestern farmers who came to grow citrus fruits wherever enough water could be pumped or diverted to make the desert arable. Farming was LA's first big industry. When the Southern Pacific and Santa Fe railroads made it possible to ship these oranges and lemons east in a few days' time, the region prospered. Railroads also promoted land development along their lines and planned new towns at convenient intervals. Not all got built, but those that were—Pasadena, Hollywood, Whittier, Glendale—generated a municipal life of their own that early on made them independent of Los Angeles proper.

The habit of long-distance commuting was also established early. From 1874 to 1887, local transportation in and around central LA depended on a few slow horsecar lines. So, as a practical matter, a businessman could just as easily travel to downtown LA each morning on a swift steam-powered train out of Santa Monica as he could by riding a plodding horsecar from Twenty-fifth Street and Figueroa.

Beginning in 1887, the first electric streetcar clanged up Pico Street. In three decades the streetcar system would extend over 1600 miles and link up all the far-flung settlements in the Log Angeles basin. It was made up of a lot of small streetcar companies that were eventually consolidated by Henry E. Huntington, whose father, Collis P. Huntington, had founded the Southern Pacific Railroad. He named the system the Pacific Electric Railroad. Wherever the PE's "Big Red Cars" ran, the adjoining land became commercially developable—often by the

PE itself—and in the words of Reyner Banham, a "diffuse and unprecedented super-community" took shape.[4]

In the early 1900s, two other important industries sprang up, oil and motion pictures, and each would affect the landscape in weird, profound, and enduring ways. The oil had been there visibly all along, bubbling up in surface seepages like the LaBrea Tar Pits. With the auto age underway, it became a much more valuable commodity. Big drilling derricks went up any old place, often in bristling clusters, creating hulking eyesores wherever they stood. When the rigs struck oil, they were replaced by the familiar nodding pumps, as common a sight around Los Angeles of the 1920s as sidewalk kiosks were in Paris. The pumps nodded next door to grammar schools, in orange groves, in vacant lots between office blocks, out by the beach, in back yards. Angelenos got used to the sight of gigantic ugly machines nodding relentlessly everywhere in the landscape. Property owners got paid handsomely for drilling rights and royalties. Elsewhere in America during this period, cities had just begun to use zoning to keep industry in its own place, but in Los Angeles the pumps went where the oil was. After a while people ceased to notice the damn things—an excellent psychological preparation for the age of the freeway.

The rise of the motion picture business had an equally strange effect on the landscape. Here was an industry devoted to the production of fantasy. It employed a large number of designers and construction specialists in the building of sets. Soon, their creations spilled beyond the movie lots and onto the streets in a fantasy aesthetic wilder than any of the hodgepodge architecture the Victorian era produced. No crazy idea or combination of motifs was overlooked, the more outlandish the better: movie theaters tarted up to look like Chinese pagodas, Mayan temples, mosques, a tire company like a Babylonian ziggurat, restaurants shaped like derby hats, hot dog stands shaped like dogs, tamale stands like tamales, an Aztec hotel, a Dutch windmill doughnut shop—you name it. The traditional Spanish Colonial architecture of California—then enjoying a revival—had something in common with stage scenery: stucco over adobe was a lot like plaster over lath and chickenwire. And the desert climate was kind to this sort of sculptural construction. The flimsiest movie sets could stand for decades on a back lot, and so could a lunchroom shaped like a pig.

Thus, Angelenos became accustomed to outlandish buildings springing up in their communities, buildings that had no physical continuity
with their surroundings, nor any continuity with the traditional vocabularies of architecture or civic art. But that was fine, because there was
plenty of room to spread out, and anyway, people were making money
from these things, improving their lives, enriching themselves, which
was what the Golden State was all about. Back East, such ridiculous
buildings were confined to amusement parks like Coney Island, and
easterners began to look upon Los Angeles with that now-familiar combination of morbid fascination and scorn expressed by observers like
Mencken, Nathanael West, and Woody Allen.

Hollywood set technicians were especially adept at creating interiors,
a talent much in demand as the Angelene landscape became more clotted with cars, oil rigs, and absurd commercial architecture, and the
insides of buildings became much more important than the outside.
This was the aesthetic of the world-as-movie-set—Katharine Hepburn
might appear to romp in the sparkling solarium of a Main Line mansion, but pan backward twenty feet and you'd see the dingy sound stage
and the grimy coils of electrical cable, and the glaring fresnel lights, and
the stage braces holding up the fake walls. Here was a new relationship
between things in the human habitat: crud on the outside and a jewelbox inside. A movie mogul's office on the studio lot might look like an
army base enlisted men's club on the outside; inside, it could be like
Louis XIV's throne room, or the Cheltenham Hunt Club, or any goddam thing.

Private luxury in counterpoint to public squalor has only become
more pronounced over time in LA. Today, in fact, the most exclusive
residences of Bel Air and the Hollywood Hills are completely invisible
from the twisting roads that are their nominal addresses. Stupendous
mansions the size of medieval monasteries lie hidden behind stucco
walls and laurel thickets, their owners dwelling in private compounds
like potentates in banana republics. And yet the most exclusive restaurants on Melrose Avenue or Main Street in Santa Monica operate out
of "taxpayer strip" buildings so dreary they don't even qualify as architecture. To design specialists these are, of course, merely "spaces"—
that is, places where things can happen inside. The outside (that is, the
public realm) means nothing. The naive might exult that this public

squalor is so democratic, that Irving "Swifty" Lazar and Elizabeth Taylor must report for supper to the same buildings as the legal secretaries who come to get their legs waxed—but if the rich can't give us public beauty, then who can?

⚓

The Pacific Electric Railroad established the basic armature for the Greater Los Angeles of today. It connected all the dots on the map and was a leading player itself in developing all the real estate that lay in between the dots. Banham calls it "a masterpiece of urban rapid transit" and points out that its very success in real estate development led to its undoing. As street traffic increased in the twenties, so did collisions between trains and cars at ever-more-frequent grade crossings. Schedules were disrupted. Service began to deteriorate.[5] As the broad areas between the transit lines filled up with homes and businesses, ever farther from the streetcar stops, the automobile became a far more convenient way to get around. Between 1919 and 1929, when the population of LA nearly doubled, automobile registrations shot up 550 percent.

The motion picture business was depression-proof, so during the 1930s, while Americans elsewhere struggled to put bread on the table, Angelenos kept buying cars and continued to build out the new pattern of a sprawling automobile city. They more or less *had* to, because downtown LA was uniquely unsuited to motorcars. The streets of its central business district were narrow and disconnected. Less total area was devoted to streets in downtown LA than in all other major American cities: 21.4 percent, compared to a range of 29 to 44 percent elsewhere. As early as 1919, traffic became so snarled downtown at Christmas time that the city had to ban on-street parking during business hours. So businesses moved elsewhere—notably to the "Miracle Mile" on Wilshire Boulevard, America's first great highway strip, with plenty of free parking in the rear. Downtown ceased to be a center of anything except court cases and a repository for public records. By 1930, 89 percent of the banks, 80 percent of the theaters, and 67 percent of doctors' offices were located outside the central business district.[6]

By 1938, General Motors along with Standard Oil of California and Firestone Tire and Rubber, through their stooge company, National City Lines, began to dismantle the Pacific Electric Railroad in order to promote private car use and sell buses. The same year, a six-mile section of the Arroyo Seco Parkway opened. It would later become the Pasadena Freeway, the first of many such superhighways criss-crossing the basin over the old streetcar right-of-ways. Only World War II, which halted private auto production entirely for four years and imposed rationing of tires and gasoline, interrupted the process.

So Los Angeles became the prototypical automobile city, the model for America's postwar Great Enterprise of building a suburban substitute for old-fashioned cities. The vast basin was like an immense laboratory for this experiment. The federal government lavishly subsidized it, footing the bill for most of the freeway construction, helping to finance the multiple thousands of single-family homes, and pouring huge sums of money into the military aircraft industry, the city's latest bonanza.

Postwar LA became the envy of the rest of the nation. And America being a free country, citizens from its bleaker corners picked up and transplanted themselves to the balmy metropolis of beaches, palm trees, unrestricted mobility, creamy young movie starlets, high-paying aerospace jobs, and other temporal niceties. LA also became the leading destination in America for immigrants from other lands. And so it grew, until finally the whole gigantic basin had filled up, and the motor metropolis spilled out into dependencies more remote than any realtor might have ever dreamed a few decades earlier. And the biggest fantasy of all in this city of fantasies was that they had built an enduring way of life, that Los Angeles was ever anything *but* an experiment.

✦

Now the results of this grand experiment are in, and the news is not good: the metropolis is strangling on its own patented brand of "growth." In the present crisis, Los Angeles has come to focus on the question of air pollution, for reasons that are rational but partly legalistic. It is quite true that LA has the worst air pollution in America. Since global atmospheric degradation may be the paramount political issue of the early twenty-first century, it makes sense that LA should face its share of the problem, and soon. But the city's approach is rather like that of a person who is addicted to cocaine, booze, and tobacco, and decides to quit smoking first.

In LA the very pattern of the city is the underlying problem, and the city is stuck with it. It is stuck with its sprawling low-density single-family house monoculture communities, with its long commutes, and its addiction to gas. Nobody can reasonably propose how to rearrange the metropolis, or downsize it, or retrofit it in a way that would be politically acceptable at this time. LA is probably at the mercy of extrinsic economic forces that have not yet come into play, like a disruption in the foreign oil supply, or a price hike. So, unable to deal with the city's inherent structural problems, Angelenos are addressing the enduring problem of their infamous *smog*. This effort is not going to save their fantasy city, but it will be an instructive exercise in making some of the sacrifices that the future will certainly require of all industrial peoples.

The legalistic part of the deal is that the city came under a federal court mandate to comply with clean air goals established by the U.S. Environmental Protection Agency, so they were forced to act, whether they wanted to or not. Had LA ignored the court mandate, the city could have lost whopping federal subsidies, plus the EPA could have stepped in and imposed some really draconian measures all on its own, such as gas rationing, or odd-even driving days based on license plate numbers.[7]

So, in 1989, after four years of study, a regional agency called the South Coast Air Quality Management District (AQMD) came up with a twenty-year plan to clean up LA's air. The plan was 5500 pages long and three feet high, and it proposed measures that seemed to signal the end of Life-As-We-Know-It in LA. The backbone of the plan was a strict set of emissions standards that would just about eliminate the gasoline engine. What might replace it was purely conjectural at this point, but none of the alternatives looked promising. A marketable electric car did not yet exist, plus it would have to charge up on electricity from power plants—and what would the power plants run on? Coal? Oil? Uranium? Power plants were already a major source of pollution in the basin.

Methanol, long touted as a gasoline substitute, was fraught with problems: burning it produced formaldehyde, a known carcinogen. It rotted the linings of storage tanks, and was half as potent as gasoline per volume, so you'd have to lug around twice as much fuel in your car.

Hydrogen was a pipe dream. Solar, for now, was a joke. In short, there was no real alternative to gasoline, but a lot of people seemed to be banking on the hope that "they'll come up with something." In the meantime, the AQMD plan would require employers to arrange for car pooling, or even operate their own jitney fleets to reduce the number of total vehicles on the road.

That was the transportation component of the plan. Next there was a whole burdensome set of new restrictions on industrial activities—and in the 1980s Southern California had become America's leading manufacturing region. Many common industrial solvents were out, because they evaporated easily. Ditto paints based on petroleum distillates. Ditto dry cleaning fluids. Commercial bakeries would have to treat their exhaust so as not to release alcohol fumes that are produced by the action of yeast. Companies making weapons for the U.S. military would have to stop using certain metal electroplating techniques. And on and on. The recommendations won few allies among business people, who predicted that industry would flee en masse for Mexico. And the new trade agreements of 1991 and 1992 suddenly made it a lot easier for U.S. companies to set up shop across the border.

Finally, the plan proposed changes in every household. A host of cleaning products were out. Spray cans would be no more. Gasoline-powered lawnmowers would go into the museum. Charcoal lighter fluid for barbecues would have to go—maybe even outdoor grilling, period. That really inflamed the multitudes. First forced car-pooling, and now this! No underarm deodorant spray! No lawns! No hibachi on the patio! Well, there goes the whole goshdarn lifestyle!

The cost of the AQMD plan was pegged at anywhere between $3 billion to $15 billion a year, depending on whether the estimator was pro or con. For instance, did you factor in lost jobs and added social service costs? In any case, the plan was conceived on the basis of conditions as they are at present, with the area's population at about fourteen million. Yet, officials at the Southern California Association of Governments were predicting in 1990 that at least four million more people would arrive in the region by the year 2010. For emphasis they liked to point out that this would be equal to the populations of metropolitan Chicago *and* Detroit all moving to LA. One could not help but feel that this introduced a note of futility into the whole matter.

A seemingly obvious solution to LA's civic crisis would be to rebuild the rapid transit lines that the city hung its growth on in the first place. In fact, the city has gone ahead and built the first 19-mile line of a proposed 150-mile light rail system—a pygmy outfit compared to the original 1600 miles of the Pacific Electric and its ancillaries. This first leg, called the Blue Line, opened in the summer of 1990. It runs from Long Beach north to downtown, along an old railroad right-of-way, through some of the city's poorest neighborhoods, including Watts. Officials predicted a weekday ridership of 5000 to 8000, but after a year of operation it was up to 27,000.

The second leg, called the Red Line, will be a 4.4-mile subway running from downtown west out Wilshire Boulevard. It is scheduled to open in the summer of 1993. A third leg, called the Green Line, is going to run down the median of the new Century Freeway, east from the airport out to Norwalk. It too would run through the riot-scarred ghetto flatlands (and criss-cross the Blue Line). The cost of building the new system is stupendous. Budgeted at $599 million, the Blue Line ended up costing $877 million. Altogether, the whole system is projected to cost $9.6 billion.

There is widespread disagreement about the usefulness of a light rail system imposed over the vast suburbia that LA has become. Critics say, things are just too spread out now. People will have to drive just to get to the transit lines. Only five of the twenty-two stations on the Blue Line have parking lots. Downtown furnishes less than 5 percent of the jobs in Los Angeles county. The rest of the jobs are widely dispersed. Anyway, the present scheme does not include transit lines to populous West LA, Santa Monica, the San Fernando Valley, Pasadena, or Orange County, all places where the Pacific Electric used to go. The old rights-of-way are gone now, chopped up into subdivisions and shopping malls. Without connecting these enormous areas, commuting by private car will still be the only way for most people to get around.

In the meantime, Angelenos have to work with what they've got—namely, the freeway system. Double-decking was seriously proposed until the 1989 San Francisco earthquake occurred and demonstrated the sort of nasty fate that might befall motorists on a double-decked freeway. An "aerial lane" (officials stress that it is *not* a double-deck) is being built over the Harbor Freeway to accommodate buses and car-pools. There are a lot of cockamamie schemes for computerizing cars and freeways into an integrated system that would permit a bunch of techno-jocks in a big central control room to regulate streams of traffic more efficiently than the present laissez-faire arrangement of mega-thousands of individuals piloting their own vehicles. But at a time when most ordinary citizens can barely afford the price of a new car, such a plan sounds implausible at best.

⚑

The underlying problem that Los Angeles and the rest of the "de-veloped" world faces is how to fashion an economy that is not an enterprise of destruction. That is, how to create sustainable economies and sustainable human habitats—cities and towns—for those econo-mies to dwell in. The transition is going to be difficult. Los Angeles is not well-equipped to make that transition. The forms imposed on its rugged landscape are already obsolete. It is a model of the city as a consumptive machine, consuming raw land, petroleum, and vast amounts of water collected from remote hinterlands. The city's present strategies for survival have little long-term intelligence. They mainly seek to protect a previous bad investment, to keep the consumption machine running a while longer.

It must have been exciting and lovely to live in Los Angeles in 1932, to motor freely out Wilshire Boulevard under that as-yet unsmoggy sky and see those bare brown Hollywood hills looming above the bright new stucco buildings on Sunset; to go to work in a factory whose product was dreams, where everyone was young and beautiful, and money just fell into your checking account. It must have seemed like heaven on earth.

A time traveler from 1932 would certainly not recognize the Los Angeles of today. If Los Angeles survives as a city of any consequence, it will be in a form that we do not yet recognize.

CAPITALS OF UNREALITY

The crisis of place in America has led to the creation of a gigantic industry dedicated to the temporary escape from the crisis. Like the three cities of the previous chapter, each of the places I call capitals of unreality operates differently. What they share is the way they represent the current condition of the public realm in America, its relation to the nation's collective fantasy life, and the ways that the public realm is packaged for sale as a commodity.

Disney World, outside Orlando, Florida, is the vacation destination *ne plus ultra* for adults with children, but its air of innocence and fun finally cannot conceal the aura of dread that underlies its attractions. Atlantic City, unlike Disney World, was once a genuine town, but has evolved unhappily into a place of the most extravagant unreality. Woodstock, Vermont, still a town, shows what can happen when our deepest psychological yearnings are reduced to a ritual of shopping for totems.

Disney World ➤➤

As the places where Americans dwell become evermore depressing and impossible, Disney World is where they escape to worship the nation in the abstract, a cartoon capital of a cartoon republic enshrining the falsehoods, half-truths, and delusions that prop up the squishy thing the national character has become—for instance, that we are a nation of families; that we care about our fellow citizens; that history matters; that there is a place called *home*.

Behind the kid stuff and the kitsch and the syrupy patriotism churns a fabulous machine for making money. It is what our grandfathers used to call an amusement park, but to leave it at that would be like calling the Vatican a Wee Kirk in the Dell, so boundless are the Disney Corp's ambitions and venality. Consider this cunning shuck: at Disney World you can trade your U.S. currency for Disney Dollars "good for dining and merchandise" all over the Magic Kingdom and its dependencies. This supposedly enhances the illusion of being in a special land. Now, imagine how many of these Disney Dollars are brought home by the kiddies as souvenirs. That is, they are never cashed in. What a nice little revenue rivulet! What do you suppose the accountants put it under on the Disney books? *Found money?*

Stripped of all its symbolic trappings and show-biz frosting, what Disney World sells is a scrap of public realm free of automobiles—or nearly so, except for a few props. In this sense it is akin to Ford's Greenfield Village, Colonial Williamsburg, and most shopping malls, but no more explicit. Ask fifty customers what they like about the place and the last thing you will hear is that they appreciate the absence of cars. There are too many other distractions. As well as being free of cars, of course, Disney World is also free of the bad relationships imposed upon things and people *by* cars. Since there are so few places of any size with this characteristic in America, the experience is understandably exhilarating.

✦

You arrive at Disney World on a four-lane entrance road several miles long. In scale it is identical to Interstate Highway 4, off which it branches. But gone is the jumble of hotels, billboards, gas stations and other architectural junk that makes the Florida landscape such a nightmare. You have entered a private corporate realm. To each side stands a wilderness of scrub pine and palmetto. By and by, rising above the foliage, you see two hotels designed by the renowned architect Michael Graves for his great patron, that *nuovo Lorenzo deMedici*, Michael Eisner, Chairman of the Disney Corp. These are the Swan and the Dolphin, hulking heaps of your basic less-is-more factory aesthetic tarted up with a lot of cartoonish surface appliqué out of the "Only Kidding" school of Postmodernism (Michael Graves, Chairman of the

Department of Irony), and surmounted by concrete swans and dolphins that, in their awkward Babylonian gigantism, evoke something like the set pieces from D. W. Griffith's epic movie *Intolerance*. Finally, you arrive at a parking lot that seems about the size of Rhode Island.

Here you gratefully leave your car behind and hop on a golf cart train to the ticket gate. After paying $32.50 for admission, you are efficiently herded onto a ferryboat for a short ride across an artificial lake to the entrance of the Kingdom. This will be the first of many crowd-control experiences—and resulting lines—that add to Disney World's air of fascism. The boat ride is also a psychological device. Making you enter the place by stages, the Disney "imagineers" emphasize the illusion of one's taking a journey to a strange land—as if driving over 1500 miles from another corner of the nation was not sufficient (and it may *not* be, for long-distance car travel on an interstate highway is literally like going nowhere fast). Anyway, this short ferry trip is fraught with archetypal death imagery so obvious that I am a little embarrassed to point it out.

What Walt Disney's personal hangup concerning death was we may never know. Company officials staunchly deny the persistent rumor that Walt arranged to have himself cryogenically frozen, hopeful of bodily resurrection in a more medically advanced future. But the fact that the rumor started in the first place is by itself rather interesting—someone was onto him. In any case, Walt's preoccupation was in tune with American provincial Protestantism's obsession with eschatology. Disney World is as death-haunted as any TV studio full of weeping evangelicals. Particulars shortly.

Even after he became a showbiz mogul, Walt Disney's world view remained that of a provincial midwestener, whether it was his idea of the jungle (*ooga-booga*), or of space travel (*gee whiz*), or of U.S. history (*I pledge allegiance . . .*). If you think of Disney World as a sort of map of Walt's imagination, it is somehow fitting that you should enter this Magic Kingdom by way of Walt's own concept of the physical surroundings of his childhood. Hence, the ferryboat from the ticket gate deposits you on Main Street U.S.A., a recreation, grossly simplified, of a provincial midwestern small town circa 1910—say, Marceline, Missouri. The Disney family lived on a farm outside Marceline around that time. If he was anything like other farm boys of the era, Walt probably only got to town on Saturdays. Marceline must have seemed like Paris to him, with its handful of shops, perhaps a soda fountain, and its sidewalks bustling with other farm folk and their children.

Farming was one of a string of occupations practiced by Walt's father, Elias Disney, over the years. He was not a lucky fellow. Before Walt was born, Elias grew oranges in Florida and got wiped out by a freeze. Then he migrated to Chicago where he worked as a carpenter on the 1893 Columbian Exposition. (Perhaps Walt heard stories about the wondrous fair at his father's knee. Something about it surely lodged in his mind.) Farming at Marceline, Mo., didn't pan out for Elias either. In 1910, when Walt was ten, his father went bust again, and the family's household effects had to be auctioned off on the lawn. When the family removed to Kansas City, Walt no doubt felt wrenched away from a smaller and more manageable world that he had loved—his father's humiliating failure adding piquancy to the loss.

There is nothing terribly mysterious about the appeal of his Main Street U.S.A. It is a well-proportioned street full of good relationships between its components, and blessedly free of cars. The two- and three-story buildings are architecturally unified, but individually various— out of an era when rooflines were interesting, when windows meant something more than holes in a wall, and when building ornament relied on pattern rather than symbolistic doodads. The street offers a terminating vista of an improbable fairy-tale castle, but the important thing is the fact that it has a focal point at all. A library, a post office, a courthouse, even a thirty-foot-tall statue of Goofy at the end of the street would serve as well to afford visual interest and a comforting sense of enclosure. The buildings along the street are designed to a five-eighths scale, the toylike appearance supposedly adding to their charm.

There's no pretense, however, that they are anything but false fronts. The souvenir shops and snack emporia within extend into a backstage retail space out of all proportion to their facades. The object is clearly to make room for as many customers as possible in order to move massive volumes of cheap merchandise off the shelves. It's revealing that Walt drew the line here in terms of verisimilitude. At Greenfield Village,

Henry Ford showed considerable interest in what people really did inside those reassembled buildings, in the ways of life that he had helped to eradicate with his cars—and it's said too that he felt pretty bad late in life about what his cars had done to the life of America. But Walt Disney practiced a more selective style of nostalgia.

Disney built his original Main Street at Anaheim in the 1950s, just when highway strips began to replace Main Streets everywhere, when small-scale agriculture surrendered to industrialized farming, and mass-merchandising started wiping out local commerce—in short, when corporate gigantism had started to kill off local economies and thereby destroy the character of small towns. Yet that was okay with Walt. If he was nostalgic about the past, for the old *feel* and *fit* of things, he was by no means opposed to the new suburban pattern of American life. He lived that way himself, Los Angeles style. Walt felt so optimistic about the way things were going in postwar America that his attitudes about the past and the future were equally sentimental. It was possible for him to believe that an organization like his own, operating freely in a free country, could only bring wonderful benefits to a free people. Thus, the underlying message of Main Street U.S.A.—for the grownups, anyway—was that a big corporation could make a better Main Street than a bunch of rubes in a real small town.

And Walt was right! Through the postwar decades Americans happily allowed their towns to be destroyed. They'd flock to Disneyland at Anaheim, or later to Disney World in Florida, and walk down Main Street, and think, *gee, it feels good here*. Then they'd go back home and tear down half the old buildings downtown and pave them over for parking lots, throw a parade to celebrate a new K Mart opening—even when it put ten local merchants out of business—turn Elm Street into a six-lane crosstown expressway, pass zoning laws that forbade corner grocery stores in residential neighborhoods and setback rules that required every new business to locate on a one-acre lot until things became so spread out you *had* to drive everywhere. They'd build the new central school four miles out of town on a busy highway so that kids couldn't walk there. They'd do every fool thing possible to destroy good existing relationships between things in their towns, and put their local economies at the mercy of distant corporations whose officers didn't give a damn whether these towns lived or died. And then, when vacation time rolled around, they'd flock back to Disney World to feel good about America.

✦

Over the long haul, the movie business proved to be rather precarious for Walt. But his amusement park was another matter, harnessed in tandem as it was with his weekly television show, which reached so many impressionable young minds. Disneyland was a cash cow from day one. There was hardly a corner of the developed world where people were not aware of the Magic Kingdom. When the Soviet leader Nikita Khrushchev toured America in 1959 and was denied a visit to Disneyland on security grounds, it broke his heart. Walt had lots more ideas for it, but no room to expand. The park at Anaheim was hemmed in on 180 measly acres in a corner of Southern California that was becoming wall-to-wall taco stands by the mid-1960s. So Walt quietly went shopping for land elsewhere. His minions located 28,000 acres of pine and palmetto scrub in central Florida and acquired it cheaply by keeping the buyer's identity a secret. In the meantime, in 1966, Walt Disney died. It is a measure of how successfully he merged his own personality with the company that even when he was bodily absent, the corporation forged ahead, implementing many of his hopes and dreams.

When the buyer's identity was revealed, Florida officials quickly figured out the potential tourist revenue from a new Disneyland and bent over backward to help get it going. For starters, the state legislature passed a special act exempting Disney from all Florida land-use laws. As one journalist said, it was "like a land grant from the king of Spain."[1] The chief benefit to Disney—as we shall refer to the corporate entity post-Walt—was that it did not have to get building permits to construct the strange kinds of buildings needed to house its rides and attractions. At issue would have been the movement of crowds through dark, confining spaces, and the potential for disaster. For instance, the "Space Mountain" ride, which was in essence an *indoor* roller coaster housed in a gigantic fiberglass shell. Imagine haggling with the county building inspector over fenestration ratios and the positions of lighted "Exit" signs in such a structure. This sort of bureaucracy could have held up things forever. So Disney was given carte blanche to build anything it liked, and if there were liability problems down the line . . . well, that's what all those attorneys were on the payroll for.

The law also exempted Disney from paying impact fees. Such fees, usually levied by counties, are supposed to offset costs incurred by the public from private development. For example, you build an amusement park that attracts eighty thousand people a day and it is going to have *some* effect on the existing roads, law enforcement, water supply, landfill, sewers, and so on. Disney World, of course, had a huge impact on all these things. Its property lay astride two counties, Osceola and Orange, and for years Disney World's attractions expanded without a cent being paid in impact fees. This does not mean the corporation paid no annual property tax. Disney paid more than the next nine largest corporations in the area combined. But the point of impact fees was to make up for *extraordinary* burdens placed on citizens who did not benefit from Disney's activities. In effect, these citizens ended up subsidizing the gigantic Disney operation. John DeGrove, a land-use professor at Florida Atlantic University, explained it nicely:

> They're bad neighbors from my point of view. As I understand it, they've always refused to pay off-site impacts for transportation. Everybody pays impact fees—every developer that comes in to do anything has to pay substantial impact fees. They won't pay a cent. Finally, the County calculated on their latest expansion that they really ought to pay about $35 million in off-site impact for transport alone. They gave their usual answer: "No, we won't. Look at all the good things we do for your economy!" Well, the County Commission, and several key members of the legislature delegation from Orange County, sat down and had a quiet meeting with the moguls out at Disney, and said, "You can take that position, but you know the special act that exempts you from all controls can also be changed. It's not in the constitution, after all. So we're going to the legislature to get your exemption from all of our zoning and land-use controls taken away if you're not reasonable about this." Well, Disney decided to be reasonable, and they negotiated, I think, $13 or $14 million. That's a first. They won't pay their fair share unless they're forced into it.[2]

If you arrive at Disney World first thing in the morning, you discover that Main Street U.S.A. opens a half hour before the other "lands" in the Magic Kingdom. You are in effect held captive on Main Street during this interval. This accomplishes a couple of things from the management's vantage: it builds more suspense for that ultimate moment of admission, and it encourages the milling captives, importuned by their pleading offspring, to spend money on souvenirs, especially articles of raiment such as the famous mouse-ear cap, without which any child under eight at Disney World feels naked and ashamed.

The entry procedure strikingly approximates the American Protestant concept of going to heaven. One leaves behind the gritty real world and mills around a pleasant and familiar outdoor place of assembly— where the climate is magically room-temperature—with a crowd of strangers all happily anticipating pleasures to come. Finally, there is that glorious moment of passing through the pearly gates! From a child's point of view, the day ahead must seem like eternity. And if the family happens to be staying for several nights at one of Disney's many on-site resort complexes, why then the illusion of eternity must be more potent still. Of course, under certain unfavorable conditions, the fantasy can seem more like a holiday in hell.

For instance, the little detail about climate. At eight o'clock in the morning, in this part of North America, the temperature is very agreeable. At two o'clock in the afternoon, however, you can fry cube steak on the hood of a car. When the little ones start shrieking and mewling under that relentless Floridian sun, you wonder what goes through the mind of a parent who has paid in advance for three more days of this.

Children also get cranky at Disney World because they must stand on long lines to get into anything. During an eight-hour visit, you can expect to be detained on lines or stuck in waiting vestibules of one kind or another for over five hours. The Disnoids are crafty about this. To eliminate the *sight* of long lines they have constructed in front of every attraction a special pavilion into which the inevitable long line is coiled and compressed. On the outside there appears to be no line. The children drag Mom and Dad inside, where they discover that the "crowd" milling around is actually a line snaking through a rat maze of velvet ropes or some such barriers. This is why so many children freak out in mid-afternoon. By then, they have waited on perhaps four lines for a total of, say, three hours, with the mercury now ranging above the ninety-degree mark. The worst thing about it from the little ones' vantage, no doubt, is the dawning discovery that this sort of tedium is mainly what they have to look forward to for the remainder of their visit, which might be several more days. What a swindle it must seem.

After waiting on line you are herded into a cable-driven boat— "Quickly! Quickly!" the attendants cry—and hauled through a series of darkened chambers where you gawk at animated tableaux. These are populated by "animatronic" puppets or robots that do various things— "cannibals" that pop up out of the "jungle" brandishing spears, pirates plundering a Caribbean port, gibbering ghouls, and so on. Because everything is programmed or scripted down to the last detail, there is an inescapable air of mechanized boredom to these goings-on. Even children seem to sense it. The narration is canned. You can hear it begin to repeat as you leave one chamber and enter the next. Machinery clanks and groans beneath the recorded soundtrack. Unlike a zoo, a circus, or even a seedy carnival, absolutely nothing is left to chance. The customer is processed through with maximum efficiency. At its conclusion, each ride debouches into a souvenir emporium selling merchandise keyed to that ride's themes: pirate swords, spears, whatever.

A recurring feature in nearly every attraction is the theme of death and mayhem. At every turn you encounter scenes of it. This is something different from the bodily thrills of speed and motion offered by ordinary amusement park rides. The cute, rum-soaked animatronic buccaneers in "Pirates of the Caribbean" are all busy ravishing women, pillaging taverns, stabbing, hacking, and shooting each other, while you just sit there floating gently by in the dark, passively taking it in. You turn down the short stretch of Disney's "western" street in Frontierland, and actors dressed as gunmen are suddenly plugging each other. You, the passersby, are supposed to be lucky to be there when this is happening. (A hundred years from now do you suppose they will re-create the drive-by shootings of LA gangs for the amusement of children? How about the spectacular fast-food store massacres of recent years?) The "Jungle Cruise" ride is garnished with skulls, shrunken heads, and intimations of slaughter. The "Haunted Mansion" ride is a celebration of organic decay, with shrieking corpses and holographic images of howling lost souls flying around the cobwebbed spaces. The amount of creative energy invested in morbid depictions of violent death is impressive.

How does this differ from past entertainments aimed at children, from the "death-defying" spectacles of the old big top (and its freak-filled sideshow) to the rancid attractions of any county fair? Mainly in this way: Disney pretends so hard to be wholesome. The customers go along with this falsehood, because it makes them feel better about themselves, the same way that Main Street U.S.A. makes them feel better about the scary places where they actually live.

↟

The most pathetic and revealing part of the Magic Kingdom is that quarter known as Tomorrowland. As a matter of design, Tomorrowland looks strikingly like the first great shopping malls of the early sixties, all parabolic woggle architecture and space-rocket imagery. The rides and attractions here mostly have to do with the worship of vehicles: cars, tramways, airplanes, spacecraft. There is even that fabulous absurdity out of the old Radiant City trick bag, the "people mover" (not to be confused with the elevated streetcar of Detroit), a moving urban footpath that eliminates the need to walk! In Tomorrowland, the oil crises of the 1970s haven't happened yet. There's no hint about global warming, acid rain, holes in the ozone shield, or any other unforeseen repercussions of our technologic heedlessness.

Tomorrowland speaks volumes about our present national predicament. Here, in all its silliness, stands yesterday's version of the future: a denatured life of endless leisure, where the only purpose of existence is the eventual permanent escape from planet Earth to colonize other worlds. It is, of course, another version of evangelical Protestantism's dull preoccupation with the hereafter, as well as its cultivated hatred for the things of this world (such as the dignity of work)—otherwise, why be so anxious to leave the planet? In Disney's future we are all consumers with our needs completely satisfied and ready to expire. And into what? Presumably to another world where all our needs will be completely satisfied. . . . Walt's spiritual life must have been a torment. Obviously, Tomorrowland has not been rethought since he took his own final rocket ride to the next world.

🜊

It happened, though, that Walt Disney had plans for a much grander exercise in utopian futurism. This was the purpose of EPCOT. The acronym stands for Experimental Prototype Community of Tomorrow. You can even hear Walt talk about his ideas for it on film in the little pavilion dedicated to his life story that is tucked away in a quiet corner on Main Street. This is what excited him more than anything about the vast acreage he had acquired in Florida. But the plan we glimpse in the film was very much a product of the sixties: a grandiose Radiant City scheme of towers and monorails straight out of Intro to Corbu. It might as easily have been the new campus of a state university, or a proposed capital for a third world republic. As a pure real estate venture, it might well have ruined the company.

The EPCOT that actually got built, in the era of corporate inertia that followed Walt's sudden death, is little more than a half-assed world's fair. There is a court of international pavilions ringing an artificial lake, which at most offer propaganda films made by national tourist bureaus, some bogus native cuisine, and the inevitable souvenirs. At the head of this court of nations stands the American Pavilion, a reproduction of Independence Hall. It is hard to imagine a more empty and embarrassing spectacle than the show they put on there, performed by animatronic robots—what a savings in actors' equity salaries and benefits! It's as if Ronald Reagan's second inaugural address had been turned into a Broadway musical, the producers thinking that if the word *America* was invoked a thousand times the heavenly spheres would ring out in tribute and gratitude. As it is, there is enough canned choral music to drown out a Super Bowl halftime show, so if the heavens answered nobody would hear them anyway. The lyrics seemed to have come straight out of the copywriting department of an Orlando advertising agency:

> *America, spread your golden wings,*
> *Sail on freedom's wind across the sky.*
> *Great bird, with your golden dreams,*
> *Flying high, flying high!*

Sitting there taking it all in, I wished I'd had a paper bag to put over my head when the houselights came back up.

Atlantic City ➤➤

Once upon a time, Americans came here to frolic by the sea, to stroll up and down an extraordinary pedestrian street called a boardwalk, to see such wonders as diving horses and strange creatures dredged from the ocean's bottom, to watch stage shows, hear band music, dance under the stars, drink beer, and eat abnormal amounts of candy. Atlantic City was one of the nation's great public places.

It was also a true city—the name was not a hopeful affectation as often it is with newly settled places. The chunky triangular island it occupies afforded more building space than the narrow barrier beaches that more typically line the Atlantic coast. When the railroad linked it to nearby Philadelphia, in 1880, the city developed rapidly into a dense fabric of gridded blocks filled with businesses, small and large, owned by the same people who ran them. And at the city's edge lay the magnificent white beach. It was like a wedge of delicious birthday cake on a plate; the town was the layers and the ocean was the frosting.

It is easy to understand how the place lost its luster. Atlantic City's heyday, from 1890 to 1929, coincided with the revolution in construction techniques that made enormous buildings possible. Hotels as big as the Traymore, the Ritz Carlton, the Ambassador, and others were a new thing in the world. To build them was one thing—structural steel and motorized equipment solved that problem—but to operate at that scale and maintain the gigantic establishments was something else, especially in a beach resort where business was sometimes bound to be slow. When the Great Depression struck, the financial equation failed and the hotels became unmanageable. Think of it: the squadrons of chambermaids, the carpeting that regularly had to be replaced in miles of corridors, the truckloads of room furnishings, the linens. To pay for all this, the big hotels had to charge high room rates. After 1929, with the economy drained of surplus cash, that was no longer possible. Still, everything was new enough to absorb a decade of neglect.

That was the thirties. And then World War II broke out. The government curtailed car travel to the Jersey shore. They blacked out the boardwalk for fear of a Nazi naval attack. Many public facilities in the city were commandeered by the armed forces. The Air Corp took over the convention center. Fifty hotels were turned into temporary hospitals or recuperation centers for wounded soldiers. The interiors were abused and never properly restored.

At the war's end, the American economy boomed—alone among the industrial nations—but by then Atlantic City had become a physically seedy place. The resort had to rely on a lumpenprole clientele. The town's attractions grew shabby, too. It had been an important show-biz venue, even through the Depression, when the big bands played in its ballrooms. By the early fifties, visitors were more likely to see lady wrestlers. To make ends meet, the town catered increasingly to a low-rent convention trade. The place was trapped in a downward economic spiral.

At the same time, American's recreational habits were changing. They had more money than ever before, and the postwar boom in manufacturing made even factory workers well-off by world standards. But this new wealth was spent on suburban houses, and on cars to get to them and appliances to put in them. It transformed American culture. The private world of home and family was everything; the public realm was out. When middle-class families took a vacation, it meant a trip by car to a national park, or perhaps to a second home by a mountain lake or beach. Most of all, it meant getting away from other people. Americans no longer wished to congregate in "playgrounds" like Atlantic City where most of the action took place in public places with crowds of strangers pressing in. Those still in the habit went to *new* playgrounds like Miami Beach, where the decor was not threadbare and the weather nicer. If you wanted the public realm in postwar America, there was TV.

By the 1960s, Atlantic City was in deep trouble. A number of its big hotels had converted themselves to rooming houses for the elderly—better full occupancy at low monthly rates than no occupancy at hotel rates—but fought a losing battle trying to maintain the buildings. Beginning in 1963, the first of several urban renewal schemes kicked off with the wholesale bulldozing of eighty-eight acres in the heart of town. What got flattened was the essence of the city's dense urban fabric: individual houses, small hotels, and small businesses. Much of this tract remains a gigantic parking lot today. Other neighborhoods followed until hardly any of the old city was left standing. By the early 1970s, boosters were still desperately promoting loony attractions like "bloodless bullfights" at the convention hall, but these were the final twitchings of a corpse. Atlantic City was technically dead. As a form of cardiopulmonary resuscitation, the state of New Jersey legalized gambling.

There is a section of Walt Disney's movie *Pinocchio* in which the gullible little puppet-boy is lured off by a gang of no-goodniks to a wonderful place called Pleasure Isle.

> *Fie fiddle-de-dee*
> *It's Pleasure Isle for me.*
> *Where every day is a holiday*
> *And kids have nothing to do but play. . . .*

As the ferryboat taking Pinocchio and his fellow victims draws close, the Isle's luridly lit-up thrill rides and fun houses rise vertiginously into the ethers of night. Gleefully, the kidnapped boys rush into the playground of their dreams. There's a pavilion that dispenses free cigars by the thousands, a fun house devoted to brawling, a "model home open to destruction," all the pies you can eat, and lots more. Pinocchio, egged on by a rather thuggish companion named Lampley, goes wild. "Bein' bad's a lot of fun!" Lampley declares. The wee hours of the morning find the two alone in a pool hall shooting eight ball, quaffing beers, and smoking cigars. Meanwhile, Pinocchio's guardian angel, Jiminy Cricket, has discovered that the rest of the boys are being transformed into donkeys. The no-goodniks are loading them in crates marked "to the salt mines." Cut back to Pinocchio and Lampley at the pool table. They have just sprouted donkey ears and tails. Yikes! The unfortunate Lampley completes his transformation, but Pinocchio, with the help of Jiminy Cricket, escapes to . . . well, I don't want to spoil it for you.

Motoring east on the Atlantic City Expressway, the skyline rose into view above the salt marshes and those creepy scenes from *Pinocchio* came vividly to mind. Ahead, the new casino hotels towered in the coastal vapors, beckoning to the credulous with their wicked promises of endless fun. A billboard along the highway said, "Poker World—More Ways to Win!," failing to mention more numerous ways to lose. Indeed, here was a place where personal transformations of a tragic kind seemed the order of the day.

The Parker Brothers' game "Monopoly" also wafted up out of deep memory, since all the streets on the gameboard were named after those in Atlantic City. And here they were! Park Place! Pacific Avenue! Marvin Gardens! Baltic Avenue, where the expressway just came to a dead stop, was apparently still the slums. A small housing project of abject red brick low-rises stood there awash in paper and plastic litter. Ahead loomed the rear end of the Trump Plaza hotel and casino, presenting a nearly blank masonry wall to the arriving visitor, except for this: a colossal escutcheon, or coat-of-arms, or some-such phony-baloney heraldic device in red, black, and gold with a crown on top (like something off a cheap rye whiskey bottle) that must have been three stories high. This escutcheon had nothing to with the architecture, as such; it was just a symbol meant to convey the message, "High Class People Here," without being so vulgar as to spell it out.

The most obvious physical characteristic of the town today was how successfully it had been transformed from a dense city of blocks into a narrow strip. Where hundreds of houses, hotels, and businesses had stood, now lay a moonscape of rubble-strewn lots. Pacific Avenue, which runs parallel to the Boardwalk and directly behind it, was little more than a service alley for the big casinos. Here were loading docks where food purveyors dropped off tons of sirloin and iceberg lettuces, and where stretch limo drivers waited stoically for their beepers to sound. On the leeward side of Pacific stood rows of dingy two- and three-story buildings that looked as though Edward Hopper had painted them into existence around 1933 and they hadn't been retouched since. Shabby storefronts housed the pawnshops that are the last resorts of the luckless here. All up and down Pacific, signs said "Cash for Gold."

I checked into a hotel at the north end of town. It was a curious establishment. Everything that a big Atlantic City hotel of the 1920s might have been, this place was not—but for its sheer bulk. A 1980s vintage thirty-story building with hundreds of rooms, it had no coffee shop, newsstand, barber shop, ballroom, or gift shop. The lobby was about the size of my living room. In short, it had almost no public spaces. It operated strictly as a storage depot for gamblers in need of sleep. The decor was on the order of what you'd find in an airport waiting room. The hotel turned out to be a Chapter 11 case, one of those real estate ventures of the Savings and Loan era that hadn't worked out.

↟

At the top of the Boardwalk the towers of the Trump Taj Mahal skewered skyward in their mogul splendor, the summation of all that Atlantic City stands for today. For example, bankruptcy. For, you see, Atlantic City is the East Coast's holiest shrine to a religion based on the idea that it is possible to get something for nothing. The idea is not new. It runs through American history. The problem with this idea is that it does not comport with the way things work in real life. Proof that it is a delusion is the fact that the gambling industry exists. The gambling industry is based on the sound idea that the odds overwhelmingly favor the house. The industry has flourished by taking advantage of those who believe that it's possible to get something for nothing. Further proof that this idea is a delusion is that even some people who run the gambling industry believe that it is possible to get something for nothing, and in their fantastic avarice, they have found themselves in the laughable position of not being able to operate their casinos profitably.

The Trump Taj Mahal opened in April of 1990 and was technically bankrupt before the year was out. It drained business from every other casino in town while failing to attract enough business to cover its own debt payments.[3] Donald Trump, the New York-based real estate developer who built it and owns two other casinos in Atlantic City, financed the Taj largely with junk bonds—the junk bond being Wall Street's way of profiting off business people who think it is possible to get something for nothing.

Standing on the Boardwalk this mild October day, one beheld the Trump Taj Mahal with that odd mixture of fascination and nausea reserved for the great blunders of human endeavor. The building is certainly large. Its architectural details are straight out of *Pinocchio*: corkscrewing minarets in cartoon turquoise, pink, magenta, purple, and gold. Much of the facade is blank wall, but the few doorways and windows that front the Boardwalk are trimmed with screwed-on moldings of a sort of metal-flake fiberglass more commonly used in the manufacture of surfboards. Ironically, the stuff hadn't held up very well in the briny ocean breezes. After only a year, it was starting to chip, fade, and warp.

The interior of the Taj was as grandiose, and the symbolism in the decor seemed pegged to a not-very-bright nine-year-old. Here was the *Gold* conference room, the *Silver* banquet room, the *Ruby* function room. The psychology went like this: a person finding himself surrounded by so much symbolic opulence must unwittingly succumb to the delusion that he was *already* rich and therefore in a position to wager any amount of money for the sheer "fun" of it. You had to admire the shamelessness of this ploy. It was so subversive of the whole democratic ideal. Every man a king! And every king a sucker!

The kings and queens who plied the corridors of Trump's Taj looked weary, old, and worn down by the storms of life. Their casual polyester attire suggested that they were more likely to be retired state highway pavement inspectors than members in good standing of the Swindon Hunt Club, or even recipients of the L. L. Bean catalog. As a matter of fact, the Atlantic City casinos have had what might be politely called a demographic problem from the start. Unlike Las Vegas, which is out in the middle of nowhere, and where most visitors stick around for a few nights, Atlantic City has attracted mostly day-trippers from the surrounding megalopolis. The majority are people on fixed incomes, retired folks on Social Security, individuals with very little money to throw away and, most important, short lines of credit—for the casinos make most of their money on high rollers who play on credit.

The casinos themselves were partly to blame for the bind they were in. To promote business they ran cheap charter bus excursions out of New York and Philadelphia for precisely this type of small fish, gave them free casino chips, meal vouchers, and show tickets. A lot of these folks would cash in their chips upon arrival, grab their free meal, stroll the Boardwalk until showtime, and climb back aboard the bus without dropping a dime at the tables. Of course, some did gamble. They mostly played the slot machines and contributed to the regular financial tidal flow that the casino bookkeepers call "the grind." The main purpose of the grind was to cushion the casino's losses to high rollers.

The casino at Trump's Taj Mahal lay deep inside the building, far from any vagrant rays of impinging daylight. It has become a cliché of casino design to eliminate all elements that hint at the passage of time. If a player looked up from the blackjack table and noticed the sun going down, or coming up, he might be inclined to stop pissing away his daughter's college tuition. Typically, there are no windows in any of the casinos. Nor are there clocks. The more disoriented the players are made to feel, the better for the casino. Cheap or free cocktails also help. The equation is simple: since the odds overwhelmingly favor the house, the longer you keep the player in the house, the more money you are certain to extract from him.

It is always twilight in the casinos. The design of their lighting must be something of an exact science, for in every casino in Atlantic City you see thousands of incandescent bulbs, neon tubes, lasers, illuminated panels, and glittering things, and yet the huge rooms remain so murky that you seem to be walking around with sunglasses in a grotto. The casino at Trump's Taj was plastered with mirrors. It might be safe to say that mirrors are Donald Trump's favorite building material, and one could see why. They make any room seem bigger, even a large room. They make it look as though twice as many lights are blazing without actually adding any illumination to the murk or jacking up the utility bill. They hold up to wear and tear much better than paint, wallpaper, or any other wall covering, especially to the most destructive force in the casino: cigarette smoke. A little swipe of Windex and they look as good as new. And they last forever, as long as people don't fling ashtrays around in fits of rage.

The casino at Trump's Taj occupies at least an acre. Half of that space is given over to the slot machines. The slots nowadays come in many more styles and models than the one-armed bandits of yore. Some have mechanical arms and tumblers, some push buttons and video screens. They all make some kind of noise—beeps, dings, gongs, whirs, gurgles, gleeps—and when you get several hundred in a room they make a lot of noise. In fact, it is something of a din, the auditory equivalent of root-canal work. The "grind" of revenue they produce is aptly named.

As the players stood before these glowing monsters performing simple repetitive physical acts—*insert coin, pull lever, insert coin, pull lever*—they reminded me of the rats we used to "run" in Skinner boxes back in the college psychology lab. A Skinner box was sort of a slot machine for a rat. The rat was "conditioned" to press a metal bar in his box. When the rat performed adequately, he was rewarded with a pellet of rat candy. You could customize your rat and make him press the bar twice. Or you could teach him to press it at the sound of a buzzer. Or you could really mess his mind up by timing the Skinner box to dispense rat candy only at three-minute intervals no matter how many times he pressed the bar. Or you could combine the time interval with some number of bar presses. It turned out that the absolutely best way to condition the rat was to reward him irregularly—that is, to dispense his pellet of rat candy only sometimes when he pressed the lever. If you gave it to him every time, he would simply press the damn bar until he was stuffed and then crawl off into the corner for a snooze. But if you frustrated him just a little, gave him that little edge of uncertainty, and now and then a small reward, why then little Hercules the Rat would stay up around the clock pressing that goshdarn bar until his sweet little pink albino rat eyes popped halfway out of his skull and his pink front paws gave out.

People do, now and then, hit jackpots at the slots. They seemed, in each case, rather bored and exhausted by it. One elderly couple hit a 10,000-coin payoff on a 25-cent machine. In such a case, the money does not pour out, as in the movies, but rather a sort of beacon lights up on top of the machine summoning a pit boss, who validates the win and arranges for a check to be issued at the cashier's window. It took a good ten minutes for the pit boss to materialize. The couple, from Philadelphia, said they lived on Social Security and the husband's union pension. They came to Atlantic City about once a month. They had won jackpots before, but never more than $1000. This day, they had been playing the slots for about four hours before they hit the big one. When asked whether this $2500 jackpot put them ahead for all their wagering over the years, they laughed. What an idea! Why then, given their admittedly modest means, did they keep playing? "Because it's fun," they said in unison.

Interestingly, their jackpot did not draw a crowd. Other slot players stood a few paces away cocooned in self-absorption, feeding coins into their own *gleeping* and *clanging* machines from the jumbo-size plastic cups that the management keeps stacked next to every slot, thank you very much. Gambling, it turns out, is an intensely private experience. The whole drama is a personal one between each player and the house— the house here being a giant corporation. That this drama is played out in a public place, the casino, is incidental. The private nature of it is essentially the same whether the player is gambling against a machine, or a live human dealer at the blackjack table. The house is still the opponent and the dealer is only an intermediary.

This perhaps helped explain why Americans dressed so badly in the casinos. For instance, in the high-roller nooks, where the smallest chip cost $25, silver-haired men with impressive bellies and yards of gold chains slouched around the baccarat tables in jogging suits and other such pajama-like get-ups. They seemed to have little consciousness of being in a public place, let alone quite a formal public place—the dealers were dressed in costumes of such weird exaggerated formality that they looked like the palace guards from *The Wizard of Oz*. But the players, absorbed in their private dreams of winning and losing, might as well have been home lounging around in their bedrooms.

⚓

The famous Boardwalk outside was a welcome contrast to the murky, smoke-filled, headache-inducing casino. It remains one of America's great public places, and for this reason: It still functions as it was originally designed to—as a marvelous buffer between civilization and the deep blue sea. Most important, it is a buffer that is also an explicit gathering place for people.

At four-thirty on a fine October afternoon, the crowds strolling up and down included many young couples with children. They looked happy in the low-slanting sunshine, and the children darted about, squealing with laughter, as children will when they are exhilarated by a place—all of which was another contrast to the dour, waxy, self-intent faces in the casino. Of course, the Boardwalk was free of automobiles, but here and there one encountered the traditional "rolling chairs." These rickshaw-like wicker contraptions are pushed rather than pedaled from behind at the rate of a brisk walk. In service, they have the comical look of overgrown baby prams. With the storms of November coming, many of the chairs were equipped with roll-down plastic windscreens. By no means did one feel sorry for the guys pushing these things around. The Boardwalk was level. The price for a ride was hefty. If anything, they seemed as hale as Amish farmers.

The ocean was always an obvious presence, but never in an intimidating way. For one thing, the beach at Atlantic City is wide and the surf breaks at a distance. With its sturdy wooden deck raised above the sand, its solid railings and street furniture, the Boardwalk was a thing *of* civilization even though it was also a place that connected civilization with the wildness of the ocean. That people felt secure and protected there was part of its charm. The other part was its physical grandeur. It was a gigantic man-made thing in proximity to one of nature's most awesome things. Yet, for all its size, everything that happened on the Boardwalk, happened at human scale. Nothing moved faster than a walk.

☀

As dusk gathered, a clammy autumn breeze blew off the ocean, prompting me to retreat indoors. The casinos all seemed so similar in layout and mind-numbing dazzle that after a while it was hard to tell whether you were at Trump's Taj, Trump's Plaza, Trump's Castle, Caesar's Palace, Bally's Park Place, Resorts International, or The Trop World. (The name of this last place fascinated me. What the heck was a *trop*? I wondered. Anything like a Trump? Was it in the English language? And why would anybody come up with a name for a hotel so devoid of pleasurable associations? It turned out that the establishment had first opened as the Tropicana—a dumb name for a hotel at nearly forty degrees of latitude, north, but no doubt it wanted to borrow a little cachet from the original Tropicana in Las Vegas. Apparently the name mutated to Trop World after a change of ownership. As places in America lose their individuality and meaning, names too mutate into meaninglessness. The American corporate mind has a moronic genius for this kind of thing.)

One of the more unnerving sights that Atlantic City offers the casual observer was of children alone or in small groups sitting on the floor in the corridors outside the casinos. The casinos admit no one under twenty-one, so there they sat while their parents were inside trying to become instant millionaires. They looked so melancholy, sprawled on the floor. A more dreadful sort of boredom is hard to imagine for a child, especially if such a child has seen its parent emerge as a loser before. As the hours crept by, they began to collect outside the casino doors, and one was apt to trip over them like the homeless on New York City's sidewalks.

In the Trop World casino, around midnight, the scene was exactly the same as it had been at two in the afternoon except that by now many of the players had developed a certain glazed expression quite different from the earlier look of intense self-absorption. With bankruptcy the small muscles of the face go slack. At Caesar's I watched one man of middle years play a slot machine for a good ten minutes. He had completely lost interest in the various fruits and gold bars that his machine displayed and was looking everywhere but at it. His head turned this way and that way, in quick jerks rather like a parrot's, but his eyes were as blank as Little Orphan Annie's. All the while, he fed silver dollars into the machine from a plastic cup and yanked the lever with a precision that was robotic. Every so often, he hit a minor payoff. He could tell without looking because the machine would noisily spit out ten or twenty coins into a steel trough below. He would reach down, scoop them into his cup, and resume robotically feeding the machine, the perfect industrial man at his leisure, having "fun."

On my way out of town at quarter after seven in the morning, a young pump jockey at the gas station on Arkansas Avenue—across the way from the disintegrating, boarded-up rail terminal—told me that he had just been cursed out by an Ohioan who didn't like the New Jersey state law that forbids motorists to pump their own gas. "Losers ain't too polite," he observed. He mentioned that another man had lost $20,000 at Trop World a few hours earlier and had to be dragged out of the casino kicking and screaming. I asked if this happened a lot. "Man," he said, "there's a whole world of losers out there, and sooner or later they all end up here. Only they don't think they're losers. When they find out, it's, like, the surprise of their life."

Woodstock, Vermont ➤➤

Here is the quintessential New England town of America's fevered imagination in all its fine-boned details: the village green bordered by streets of white clapboard houses, stolid churches, and a handsome red-brick inn; the charming little commercial district with well-kept shops and cozy restaurants; the dignified old civic buildings unsullied by the affronts of Modernism; the brook that burbles through the heart of the village crossed by several quaint iron-railed bridges; the whole community of buildings wedged into a narrow valley between abrupt wooded hills so as to afford a pleasing sense of compactness and enclosure.

On a crisp October afternoon the scene was rich with paradoxes for a student of human ecology. Here were the weekending corporate warriors, plying the sidewalks with their burnished wives, hunting for hand-crafted totem objects of hearth and home: the country quilts, the $38 carved birchwood salad forks, the whimsical pieces of "folk art" made twenty minutes ago. You knew these people were high-flyers because they stepped out of immaculate four-wheel-drive Jeeps, or else sedans of German manufacture, and they dressed in a kind of uniform: mint-condition expeditionary togs that had never been exposed to so much as a raindrop. The bull-like, middle-aged men also wore a slightly embarrassed, bewildered, and furtively resentful look on their faces, as though harboring deep doubts that shopping for handmade knickknacks was a virile pastime. And yet this is what their culture had reduced them to in their hours of leisure. They seemed especially doleful late in the day as they dutifully toted around the little twine-handled shopping bags that contained their wives' ceremonial purchases.

One sensed they saw in Woodstock some assemblage of symbols that spoke to them of a more spiritually gratifying way of life than the one they lived back home in the CEO enclaves of suburbia. I would even presume to summarize what it all signified to them: the idea of a true community organized at the human scale, along with a feeling of secure remoteness from the so-called modern world and all its terrors of giantism and discontinuity. In short, Woodstock was more like home ought to be than their own homes were. As a legitimate yearning for a more humane living arrangement, this went beyond nostalgia—but it tended to express itself in sentimental terms.

For instance, there were quite a few art galleries in Woodstock filled with paintings that in one way or another tried to depict small town and rural life. Some of the paintings were very accomplished; some were amateurish. Some obviously tried to capture a contemporary scene (often of rural desolation) in a contemporary way; others blatantly resorted to clichés (covered bridges in the snow, et cetera). But they all had this in common: not one included an image of a car.

I asked the gallery owners what this signified and got a set of explanations ranging from "Beats me," to "Paintings with cars don't sell." Yet the village of Woodstock was jam-packed with cars, cars not just of great monetary value, but of great symbolic value to their owners—Mercedes Benzes, BMWs, Land Rovers. The rural landscape around Woodstock was infested with cars. Every half-million-dollar vacation home, ancient or modern, had three or four parked in the driveway as did the few working farms that remained in the area. It was much easier to spot a car in Vermont than a cow.

Of course, the paintings were totem objects, invested with a specific set of symbolic meanings, in this case relating to the sense of place that is a part of every person's emotional equipment. People bought the paintings in order to bring a little sense of place home with them—home being somehow deficient in this quality.

All this is probably more or less obvious. But what is less obvious is the confusion that Americans feel about the entire issue of *place* and the abstract quality of their thinking about it. Hence the sentimentality. Everywhere in America, cars had destroyed the physical relationships between things and thereby destroyed the places themselves, and yet Americans could not conceive of life without cars. They couldn't imagine any modifications in their living arrangements that would make their home places more humane—for example, changing their zoning laws. They didn't want to challenge the status quo, or their own ideas about it. Undoubtedly, many of these visitors to Woodstock made money in the very enterprises that ruined places—like shopping plazas, or mass retailing, or any number of other endeavors that had the final consequence of making America ugly and killing local economies. This left them in quite a psychological pickle. What they did in the world and what they yearned for were at odds with each other. Unwilling to think clearly about the meaning of place in their lives, or their responsibility for making good places, they sought comfort in paintings of places with the cars deliberately left out. They finally reduced the whole question to just another commodity for consumption—shopping being one thing they could understand. This made them ridiculous and perhaps a little evil.

᛭

Unfortunately, what they yearn for—a place that feels like home ought to feel—is in short supply these days, and it can't really be bought, anyway. If it could be packaged and sold to individuals, then all the corporate warriors would live in better places than the jive-plastic residential enclaves where they return each night to watch TV, after a day's work in some distant elsewhere. But a community is something different from a commodity. As we saw in an earlier chapter, a community is an economy: the two are one and the same. The kind of economy that visitors to Woodstock imagine the place having is a local economy, a web of practical interrelationships between neighbors who understand their mutual dependency and honor it by competently caring for their work, their town, their offspring, and each other. The truth is that this sort of economy doesn't exist in Woodstock now, and hasn't for a very long time.

᛭

Woodstock was a dreary frontier settlement of less than a hundred souls until after the American Revolution, when it evolved into a trading center for farmers in the surrounding hills. It soon came to enjoy a great deal of pure luck. In 1787 the state decided to locate the Windsor County court there. The need to accommodate a constant stream of visiting lawyers led to the building of several inns, and some lawyers settled in the village permanently, building impressive houses. In 1806, Vermont established a state bank and put one of its two branches at Woodstock. The lawyers and bankers brought to town the felicities of higher culture. They owned books, founded schools, bought fancy goods, formed musical, poetic, and dramatic clubs, built churches and public buildings to dignify their spiritual and civic life, and supported several newspapers.

The period, roughly from 1800 to 1860, was Woodstock's golden era as a self-sustaining community *and* economy. The town enjoyed a source of water power in Kedron Brook, and along it sprang up small factories which sent all sorts of useful products into the world: pottery, chairs, linseed oil, liquor, and pianos. Farming then was quite different from the dairying monoculture of today. Hills now deeply wooded were then open sheep pastures. With wool in ready supply, a carding and spinning mill was established, adding value to this local product. Farmers grew wheat until flatlands more easily cultivated opened in western New York and Ohio. They raised hops, kept bees, cultivated silkworms, and grew market vegetables. Altogether, it was a more diversified agriculture, and it furnished most of the town's food needs.

After the Civil War, though, the state became a backwater. The war decimated a generation of Vermont's young men, who were not replaced by newcomers—immigrants settled in the rising cities, whose great factories surpassed Vermont's little water-powered mills, or else headed west. The hill farms became hardscrabble subsistence operations as railroads linked the East to cheaper food products in the Midwest. Sheep-raising ended when the vast range lands of the Far West opened to settlement. As a result, time stood still in Vermont. Physically, her towns changed little. The old buildings and the relationships between them remained preserved, as if in cold storage, into the twentieth century.

Woodstock remained lucky. While other towns slept, it became a resort. Its rustic inns for country lawyers evolved into proper hotels for families, and city folk of means would come to stay for weeks at a time, or even for the summer. Men who had made fortunes elsewhere bought homes in the village, most notably Frederick Billings, a Woodstock boy who went west in the California gold rush, learned law out there, and ended up President of the Northern Pacific Railroad. He returned to his hometown in his later years and became its great benefactor. The Billings connection persists to this day, since his granddaughter married Laurance Rockefeller, grandson of John D. the first.

†

When people visit Woodstock today, what they see there is a community much influenced by two great family fortunes, and an economy based in almost every way on resources that are not local. The crackerbarrel ambience is an artifice of wealth, as is the ability to maintain a lot of fragile old wooden houses in something close to their original condition. (Visit a Vermont town inhabited by native Vermonters and you are liable to encounter as much dingy vinyl siding as you would in a working-class neighborhood of Schenectady, New York.)

Ironically, though, it was Laurance Rockefeller who perpetrated one of Woodstock's worst building desecrations. His company owns the Woodstock Inn, the town's poshest hotel. When he bought the place in 1968, the inn that stood there was a five-story wooden colossus in the Shingle Style dating from the 1890s with an enormous porch, individual balconies, and a fantastic observation tower at one end—a gorgeous building, lining the entire block on the south side of the village green. Rockefeller tore it down and replaced it with an ersatz Georgian building that looks rather like an overblown suburban bank. It is set way back off the street and as a result the whole relationship between the building and the village green was spoiled. Mr. Rockefeller also owns the Woodstock Country Club, the town ski area, Suicide Six, and the Billings Farm Museum—where, in the 1880s, Frederick Billings had run a "model" farm to promote dairying as a way to uplift the state's demoralized farmers.

Woodstock no longer produces useful goods for local consumption or export. It relies on what we call a service economy, meaning essentially shops and restaurants. The shop clerks and waiters who work in these establishments live elsewhere, because they can't afford the housing in town, a predicament common in resort towns. It is a fifteen-minute drive to White River Junction and Lebanon, New Hampshire, where rents and house prices are much lower. During the 1980s, dairying collapsed and the farms were carved up into vacation parcels. Twenty-five percent of the property in and around Woodstock is owned by out-of-staters. Yet there remained a class of native Vermonters out in the hills, the sons and grandsons of farmers, who struggled to make a living at odd jobs—fixing cars or cutting cordwood for all those woodstoves in the half-million-dollar weekend hideaways owned by mall developers from Connecticut.

The Woodstock that the tourists love is largely a figment of the collective national imagination. Americans are a people lately given to abstraction, and little wonder, given the alienating discontinuities of daily life. Yet, for all its fakeness, it is a good thing that Woodstock is there for people to see, and however pathetic their shopping fetishism may be, it is a good thing that people come to see it. It would be better if they understood what they were looking at.

When I asked people on the street what they liked about the place, they replied overwhelmingly, in one way or another, that they liked the town's "old-fashioned feeling." Urged to cite specifics, they quickly got mired in circular reasoning: They liked the buildings because they were old-fashioned, and they liked old-fashioned things because they were old and antiquey, and . . . It was like Greenfield Village, where nobody seemed to notice that there were no cars around. These were educated people for the most part, but they were members of a culture that had long ceased to value place except as a sales gimmick, and they had no vocabulary with which to think about it. Whatever they took from the experience of walking around Woodstock on a fine fall day was not apt to make their hometowns better places.

BETTER PLACES

The great suburban build-out is over. It was wonderful for business in the short term, and a disaster for our civilization when the short term expired. We shall have to live with its consequences for a long time.

The chief consequence is that the living arrangement most Americans think of as "normal" is bankrupting us both personally and at every level of government. This is the true meaning of the word *deficit*, which has resounded so hollowly the past ten years as to have lost its power to distress us. Now that we have built the sprawling system of far-flung houses, offices, and discount marts connected by freeways, we can't afford to live in it. We also failed to anticipate the costs of the social problems we created in letting our towns and cities go to hell.

A further consequence is that two generations have grown up and matured in America without experiencing what it is like to live in a human habitat of quality. We have lost so much culture in the sense of how to build things well. Bodies of knowledge and sets of skills that took centuries to develop were tossed into the garbage, and we will not get them back easily. The culture of architecture was lost to Modernism and its dogmas. The culture of town planning was handed over to lawyers and bureaucrats, with pockets of resistance mopped up by the automobile, highway, and real estate interests.

The average citizen—who went to school in a building modeled on a shoe factory, who works in a suburban office park, who lives in a raised ranch house, who vacations in Las Vegas—would not recognize a building of quality if a tornado dropped it in his yard. But the professional architects, who ought to know better, have lost almost as much ability to discern the good from the bad, the human from the antihuman. The consequence of losing our planning skills is the monotony and soullessness of single-use zoning, which banished the variety that was the essence of our best communities. Most important, we have lost our knowledge of how physically to connect things in our everyday world, except by car and telephone.

You might say the overall consequence is that we have lost our sense of consequence. Living in places where nothing is connected properly, we have forgotten that connections are important. To a certain degree, we have forgotten how to think. Doesn't this show in our failure to bring these issues into the political arena? There *is* a direct connection between suburban sprawl and the spiraling cost of government, and most Americans don't see it yet, including many in government. Likewise, there is a connection between disregard for the public realm—for public life in general—and the breakdown of public safety.

These issues will not enter the public discourse until something of a paradigm shift occurs in American society. By paradigm, I mean a comprehensive world view shared by a critical mass of citizens. At any given time, enough people agree upon a particular model of reality and do whatever is necessary to sustain it. Ideas themselves may evolve slowly or rapidly and credible proofs may lag behind hypotheses. But a collective world view is made up of many ideas, all operating dynamically, and when the consensus about what they all add up to is shaken, the result can be convulsive social change. Enough people move to one side of the raft and suddenly the whole thing flips over. The rapid demise of Leninist communism as a believable model of economic reality is an example.

When I suggest that something similar may happen here, I do not anticipate the demise of capitalism. Capitalism in some form is likely to endure, whatever its shortcomings, for it is the only way known for managing accumulated material assets. I do foresee a necessary change, however, in our effort to create a capitalist economy appropriate to our circumstances—namely, a *sustainable* economy as opposed to our present *exhaustive* economy. And we can't have a sustainable economy unless we build a physical setting to house it. The physical setting we presently dwell in itself exhausts our capital. It is, in fact, the biggest part of the problem. The future will require us to build better places, or else the future will belong to other people and other societies.

Even after 1990, when the savings and loan catastrophe left the commercial real estate market in shambles, and the American economy began to slide into a malaise resembling the Great Depression, developers were still building some major projects in the same old foolish manner: single-family detached homes on half-acre lots out in the hills, minimalls along the connector roads, accountants' offices out in the old cornfields. But these are the mindless twitchings of a brain-dead culture, artificially sustained by the intravenous feeding of cheap oil. Indeed, the continuation of a cheap oil supply through the 1980s—a temporary quirk of politics and history—has been a disaster, allowing us to postpone the necessary redesign of America.

The longer we fail to act on this redesign of our everyday world, the more mired we are apt to become in a psychology of previous investment. So much of the nation's wealth is tied up in badly designed communities, inhuman buildings, and commercial highway crud that we cannot bring ourselves to imagine changing it. But time and circumstances will change our ability to use these things, whether we choose to think about it or not. What will become of all the junk that litters our landscape?

Things that were built in absurd locations, like the vast housing tracts outside Los Angeles on the fringe of the Mojave desert, may have to be abandoned. Ill-conceived building types, such as the vertical slum housing projects of the big cities, will have to be demolished on a wholesale basis. Today's posh suburbs could easily become tomorrow's slums. If it seems unthinkable, go to Detroit and check out the square miles of mansions-turned-slums off Woodward Avenue. It is a good bet that many of the suburban office buildings put up in the 1980s will never be used as intended—by corporate enterprises that employ hundreds of drones in the arrangement known as "back office"—and what they might be converted to, if anything, is anybody's guess. Many houses and shopping plazas built in the postwar era were so poorly constructed in the first place that they will reach the end of their "design life" before they might be eligible for reuse. In all, a lot of property is apt to lose its value.

There are some things we can predict about the physical arrangement of life in the coming decades. The most obvious is that we will have to rebuild our towns and cities in order to have any kind of advanced economy at all. In fact, this enterprise may turn out to be the engine that powers our economy for years to come, much the same way that the suburban build-out did—with results, one hopes, of more lasting value. To accomplish it, we will have to reacquire the lost art of town planning and radically revise the rules of building, especially the zoning codes that impoverish our present townscapes.

This implies that we shall have to give up mass automobile use. By this, I do not mean an end to all cars but rather, that every individual adult need not make a car trip for every function of living: to go to work, to buy clothes, to have a drink; that every adult need not be compelled to bear the absurd expense of car ownership and maintenance as a requisite of citizenship. The adjustment may be painful for a nation that views car ownership as the essence of individual liberty. Indeed, it is estimated that one sixth of all Americans make their living off of cars in one way or another. But the future will require us to make this adjustment. If we are wise, we will enjoy the compensations of an improved civic life that rehabilitated towns and cities can provide.

Reviving our towns and cities also offers a chance to rehabilitate our countryside. In the future, when we practice a different kind of agriculture than the heavily subsidized, petroleum-intensive, single-crop system we follow today, farming may be down-scaled and regionalized, more food grown and consumed locally. American farmers may learn to produce value-added products—for example, cheese—instead of supplying tons of raw milk to distant cheese factories. European farmers produce an array of value-added products from champagne to Parma hams. They have a richer agriculture *and* a richer food culture. They even live more comfortable, civilized, middle-class lives than many American farmers, though they operate on a far smaller scale.

Having turned farming into just another industrial enterprise, Americans have lost the *culture* of agriculture. Where I live there are still dozens of dairy farms in operation. On hardly any of them will you find a household vegetable garden. The farmers have vinyl swimming pools in their side yards, recreational vehicles parked next to the house, motorcycles, TV satellite dishes, but no gardens. Like the rest of us, they get their food at the supermarket. The pathetic thing is that in recent years these dairy farmers have seen their profits dwindle because of state-subsidized overproduction. Many teeter on bankruptcy from one year to the next, barely scraping by, their barns collapsing and expensive machinery (bought on time payments) rusting in the rain. Yet they will not grow any of their own food. Perhaps they are ashamed to put in a garden—afraid the neighbors might take it as a sign that they are too poor to go to the supermarket. Perhaps they have lost the knowledge and skill to garden. Perhaps they are lazy. In any case, their behavior is a symptom of a degraded agriculture.

In a culture that views *ecology* as the antithesis to *economy*, it is difficult to think clearly about how we live in relation to where we are. So we drop the subject from the political debate entirely. We have witnessed the collapse of the communist economic system with a strange smugness, unaware that our own vaunted way of life is in the process of bankrupting us, too. Even environmentalists, committed to the rescue of wild places, have failed to address the problem of human ecology in the places where we live and work. Yet, a few lonely figures around the country have sent out intelligent signals about redesigning the human habitat in America, and I would like to discuss some of their ideas in this last chapter. Their work varies widely from the theoretical to the practical, from the idealistic to the commercial, but all are making a valuable contribution to a field that barely exists anymore in America: the art of making good places.

A Pattern Language ➤➤

Back in the 1970s, a gang of architects, planners, academics, and artists led by Christopher Alexander of the University of California at Berkeley, published a gentle manifesto challenging the wisdom of the mid-twentieth century building establishment with a startling alternative vision. The essence of their vision was this: all the stuff in the man-made landscape—towns, streets, buildings, et cetera—had to be viewed as orders of connecting relationships rather than as mere objects in space. Though this may sound both overly abstract and simpleminded, it had deep implications.

They argued, for example, that the front of a house had to be understood not just as a wall with holes in it, but as a connection between the house and the street. Taking the argument a step further, the front of the house had no meaning *except* as a relationship between two places. Carried to its furthest limit, the argument implied that the whole built environment consisted not of things at all but only of relationships between and within other relationships. A window was not a hole in the wall, but a relationship between the outside and the inside, between darkness and light, warmth and cold. By viewing a window as an isolated *thing* we turned it into a mere hole in the wall—and treat it accordingly. This was precisely why the windows on suburban houses were so boring and banal, why many office buildings seemed to have no windows at all—why, in short, we lived surrounded by failed building relationships.

Alexander's concept sounded very Zen-like, and no doubt it was. It certainly went against the mechanistic, bottom-line, hyperrational dogmas of the architectural establishment. Alexander and Company refuted its bombastic pretensions in their gentle Zen way. All these things we build are illusions when viewed as isolated objects, they said. Take a picket fence. Sure, it had material existence. But it only made sense as something that ordered the relationship between the yard and the sidewalk. The wooden pickets had meaning only in relation to the spaces between them, which allowed a person on the street to see through the fence and yet still be informed that the private yard beyond it was a separate place from the public street. For that matter, the house was only the sum of fifty big and little relationships between the inside and the outside, the family within and mankind without. It was our very inability to see past objects in the landscape and understand the relationships at work between them that had led us to create such a symbolically impoverished everyday environment.

Ignoring the relationships between things and fetishizing buildings, the cult of Modernism promoted all the discontinuities of the common sprawlscape. The relationships created there were horrible because no thought went into them. At best, they were haphazard. An office tower gets built in the middle of a five-acre parking lot on a boulevard lined by similar isolated office buildings—who cares how it relates to the rest of Fairfax, Virginia, as long as the cars can get to it? And say, won't ten stories of greenish mirrored glass look spiffy from the Beltway! Building on that philosophical premise was a disaster.

Alexander and his colleagues concocted an antidote to this cultural poison. They called it "A Pattern Language." Here they summarized it nicely in clear prose refreshingly free of jargon.

> The elements of this language are entities called patterns. Each pattern describes a problem which occurs over and over again in our environment, and then describes the core of the solution to that problem in such a way that you can use this solution a million times over, without ever doing it the same way twice.[1]

This pattern language was a vocabulary for building. It derived partly from building traditions thousands of years old, partly from common sense, and it found humane solutions to the problems caused by such new, disruptive elements as cars, without eliminating them altogether from the general scheme. Alexander ordered his pattern language as a logical sequence beginning with the largest places, regions and towns, and then working down through neighborhoods, streets, buildings, rooms, ending with the details of construction. Each pattern was given a simple, comprehensible label in plain English—for example, "Promenade" to describe the sort of street where people go to relax and see other people, or "Light on Two Sides of Every Room," which describes a pattern for designing the placement of windows in houses. Each of these patterns was presented as a brief set of instructions—for example, "Six-Foot Balcony":

> Balconies and porches which are less than six feet deep are hardly ever used. . . . Therefore, whenever you build a balcony, a porch, a gallery, or a terrace, make it at least six feet deep. If possible, recess at least part of it into the building so that it is not cantilevered out and separated from the building by a simple line, and enclose it partially.[2]

All the patterns had certain qualities in common. They were based consciously on deep human emotional and psychological needs: the need for greenery, sunlight, places to be with other people, spaces to be alone, spaces for the young and the old to mix, for excitement, tranquility, and so on. Particularized in this manner, one could begin to see how dismally the modern milieu failed to provide for the variety of human nature. Everything had been ruthlessly but rationally edited out until the final result was the "function" room of a Holiday Inn: a room designed for any function, in which no one function felt right.

The best patterns also held in common a quality Alexander called "aliveness." They *supported* the good qualities in patterns they were connected with. A garden gate that is "alive" supports the good qualities of the garden and also of the path leading to it, because it defines the entrance in a delightful way at the same time it allows you to peer over and see the roses within a partially hidden place. "Deadness" was the result of bad connections. For instance, a stockade fence in front of a house would disrupt the visual connection between the house and the street. It wasn't a fence at all, really, it was a wall. A steel cyclone fence would also be a "dead" pattern, but for different reasons. You could see through it okay, but it lacked visual substance of its own. It pretended to be invisible when in fact it was only thin and brutal. Alexander's Pattern Language made it possible to understand these things.

Patterns that were alive promoted stability. They helped buttress all the other good patterns in a universe of living patterns. Patterns that were dead caused instability and disintegration. They spread a poison that infected and weakened other patterns. The entrance to a house was a system of lesser patterns: it required some ornament around the opening to mark it as ceremonially distinct; it called for a roof overhang to shelter someone coming in out of the rain fumbling with his house key; it needed a certain depth of penetration to mark the difference in light between the inside and the outside; a set of stairs would add dignity; it might include benches or seats flanking the door. Notice that these design considerations were elements common to houses built before World War II. Having lost the culture of design since then, we dispense with all these elements or patterns, and the result is a typical American house with a blank garage door facing the street. Multiply it by millions and you begin to understand the scope of the spiritual problems caused by bad building.

Alexander's Pattern Language was a great achievement in resurrecting building traditions on the verge of extinction. Unfortunately, America was not ready to pay attention to it. In fact, a great many of the patterns, and especially those pertaining to good town planning practices, contradicted the reigning zoning laws, and hence were illegal and unusable. Somebody had to carry this message to the people who voted for the zoning ordinances, and so along came Andres Duany.

Traditional Neighborhood Development (TND) ➤➤

I went down to Seaside in the Florida panhandle because stories about it had appeared in so many magazines that the place began to seem more like a force of nature than a work of architecture. Why had it gotten so much attention? Because it was a real estate development that was designed to look and function like a small town. The audacity!

To get to Seaside you drive an hour west from Panama City on Route 30-A along the "Redneck Riviera," an appalling stretch of beachfront highway crudscape that runs between two enormous military installations—the strip's attractions are geared to the tastes of servicemen. All of a sudden, there comes a strange break in the awful cavalcade of cheap motels, grog shops, souvenir sheds, and tombstone condo towers, and you find yourself in what appears to be a drowsing southern small town circa 1918.

At Seaside, all the houses are made of wood with peaked tin roofs and deep porches. No two are alike, but all share a congruity of design that is soothing to eyeballs scalded by the chaotic squalor of the strip. The pastel-colored houses stand along a coherent network of narrow streets paved with brick. Cars parked parallel-wise line these streets, as they might in any small town. Otherwise, there are no parking lots or special accommodation for cars. Picket fences enclose small front yards. At the center of the town stands a grocery store, an open-air market, a couple of beer joints, an upscale eatery—no illuminated plastic signs, thank you—and a little Greek temple-style post office. At spacious intervals along the crest of the dunes stand three columned pavilions with graceful wooden steps leading down to the Gulf of Mexico. They look like gateways to the sea, which is just what they are—it's that simple.

At first, one catches a fugitive whiff of theme park cutesiness on the balmy salt breeze. This must be a common mental reflex among people, like myself, accustomed to a constant ambient dissonance in their surroundings. If Seaside seems a little too perfect, it is only because everything there is so spanking new. The patina of age is absent, and of course there is no cure for that except time. Nobody was more keenly aware of this than the developer, Robert Davis, and the architects who planned the town, Andres Duany and his wife and partner, Elizabeth Plater-Zyberk.

Davis, lean, bespectacled, and preppy-handsome, a self-styled "political radical" in college, started his career as an idealist working on subsidized housing in Washington, D.C. The job left him "totally disillusioned" as he began to understand the futility of isolating the poor, with all their social problems, in oversized, unmanageable "projects." After a while, he gravitated to Miami and developed town houses that garnered some design awards, becoming an entrepreneur in the process. In the late 1970s, his grandfather, a department store mogul, died and left him eighty acres of beachfront along the Redneck Riviera. What to do with it?

Davis scorned the typical Florida beachfront development as much as he had learned to loathe typical housing projects for the poor. He had a vague desire to revive the local North Florida building traditions that had been lost in the era of air conditioning and interstate highways. Most of all, he wanted to build a real place, not just a bunch of buildings. So he approached Duany and Plater-Zyberk, who had lately broken away from the cutting-edge Miami design firm Architechtonica. Duany was a suave, handsome Cuban-American. Plater-Zyberk came out of the Philadelphia Main Line suburbs. Both were Ivy Leaguers: Princeton and Yale.

Together, they toured the south with cameras, sketchpads, and measuring tapes, gradually realizing that the classic southern small town was the correct model for what Davis wanted to build. Such towns were made up of so-called "cracker cottages," wood-framed dwellings with deep roof overhangs, ample windows, and broad porches, designed for ventilation and shade in a hot climate.

Duany and Plater-Zyberk, then in their early thirties, had become obsessed with classic town planning of the early twentieth century, especially as practiced in England by Raymond Unwin and in America by John Nolen. Unwin and Nolen had raised town planning to a high art in the days of the City Beautiful movement. What's more, their ideas actually got built. Nolen designed hundreds of major civic projects, including Madison, the Wisconsin state capital. Automobiles entered the scene at the height of their careers and they found ways to accommodate them without compromising their standards of good civic design.

"Urban planning reached a level of competence in the 1920s that was absolutely mind-boggling," Duany told me.[3] "We're not up to their ankles. But what happened to these people is that they were hit by the crash of '29 and they never worked again. And then World War II happened." And after that, of course, the cars completely took over.

This culture of urban design, which respected the human scale and the complexity of human needs, had been lost, forgotten, consigned to the ash pit of history. It certainly wasn't part of the curriculum anymore in the graduate schools of design. If you were interested in the subject, you had to root out the dusty old texts yourself. Which Duany did, and he began to realize with alarm that, under today's zoning regulations, most of the standard practices of good town planning were against the law. For instance, something as traditional and commonsensical as allowing people to live in apartments above shops—this was no longer allowed in America, as evidenced by every one-story minimall from sea to shining sea. And how could you build a proper town center without such an arrangement? Even if you educated yourself in the lost art of town planning, Duany realized, you couldn't obtain the necessary permits to build good towns. And so with Seaside, Duany set out to prove a point.

Robert Davis enthusiastically embraced the idea of making Seaside a demonstration project. Someone had to show America that it was possible to build coherent communities. Besides, he was sure that it would make money as a business venture. People longed to live in places like the town he had in mind. Finally, the team brought in Leon Krier, the London-based architectural theorist, as a consultant. Krier, an eloquent critic of the modern crudscape, had proposed in his writings that the ideal size for a small town, or a city quarter, was eighty acres, exactly the size of Davis's property. It encompassed an area with a quarter-mile radius, which happened to be the distance that a healthy person would be willing to walk on a routine basis to go to work, shop, or go out to eat.

They drafted a master plan for Seaside in 1982. It was a modified neoclassical grid, straight out of John Nolen, with a semielliptical commercial district, a diagonal grand boulevard, and blocks of houses intersected by little alleyways and footpaths. The plan was highly unconventional by modern standards. It had a coherent town center, which included plenty of apartments that could serve as affordable dwellings for people who worked in the stores below. Houses were close together, and arranged in a manner that helped to define the street as an attractive public space. Outbuildings were encouraged to create odd little rental units—again, to promote an income mix of residents so that not everybody had to be an orthopedic surgeon to live there. Lots for civic buildings were reserved in places where they would look good and enhance public spaces. The post office was sited smack at the town center, where it might logically promote casual socializing. Streets were detailed for human delight rather than ease of motoring. Gazebos were placed at some intersections—they made the cars slow down, and they were magnets for pedestrians.

Perhaps the most unconventional aspect of the plan was that they did not sell off the beach. Typically in America, beachfront is sold off and privatized, denying access to anyone but the owners. Land without frontage thus becomes valueless, even if it is only across the road and 200 yards from the tide line. This is the reason that American beach towns tend to become linear one-sided strips. At Seaside, it was assumed that the beach was the reason for the town's existence, so the planners reserved the length of it for public access. They arranged streets perpendicularly to the beach, so that no one would live more than a five-minute walk from the ocean, and yet every town resident was free to enjoy it. This allowed them to build a community of much greater physical depth in which many more houses would have value. Finally, they built those graceful pavilions on the dunes, symbolizing the public sharing of this great resource.

Fortunately, when Davis, Duany, and Company got underway, Walton County had no building codes, nor even an official inspector, so they were able to write their own rules. The Seaside code is a simple graphic document; it explains itself in pictures so that the layman can understand it. Duany has said of the code: "It works even with the most horrifying incompetent architects; it pulls them into shape so, at least, they don't destroy a town." The code is designed to promote a common vocabulary of building forms. Wood is the preferred building material for houses; cement and stucco for commercial buildings. Vinyl siding is not allowed because ultraviolet light from the fierce Floridian sun makes it look crappy in only a few years. Rules mandate roof pitches, types of fencing, porch dimensions, and how lot frontage must be treated in order to maintain the spatial definition of the street. Small towers are encouraged so that every house can have a view of the sea. To promote variety within the unity of the code, the designers wrote a rule saying that no single architect could design more than twelve buildings in town, and another rule granting variances on the basis of architectural merit.

By the spring of 1990, 150 houses had been built in Seaside. Some business establishments were also up, but the main elliptical commercial district, which was to include offices and warehouses, existed only as a street with waiting lots. It seemed foolish to fault the developers for that, though critics carped because the whole scheme hadn't fully blossomed overnight.

"To make a stew you put in the potatoes and the beef, but you still have to cook it for two hours," Duany said. "You can put these elements in place, but it's only over time, over a generation maybe, that people will actually work there. Also, the civic institutions aren't going to be in place for a generation. We reserve the sites and we build a few of them, but the churches, the clubhouses, will only emerge over time. It's not instant."

Critics also complained that Seaside, being a resort town, was a completely artificial place inhabited only by yuppies, with none of the nitty-gritty problems of a real town with a diverse population, real economic concerns, and a history. It is inarguable that Seaside lacks history. But that is hardly the point. Its aim is to demonstrate how good relationships between public and private space may be achieved by changing a few rules of building. It never pretended to be anything else. It did make the important point that if you change the rules of building, you can reproduce these good relationships anywhere.

It's no exaggeration to say that Duany and Plater-Zyberk are out to change the physical arrangement of American life, and to do so by changing the rules of building. As Seaside took off in the 1980s and confirmed their belief that, given the choice, many people would prefer to live in coherent towns, they systematized what they had learned and came up with a program that they called Traditional Neighborhood Development, or TND. It was good old-fashioned urban planning repackaged for developers.

After Seaside, and all the publicity it generated, the firm was swamped with work. One project that got built is the 352-acre Kentlands, in Gaithersburg, Maryland, a further refinement of the TND approach in a place that can't be written off as a mere resort. All the elements are in place: a coherent grid of intersecting streets, houses closer together to define the public space, back alleys, garage apartments, an architectural code, the whole schmeer. But Duany and Plater-Zyberk ran into some pretty demoralizing problems with the local zoning officials along the way. The planned elementary school was supposed to be a focal point at the termination of a major street, but the Gaithersburg Board of Ed kept insisting on an off-the-shelf design with a flat roof and a ceramic-tiled exterior that made it look like a sludge-processing plant. Worse, they wanted to put the loading dock where the front of the building was supposed to be. Duany got them to agree on red bricks instead of the tile, and a columned and pedimented entrance with a cornice and sloping roof—if the developers paid for it—but they lost on the positioning of the loading dock. Other tussles over street dimensions and tree planting entailed some necessary compromise. Still, Duany was not demoralized about it. Rather, he argued that design imperfections would make the town more memorable, reflecting that it is, after all, part of the real world. He cited nearby Annapolis as an example: "Annapolis is full of lessons. One of them is how imperfect urbanism can be and still make a really great town. Everywhere you look in Annapolis things are off, things are imperfect. Yet it all adds up to a really magnificent place."[4]

The firm has also designed some enormous projects that are still in the tedious permitting stage. One, called Avalon Park, in central Florida, may reach the size of a small city, comprising sixteen coherent "neighborhoods" on the TND pattern. Another project, in California, would, at 20,000 acres, eventually be larger than Washington, D.C. At Mashpee, Massachusetts, on Cape Cod, where bad development ran completely amok for forty years, the firm redesigned a hideous shopping plaza and turned it into an authentic town center, with real streets and places to live above the shops. And all along their chief obstacle has been the by-the-book mind-set of local planning and zoning officials.

It is very hard to convince zoning board members that there are advantages in smaller lots arranged intelligently around public open space. The usual practice for suburb-building is to place individual houses on large lots. To zoners, public open space means a parking lot. So when you suggest shrinking house-lot size and doing something else with the land that would otherwise just be lawns, they see only the loss of privacy and the squalor of urban congestion. To recognize the benefit, they would have to understand public space. You would have to show them pictures of the houses in Savannah standing around the lovely tree-filled squares, or of the beautifully detailed streets on Beacon Hill—which Duany does in elaborate design meetings called charrettes. Even then, they don't always get it. There are so few good models in America, and most of our public places *are* squalid.

"For a long time now, zoning codes have been written in words, primarily by lawyers," said Plater-Zyberk. "In the past, town planning involved *design*. If you look at the plans from the 1920s you can see very clearly the concern for public space, where the civic monuments were, the focus on neighborhoods. Today it has become totally a matter of words and numbers, like an abstract painting."

"When we design a town, we need twenty variances to do it," Duany said.

"In general, most zoning codes are *pro*scriptive," Plater-Zyberk said. "They just try to prevent things from happening without offering a vision of how things should be. Our codes are *pre*scriptive. We want the streets to feel and act a certain way. Our codes are primarily related to how private property defines public space."[5]

Over the past decade, Duany has lectured at every venue where a crowd could be mustered to listen, be it the Boston Museum of Fine Arts or a town meeting in rural Florida. He is the front-man of the operation—Plater-Zyberk holds down a professorship at the University of Miami, and is less free to travel. Duany speaks with a persuasive combination of sardonic humor and messianic fervor about what's wrong with our surroundings today and the kinds of places the future will require us to build if we are to remain a civilized nation. Lately, municipal leaders and officials in charge of the present zoning laws have heard the message and come to Duany in search of some direction.

Louden County, Virginia, threatened with overwhelming sprawl from nearby Washington, invited Duany to rewrite its codes. Trenton, New Jersey, was another customer. Rockport, Maine. St. Louis, Missouri. Orange and Palm Beach Counties, Florida. The TND, in fact, is now being used as the model for future development across Florida.

"We get dozens of requests a week," Duany said. "The fight hasn't been terribly difficult because the world is ready for change. Over the past twenty years, enormous strides have been made in preserving the environment. Where we've failed is in the human ecology. It's this human ecology movement that must really be the agenda for the years ahead."

Pedestrian Pockets ➤➤

Peter Calthorpe, the San Francisco architect and planner, is the main figure behind Pedestrian Pockets, a scheme to retool the suburbs.[6] Calthorpe and his colleagues bring a distinctly West Coast point of view to the task. In their part of the country there is very little traditional town fabric dating from before World War II, so good models are few. Rather, most people on the West Coast have always lived in sprawling automobile suburbs, and never experienced an alternative to it. Lately, though, as the commuting distance increases, and speeds drop below twenty miles per hour, and the freeways back up, life on wheels becomes increasingly intolerable and people go mad with ennui. "The story of the West in the last forty years is a strange paradox—a period of intense urbanization based on images and aspirations that are non-urban," wrote architect Daniel Solomon, who helped articulate the philosophy behind Pedestrian Pockets.

Solomon went on to identify five major problems with West Coast suburbia: (1) It devours vast amounts of rural land, including some of the best farmland. (2) It squanders energy. (3) It wastes people's time, condemning them to solitary imprisonment in their cars for hours each day. (4) It is by nature homogenizing and intolerant of diversity, both economic and social, failing to provide "odd little corners for people with odd little lives." (5) It fails to provide decent public places that bring people into casual face-to-face contact.[7]

The need for an alternative everyday environment is particularly acute out West, where population growth is projected to continue at high rates. The Sacramento area, for instance, is expected to gain 700,000 people in the next twenty years—a figure equal to the present population of metropolitan San Francisco. Since there isn't enough old abandoned urban fabric to redevelop, the future presents West Coasters with a stark choice: more sprawl or something better.

The Pedestrian Pocket scheme depends on a coherent network of rail or trolley lines. Sacramento County has the beginnings of a light rail system in operation. So do Portland, Oregon, and San Diego. Calthorpe's firm has been active in development schemes and regional land-use plans in all three places. Each Pedestrian Pocket is conceived as a node along these rail lines. Each would be on the order of 100 acres, with housing for some 5000 people. The Pockets are not intended to be entirely self-sufficient—though the necessities of life would all be within walking distance. Rather, every pocket in a greater region would emphasize some aspect of life, such as manufacturing, major retail, warehousing, office work, museums, performing arts, while the inhabitants would "see themselves as citizens of the larger region."

I think it is fair to say that Calthorpe aims at a level of urbanism that is, at least, on a par with Duany and Plater-Zyberk's TND. In fact, looking at a set of drawings, it might be hard for the average person to tell the difference. Both employ coherent street grids modified by radial avenues, plazas, and parks. Calthorpe grew up in the sprawling suburbs south of San Francisco, and his revulsion for the "spaghetti streets" of the cul-de-sac subdivisions is heartfelt. If anything, his street plans may be even more formal and baroque than Duany and Company's. He is equally attentive to the creation of good public space and walkable relationships, and his Pedestrian Pockets include service alleys, well-placed civic buildings, and auxiliary apartments. Calthorpe is arguably less interested in the question of architectural unity than Duany is.

Calthorpe's ideas have been warmly accepted in official quarters. Sacramento County invited him to help rewrite their entire code of design regulations for future development. Closer to home, in Marin County, where he lives on a houseboat, Calthorpe knocked heads with environmentalists who favor a simple "no growth" policy. The problem with the "no growth" approach, Calthorpe insists, is that the pressure doesn't go away; if you don't make some kind of provision for growth in the form of good planning, development just leapfrogs farther out into the hinterlands, resulting in longer commutes and more mindless sprawl.

Calthorpe's best-known project to date is the Laguna West development, twelve miles south of Sacramento. At 800 acres, it is ten times larger than Seaside. The plan focuses five park-centered neighborhoods around a sixty-five-acre artificial lake. Public esplanades line most of the lakeshore. Three grand causeways run across the lake (over large islands that also function as neighborhoods of houses) and converge in a town center of stores, schools, civic buildings, tree-filled plazas, low-rise apartment buildings, and town houses. Everything is walkable. Houses are pushed forward to the front lot lines, with porches providing "a public face" for the street. Cars may be parked along the tree-lined streets. Garages are located off back alleys, where they belong. Calthorpe's colleague Doug Kelbaugh, who is chairman of the architecture school at the University of Washington, says of Calthrope's design for Laguna West: "It is a geometry where the whole is greater than the sum of its parts." The first batch of building sites came on the market late in 1991 and sold out in a matter of days.

Calthrope's overall aim is to create a decent public realm so that Americans can have a decent public life, to redress the extreme over-privatization of life in postwar suburbia. He also quite clearly believes that we can no longer afford suburbia, either economically or socially. "The notion of creating real places is the challenge of the nineties," he has said. "The whole structure of our suburban environment has to be rethought." Critics accuse him of indulging in nostalgia, but in his own writing, Calthorpe takes care to make a distinction between sound building traditions and nostalgia: "Tradition evolves with time and place while holding strongly to certain formal, cultural, and personal principles. Nostalgia seeks the security of past forms without the inherent principles."[8]

Saving the Countryside ➤➤

I found Randall Arendt, after some considerable trouble, at his office on the campus of the University of Massachusetts in Amherst. The campus was a masterwork of bad design in the classic postwar mode, a monstrous assemblage of throwaway buildings, Modernist mausole-ums, and incongruous Radiant City high-rises planted at a gaping scale in no meaningful relation amid a yawning wasteland of parking. It looked more like Monument Valley than New England. Nobody I asked seemed to know where anything was.

Arendt runs a program called the Center for Rural Massachusetts, and his mission is to try to prevent the creeping crud of suburbia from overwhelming what remains of the open country in that little state—so perhaps it is a good thing that he has to come to work at this ghastly place every day. His office was in the basement of one of the few old buildings on campus, a red-sandstone Romanesque structure that houses an obscure branch of the university called the College of Food and Natural Resources. Dark-haired and lean, a youthful-looking for-tyish with a somewhat impatient, perpetually exasperated manner, Arendt talked in rapid bursts about the need to change the rules of land development so that good farmland and "working landscapes" are not lost to the generations that will follow ours.

"I trained in England, and coming back to this country was a real culture shock. The first zoning ordinance I ever read, I read after I came back here, after I had my degree in planning and had worked in plan-ning for two years. They don't have subdivision regulations or zoning ordinances in Great Britain. Then, a lightbulb went off inside my head: *This is why America looks the way it does!* The law is the major problem with the development pattern. Developers don't fight it, they go with the flow."

Arendt is chiefly concerned with the landscape of the Pioneer Valley, which is that section of the Connecticut River Valley that runs north to south clear through the western part of Massachusetts. It is an old and beloved landscape, commemorated by the painter Thomas Cole, cele-brated in literature, but lately very much at risk of being lost to sub-divisions and convenience marts. Here was some of the richest farmland in New England, deep loam laid down by eons of floodborne silt and cared for by careful farmers. When Arendt calls it a "working land-scape," he means that the qualities we value in it come not just from its physiography but from the gentle imprint that agriculture has left on it over time—open pastures, fields of crops, cows, hedgerows, stone walls, barns, woodlots, narrow roads.

The population of the valley surged in the postwar period, especially after Interstate Highway 91 opened in the 1960s. In the town of Amherst alone it spurted from 8000 to 38,000 between 1950 and 1990—the same period in which more than three quarters of the farms in Massachusetts disappeared. Until the 1980s, the long sheds of the tobacco growers were a common sight through the valley, but the land became more valuable for tract housing and minimalls than it was for farming. These things were expressions of a new economy, a cheap oil economy of gold-plated roadways and throwaway architecture.

As sprawl spilled over the countryside, alarmed town officials passed laws designed to mitigate it, which had the unforeseen consequence of making it worse. One common response was to increase the minimum lot size in the mistaken belief that spreading houses farther apart would preserve the open character of the landscape. In fact, it had the opposite effect: it ruined rural landscape in larger chunks. A two- to five-acre-minimum lot requirement meant houses were being plopped down in the middle of every cow pasture. The scraps of land left between the houses weren't used for anything. They were "too big to mow, and too small to plow," in the words of Robert Yaro, Randall Arendt's former boss, now an officer with the Regional Plan Association in New York City.[9]

The deeper truth, as Randall Arendt realized, was that typical zoning laws not only failed to protect the landscape, they virtually *mandated* sprawl. To reproduce anything resembling a traditional New England village had become illegal, a violation of all codes, acreage requirements, setbacks, street widths, and laws insisting on the separation of uses. So, towns ended up splattered all over the countryside while the countryside completely lost its rural character. All you could build in present-day New England was Los Angeles.

In the mid-eighties, Yaro and Arendt, along with landscapists Harry Dodson and Elizabeth A. Brabec, put together a strategy to alter this outcome. They published their ideas under the somewhat unwieldy title *Dealing with Change in the Connecticut River Valley: A Design Manual for Conservation and Development*. It offered many specific remedies, in the form of a comprehensive new set of model laws and codes, and the team devised a very effective way to make their points using illustrations. The four-color drawings were presented as triptychs. They showed a bird's-eye view of a rural landscape, then the same place as developed under the typical zoning laws, and finally as developed under their proposed new rules. Even the casual reader got a very vivid picture of each outcome.

"The first 5 percent of development ruins 50 percent of the countryside," Arendt explained. "What it means is that you can take a small amount of development, say three buildings, and if you put them in the middle of a farm field you've completely screwed it up, whereas if you put them on the other side of the street, or at the edge of the field, or behind some trees you can do a lot to preserve the character of that landscape."

The cornerstone of the new code was something called a "Farmland/ Open Space Conservation and Development Bylaw." It allowed developers to buy farmland and build houses on it, but required them to set aside half the buildable acreage for agriculture or scenic or recreational open space under perpetual deed restrictions. This was as close as you could get to locking land up and throwing away the key. The developer could build the same number of houses as under the old laws, but he had to do it on smaller lots, in village-like clusters. Houses also had to be built on "the least fertile soils" and "in a manner that maximized the usable area remaining for agricultural use"—meaning, keep them off the established fields and pastures and try to put them at the fringe of the woods.

Another set of bylaws for commercial growth required that business establishments be built in clusters, or "nodes," rather than along highway strips. All parking lots were to be placed in the side or rear. Highway access or curb cuts would be strictly limited so that, in effect, each node would be served by a single access road. Outdoor lighting had to be shielded. Signs would be controlled as to size, material, and manner of illumination. In fact, the overall package included an extremely rigorous set of design bylaws intended to make New England look more like New England. Flat roofs were out. Where new buildings went up alongside old ones, the new had to "harmonize" with what was already there in terms of scale, setbacks, roofline, and building materials.

In my view, the bundle of proposed new rules and regulations had some signal weaknesses. It did little to address the extreme separation of uses—residential, commercial, et cetera—that makes people so dependent on their cars in the first place. Somebody living in a rural cluster of houses would still have to drive to a commercial node to pick up a loaf of bread. The scheme insisted on concentrated development without a concomitant measure of detailed town planning.

Some of the aesthetic considerations, I thought, depended on a public consensus that doesn't really exist. Our buildings look ridiculous largely because they are built to serve cars, not people, and because they stand in isolation, unconnected with communities of other buildings. To get hung up on building materials without repairing underlying bad relationships would result, it seems to me, in just the sort of exercise in nostalgia that Peter Calthorpe was talking about: using old forms without the supporting principles, hamburger joints dolled up to look like little white churches, in the middle of a parking lot.

I aired these doubts with Randall Arendt over lunch in the UMass faculty club. We talked about the town planning ideas being pushed by Duany and others, and how, if implemented, these ideas could go a long way toward saving rural land by putting development where it belonged: in coherent towns with walkable streets, housing for all income groups, and places to shop and work, all mixed together.

"We're starting from the countryside and working back to the village," Arendt said. "We [he and Duany] don't quite meet in the middle. We do little in terms of town-centered development. He does very little in terms of land conservation. Both are equally important. I think we'd both like to move in each other's directions. Our whole focus has been on open space development design rather than mixed use. We felt that was the issue that people really were more concerned about. They're not too unhappy with the situation as it exists. It's an easily accomplished task to greatly improve the development pattern."

Arendt, like Duany and Calthorpe, does a lot of road shows, lecturing to town officials and ordinary citizens wherever they will let him set up his slide projector, and insofar as his program seeks mainly to halt the loss of landscape, whether it is woods, or hills, or age-old corn fields, he has been relatively successful in persuading Pioneer Valley officials to try his new way for regulating growth. Anyway, the continued glut of cheap oil has postponed a tougher general reassessment of the way we live in America.

On the way back across campus to his office, we passed one of the wonders of modern American architecture: the UMass library. It was a stand-alone twenty-eight-story red brick high-rise completed in 1973. A conspicuously ugly chain-link fence ringed the base of the building—except where a sort of temporary canopy of wood planks and iron-pipe scaffolding shielded the entrance. It looked as though the building had acquired some contagious disease and school officials didn't want anybody getting near it. This proved close to the truth. Arendt explained that the architects hadn't taken into consideration the extreme weight of the books in the stacks, which had exerted pressure in such a manner as to make the exterior walls bulge slightly. As a result, some of the bricks were beginning to *spall*, or break apart, sending brick fragments hailing down into the crowded quadrangles below. Administrators were nervous that sooner or later a big chunk, or maybe even a whole brick, would pop out and brain some poor, innocent sophomore.

Back in the cavernous basement office he occupies with his small staff, Arendt told me, "We promote *mandatory* open space zoning. Optional doesn't work. The towns that have tried optional zoning, nine times out of ten the developers come in with the same old worn-out pattern of big lots and streets taking up the entire parcel, offering nothing more. We've moved, since 1986, from having zero towns with mandatory open space zoning to having eight or nine today. We're not trying to turn the system on its head or radically reform it. We're trying to reshape it so that towns on their own, without professional planning consultants, can implement it."

There were other moments during the afternoon when Arendt, who grew up in the New Jersey suburbs, seemed to wax a little less optimistic about the task he had set for himself.

"When you've done some planning in England and you come back over to this country, you realize how futile it is, because no one's really looking at the big picture. I admit that what we're doing here is looking at some individual pieces of property and trying to make sure they don't get paved over. But where is the big picture? It doesn't exist."

Bob Yaro, since departed for his new job with the NYRPA, offered this final assessment in a phone interview: "When they come to chronicle the decline of this civilization," he said, "they're going to wonder why we were debating flag burning, abortion, and broccoli eating instead of the fundamental issues of how we live and use the environment."

In Land We Trust ➤➤

Between 1950 and 1990, Vermont quietly lost 90 percent of its farms, from roughly 20,000 down to 2000. Though the state had some progressive land-use laws in place—an antibillboard act, a prohibition against building on mountainsides above 2500 feet—it was ceasing to be a working landscape and stood in danger of losing its physical character altogether. Think of Vermont and you picture barns, cows, hayrolls standing in meadows, pastures bordered by woods. But without the farmers working day by day to maintain that landscape, it would soon be doomed to disappear, with dire consequences for Vermont's leading industry: tourism.

In the 1980s, the subdividers had a field day buying up Vermont farms. The amount of cash unleashed by banks into the real estate market was supernatural—it would come back to haunt us in the 1990s as bankruptcy and unprecedented debt—and Vermont farms were ripe for the picking. The economics of dairy farming had sunk to a miserable level. Milk prices were depressed by a cockamamie system of government regulations that gave consumers (i.e., most voters) cheap milk at the expense of the farmers, who couldn't make a dime. What's more, dairying was very hard work. You could never leave the farm for even a couple of days because the cows *had* to be milked, no matter what, and hired help was a thing of the past. Young people wouldn't consider dairying as a vocation—the very few who might, couldn't afford to buy farms at market prices—while aging farmers wanted to cash in on their biggest asset, their land, and retire to some sun-baked strand in Florida.

To make matters worse, the farmer's property taxes were eating him alive. His taxes were calculated on the basis of the land's *potential* for development, not its value for agriculture. That is, a 250-acre farm a man might have bought for $38,000 in 1959 was now assessed at $1 million, because that was its fair market value—to developers who could chop it up into ten-acre parcels and sell it off for homesites, or condos, or strip malls. So the farmer was paying a tax all out of proportion to his actual income, or to what he was doing with the land. And the high taxes were just another thing that kept young people from starting out in farming.

No wonder, then, when some out-of-state sharpie offered an elderly farmer a cool million in cash for his land, well, the farmer's head might swim with visions of swaying palms and frosty drinks out in the bass boat cruising off his new place on Lake Okeechobee—and could you blame the guy, after getting up at four-fifteen in the morning for thirty-two years to plug fifty Holstein cows into their electric milkers?

The catastrophic farm sell-off was followed by many in the conservation movement, and they devised a strategy to fight it. Their chief weapon was a legal instrument called a land trust. The basic idea was this: if development was ruining the agricultural landscape, then buy up the development rights from farmers so that the land could never be used for anything *but* farming, though it could still be bought and sold. About half the money to make purchases came from Vermont's Housing and Conservation Board, the rest came from private foundations and individual donations. Here is how it worked.

Let's say Farmer Jones, age sixty-four, has a 100-acre dairy farm with a market value of $310,000. He is determined to sell, and he views the $310,000 as his retirement fund. Much as he would like to sell his farm to a younger farmer, the asking price makes that outcome highly improbable. A realtor he talked to down at the Koffee Kupboard came up with the figure $310,000 knowing that, minus some wetland and steep hillside, the property could be legally subdivided into eight ten-acre vacation homesites worth $45,000 each, according to the "comparables," leaving a tidy profit for the subdivider. Six other farmers in the township have sold out since 1983 and the demand for developable farmland remains strong because a major ski area beckons twenty minutes away by car. In fact, a developer from Westchester County in New York has already stopped by Farmer Jones's house and pitched an offer, leaving his card on the kitchen table. Every time he goes out to milk the cows before dawn, Farmer Jones sees the card taped to his refrigerator and starts thinking about that bass boat in Florida.

In steps the land trust. It says, "Wait a second. We'll buy the development rights from you, Farmer Jones, for $150,000. Then, with those rights 'stripped,' you can turn around and sell the farm for $160,000 to an enterprising lad on our list of young men who want to be farmers, with the explicit understanding that it can never be used for subdividing into homesites, or a miniature golf complex, or a shopping plaza." Altogether, Farmer Jones realizes $310,000 for his retirement—the same as he would have gotten in a straight sellout. He can go and buy that bass boat in Florida with a clear conscience now, because he truly *loves* the farm and deep down the thought of ski chalets going up on the old pastures makes him ashamed of himself, as if he were dishonoring the decades of work his family put into the place.

The Jones farm is now both protected from any future development and kept in active farming. Moreover, the deal has the additional *public* benefit of saving the landscape for Farmer Jones's neighbors and for the tourist industry, which needs Vermont to preserve its rural character—for when it starts to look like New Jersey the tourists might as well stay home. The development restriction will carry forward in the deed as a permanent condition, no matter how many times the farm is bought and sold in the future. Finally, the land has been made affordable so that a young person might take up farming. Dairying may not pan out, but when it becomes too expensive to truck pears from California, or onions from Mexico, as is likely to happen in the years ahead, then Vermont farmers will learn to grow more diversified crops. The land trust is an elegant solution.

Of course, it didn't always work out so smoothly in practice. For one thing, the land trust idea tended to sound abstruse and confusing to weary farmers, who often just wanted to take a big wad of money and run. The land trust staffers would go to talk to them, and the farmers' eyes would glaze over. Or, when they managed to listen, the whole scheme rubbed them the wrong way at a deep philosophical level. Farmers tend to be politically conservative. Terms like *permanent restrictions* smacked of the government's telling you what to do with your land. In some areas, the land trust idea bred an "us-versus-them" atmosphere.

There were also financial complications, because not all farmland was valued equally. In some towns, like Woodstock, where a lot of wealthy city people had summer places, you could strip the development rights from a farm and it would still possess what they call "estate value," meaning other rich people would bid up the price, no matter how restricted the deed, because it was such pretty land—the net effect being that it was still beyond the means of an ordinary farmer, and hence might be taken out of agriculture anyway. This was a problem from the scenic point of view too, because in twenty years or so the pastures and corn fields would grow into woods, blocking vistas and obliterating the gentler imprints of man's presence over time that gave richness to the rural landscape.

But on balance, the land trust idea proved to be an effective strategy. It saved farms at a time when little else was being done to challenge the hegemony of the realtors, or to change land-use laws, or bad zoning, bad tax arrangements, and bad agricultural policies. No other institution, public or private, has yet proven up to the task.

⚓

One snowy day just before Christmas last year, I drove across the border from New York into a quiet corner of Vermont called the Mettowee River Valley, where the Vermont Land Trust had set up an exemplary project to save farms. The project director and sole paid employee was Jacki Lappen, thirty-nine, a handsome, dark-haired woman originally from Boston, with a master's degree in resource management, who was married to a professional bookbinder and had a six-month-old baby.

Lappen operated out of a one-room office heated with a woodstove in the microscopic village of Pawlet. Her first two years on the job had all been groundwork, getting to know the local farmers, explaining to them how the land trust idea worked, striving to gain their trust. She didn't put together any deals during that period.

"They had lots of trouble understanding what we're doing," Lappen told me while large snowflakes swirled outside her office windows. "We're perceived as an outside organization. It's true, this land trust idea didn't emerge from the farm community, but from people who wanted to protect farms because they're pretty. So it's looked on as elitist, as something being imposed on them, even though it's a voluntary program. It took a long time to convince farmers that we're not the government. One farmer, when she first heard of *development rights*, thought we wanted to buy her farm and develop it."

The Mettowee Valley lies ten minutes up Highway 30 from Manchester, a town thick with ski lodges and summer mansions that had grown positively clotted with factory outlet stores in the 1980s. An accompanying real estate boom sent shock waves thundering through all the nearby towns. Developers and their agents from Manchester made regular forays up into the Mettowee Valley, ringing farmers' doorbells, searching for buildable land. Being a rather narrow, steep-walled valley, most of the farms stood right along Highway 30, which paralleled the Mettowee River, a good trout stream, and if the farms were lost, the landscape character of the valley would have changed drastically.

"As the developers were rotated out the door, I'd come in and say, 'Hey, there's another option,' " Lappen recalled. "The farmer would say, 'The guy before you offered me a million dollars. What can you do for me?' "

Since she took over the Mettowee Valley Project in 1988, Lappen has protected six farms in one way or another. The first was a deal to put the 198-acre Moore Farm into the hands of the farmer who had been renting pasture and crop land on the place for eighteen years. To start, the Vermont Land Trust had to buy the whole farm because the owners wanted to cash out. Lappen knew that even with the development rights stripped, the farmer, Fred "Shorty" Stone, still couldn't afford to buy the whole place and also make necessary improvements in the barns, so the Land Trust sold him back only that portion of the land where his buildings stood. Then they wrote up a long-term lease for the rest. Under these terms, Stone was able to put up a new barn. Bottom line: the farm was kept in active agriculture.

The five other farms involved the straight purchase of development rights on a total of 1558 acres of prime valley land along Highway 30. The largest, the 376-acre Leach Farm, had been in the hands of the same family for 223 years. The project has also protected an additional 1500 acres of forest and wetland, and almost three miles of the Mettowee River's frontage. Altogether, this represents 3.5 percent of the valley's land area, and 10 percent of its farms, quite an accomplishment for four years' work. Lappen recognizes the difficulty of finding young people to replace the farmers who are leaving the land, and the uncertain course of the nation's economy in the years ahead, but she views her work with quiet satisfaction.

"We're trying to keep a community tradition going by preserving these viable farms," she said, "but failing that, we'll end up with land that's kept open, which is a legitimate end in itself."

Credo ➡

Born in 1948, I have lived my entire life in America's high imperial moment. During this epoch of stupendous wealth and power, we have managed to ruin our greatest cities, throw away our small towns, and impose over the countryside a joyless junk habitat which we can no longer afford to support. Indulging in a fetish of commercialized individualism, we did away with the public realm, and with nothing left but private life in our private homes and private cars, we wonder what happened to the spirit of community. We created a landscape of scary places and became a nation of scary people.

As a young newspaper reporter, some twenty years ago, I used to drive each day up a new six-lane commercial boulevard near the office where I worked, my heart filled with cold, spreading horror at the sight of the mall buildings, the fast-food huts, the auto-lube joints, and the other monuments of sprawl, all rising out of what had been corn fields and apple orchards ten miles outside the capital city of New York State. I felt that there was something profoundly wrong with the place that was being created there, though my reasons were inexact. Just being there weighed me down with intimations of doom.

It also troubled me to realize that all over America places like this were being duplicated by the tens of thousands, and that this was to be the world of my future. I wanted "them" to stop building all that stuff, though I sensed it would take some catastrophe—war, depression, pestilence—to stop it, and I didn't relish the prospect of that either. Then the Arab Oil Embargo struck in the fall of 1973, and the traffic vanished from the big new shopping boulevard, and the bottom fell out of the economy for a while—though not long enough for America to get the message—and I began to dimly discern that the place itself, this new everyday environment, *was* the catastrophe.

As a child of my times, I was naturally ignorant about the culture of place-making which America had thrown away in its eagerness to become a drive-in civilization. It simply wasn't there anymore, especially for someone unconnected to the formal study of architecture. Nobody I knew, or even knew of, talked about building good towns. Cities were considered hopeless—the official policy of urban renewal was a sick joke, and individual acts of urban gentrification were commonly sneered at as an offense to the poor. To be against cars was more un-American than being against the Vietnam War—even hippies loved their Volkswagen microbuses, and every guitar player had his song of the open road. It took me twenty years of searching to begin to understand my own emotional response to the places I lived in in America.

Lately I am impressed by the number of educated people I meet who don't think about these issues and their implications. They may feel that there is something vaguely wrong with their homes, their neighborhoods, their cities, the whole physical arrangement of their lives. They may quietly yearn, like homesick children, to belong somewhere, to be members of real communities. But their feelings aren't moored to specific positive ideas about what it takes to make a good place. When I mention the things I have been writing about to my friends—middle-aged people advanced in serious careers—they say, "Huh . . . ?" as though I were describing life on another planet.

I am concerned because I don't think we will be able to have much of a civilization in the future unless we build proper places in which to dwell. And it seems unlikely that we will move to do this anytime soon in a conscious and systematic way. Sooner or later, absolute necessity will compel us to give up our present habits, but by then the cost of rebuilding may be more than we can bear. In the meantime, the standard of living in the United States is apt to decline sharply, and as it does the probability of political trouble will rise. It may become too expensive for ever-broader classes of people to own and operate cars. Decent housing is already beyond the reach of many "average" families and individuals, and unless we change the rules of building, the situation will get worse. Imagine the resentment this will breed. Some talented mob-master may arise among us, promising the American people that he can bring back the good old days—if only we have the guts to invade some region with deep oil reserves. Or maybe he will promise to confiscate the property of the dwindling "haves" for the benefit of the increasing "have-nots."

Winston Churchill once said that Americans could be counted on to do the right thing after they had exhausted the alternatives. We are a paradoxical people. In the nineteenth century, we were renowned for our ingenuity, for our ability to solve so many of the practical problems of existence. Today, the world views us as a nation of bumbling crybabies. During the Reagan and Bush years, we had to be dragged kicking and screaming to every venue where the planet's worst problems were openly discussed. Global warming? If it means changing our behavior, we're not interested. Ozone depletion? Only if you twist our arm. Acid rain? Run some more tests. Population control? Tell the little wogs to give up sex.

But let's assume we now face the future with better intentions. The coming decades are still bound to be difficult. We will have to replace a destructive economy of mindless expansion with one that consciously respects earthly limits and human scale. To begin doing that, we'll have to reevaluate some sacred ideas about ourselves. We'll have to give up our fetish for extreme individualism and rediscover public life. In doing so, we will surely rediscover public manners and some notion of the common good. We will have to tell some people, in some instances, what they can and cannot do with their land.

We will have to downscale our gigantic enterprises and institutions—corporations, governments, banks, schools, hospitals, markets, farms—and learn to live locally, hence responsibly. We will have to drive less and create decent public transportation that people want to use. We will have to produce less garbage (including pollution) and consume less fossil fuel. We will have to reacquire the lost art of civic planning and redesign our rules for building. If we can do these things, we may be able to recreate a nation of places worth caring about, places of enduring quality and memorable character.

There is a reason that human beings long for a sense of permanence. This longing is not limited to children, for it touches the profoundest aspects of our existence: that life is short, fraught with uncertainty, and sometimes tragic. We know not where we come from, still less where we are going, and to keep from going crazy while we are here, we want to feel that we truly belong to a specific part of the world.

CHAPTER 2

1. Roderick Nash, *Wilderness and the American Mind*, p. 15.
2. Hawke, *Everyday Life in Early America*, p. 17.
3. Warner, *The Urban Wilderness*, p. 10.
4. Ibid., p. 11.
5. David M. Ellis, James A. Frost, Harold C. Syrett, and Harry J. Carmen, *A History of New York State* (Ithaca: Cornell University Press, 1957).
6. Hawke, *Everyday Life in Early America*, pp. 28–29.
7. Ibid., pp. 28–29.
8. William H. Whyte, *The Last Landscape* (New York: Doubleday, 1968), p. 78.
9. Warner, *The Urban Wilderness*, p. 15.

CHAPTER 3

1. Johnson, *The Birth of the Modern*, p. 211.
2. Kostof, *America by Design*, p. 297.
3. Solomon, "Fixing Suburbia," in Peter Calthorpe, et al., *The Pedestrian Pocket Book*, p. 23.
4. Stern, *Pride of Place*, p. 297.
5. Ibid., p. 302
6. Silver, *Lost New York*, p. 4.
7. Lewis, "The Galactic Metropolis," p. 29.
8. Stilgoe, *Borderland*, p. 75.
9. Mumford, *The City in History*, p. 447.
10. Ibid., pp. 450–51, 461.
11. Warner, *The Urban Wilderness*, p. 27.
12. Mumford, *The City in History*, p. 433.
13. Ibid., p. 302.

CHAPTER 4

1. Matthew Baigell, *Thomas Cole* (New York: Watson-Guptill Publications, 1981), p. 54.
2. Stilgoe, *Borderland*, p. 73.
3. Ibid., p. 53.
4. Author's interview with civil engineer Chester Chellman, White Mountain Survey, August 1990.
5. Stern, *Pride of Place*, p. 135.
6. Caro, *The Power Broker*, p. 151.

CHAPTER 5

1. Quoted in Hegemann and Peets, *The American Vitruvius*, p. 101.
2. Quoted in Roth, *McKim, Mead & White, Architects*, p. 179.
3. Banham, *A Concrete Atlantis*, p. 46.
4. Rybczynski, *Home: A Short History of an Idea*, pp. 187–189.
5. Alfred H. Barr, Jr. Preface to Johnson and Hitchcock, *The International Style*, p. 11.
6. Quoted in Handlin, *American Architecture*, p. 208.

CHAPTER 6

1. Jackson, *Crabgrass Frontier*, p. 108.
2. M. F. K. Fisher, "The Gastronomical Me," collected in *The Art of Eating* (New York: World Publishing Company, 1953), p. 356.
3. Flink, *The Automobile Age*, p. 43.
4. Flink cites Robert Walker's 1939 study of urban planning in thirty-one of the nation's largest cities. *The Automobile Age*, p. 153.
5. Ibid., pp. 364–67.
6. For the complete story, the author recommends Robert Caro's enormous and excellent biography *The Power Broker*, from which much of this information was drawn.
7. Author's interview with Lee Koppleman, January 1990, at the State University of New York at Stonybrook.
8. Jackson, *Crabgrass Frontier*, p. 193.

CHAPTER 7

1. Author's interview with civil engineer Chester Chellman in October 1990. Chellman, who specializes in traffic management and road design, is a maverick in his field. He derived this fragment of engineering culture from original papers in the archives of what today is called AASHTO, the American Association of State Highway and Transportation officials.
2. Author's interview with J. B. Jackson, July 1989.

3. Lewis, "The Galactic Metropolis," pp. 141–42.
4. I am indebted to the firm of Duany, Plater-Zyberk for making available to me tapes of Mr. Duany's Lecture on Principles.

CHAPTER 9

1. National Association of Homebuilders.
2. Jackson, *Discovering the Vernacular Landscape*, p. 94.
3. Scully, *American Architecture and Urbanism*, p. 38.
4. Rybczynski, *Home*, p. 127.
5. Handlin, *American Architecture*, p. 46.
6. Scully, *American Architecture and Urbanism*, pp. 65–66.
7. Downing, *Cottage Residences*, p. 5.

CHAPTER 10

1. Wendell Berry, "Property, Patriotism, and National Defense," included in his collection of essays, *Home Economics*, p. 103.

CHAPTER 11

1. Davies, *Conspicuous Production*, p. 171.
2. Golden, *The Quiet Diplomat*, pp. 389–90. I am indebted to Mr. Golden for letting me share his primary source information about the RenCen project, including interviews with Mayor Coleman Young and Detroit industrialist Max M. Fisher.
3. The speaker was Mike Ragsdale, senior marketing consultant for Grubb and Ellis, a national commercial real estate company. He had served in the Oregon legislature from 1972 to 1980. His remarks were part of a panel discussion held as part of the 1990 Regional Growth Conference, "Planning a Livable Future: Growth Strategies for the 21st Century." The conference was sponsored by the Metropolitan Service District. The quoted remarks were taken from a transcript of the conference proceedings, published by Metro.
4. Banham, *Los Angeles: The Architecture of Four Ecologies*, p. 31.
5. Ibid., pp. 82–83.
6. Flink, *The Automobile Age*, pp. 143–45.
7. Alan Weisman, "A Matter of Life and Breath," *The New York Times Magazine*, July 30, 1989.

CHAPTER 12

1. Andrew Holleran, "The Virgin and the Mouse," *Wigwag Magazine* (August 1990), p. 24.

2. Author's interview with John DeGrove, Director of the Florida Atlantic University/Florida International University Joint Center for Environmental and Urban Problems, April 1990.

3. "The Tables Have Turned on Gaming in Atlantic City," *The New York Times*, Sunday Business Section (December 9, 1990), p. 1.

CHAPTER 13

1. Alexander, et al., *A Pattern Language*, p. x.

2. Ibid., pp. 783–84.

3. Author's interview with Andres Duany, May 10, 1990.

4. Edward Gunts, "Plan Meets Reality," *Architecture Magazine*, December 1991.

5. Author's interview with Elizabeth Plater-Zyberk, May 12, 1990.

6. The other architects involved were Doug Kelbaugh, chairman of the University of Washington School of Architecture; Robert Small, also of the University of Washington; Harrison Fraker, University of Minnesota; Mark Mack and Daniel Solomon, University of California, Berkeley; Don Prowler, University of Pennsylvania; and David Sellers, in private practice in Vermont (formerly Yale University). The idea was formally developed at a charrette, or design workshop, held at the University of Washington in the Spring of 1988. The documents were subsequently published under the title, *The Pedestrian Pocket Book*, edited by Mr. Kelbaugh.

7. Solomon, "Fixing Suburbia," Peter Calthorpe, et al., *The Pedestrian Pocket Book*, p. 29.

8. Peter Calthorpe, "The Post-Suburban Metropolis," *Whole Earth Review*, Winter 1991.

9. Hiss, *The Experience of Place*, p. 214.

Alexander, Christopher. *The Timeless Way of Building.* New York: Oxford University Press, 1979.

Alexander, Christopher; Ishikawa, Sara; Silverstein, Murry; et al. *A Pattern Language.* New York: Oxford University Press, 1977.

Arendt, Randall G.; Brabec, Elizabeth A.; Dodson, Harry L.; Yaro, Robert D. *Dealing with Change in the Connecticut River Valley: A Design Manual for Conservation and Development.* Cambridge: Lincoln Institute of Land Policy, 1989.

Banham, Reyner. *A Concrete Atlantis—U.S. Industrial Building and European Modern Architecture 1900–1925.* Cambridge: MIT Press, 1986.

———. *Los Angeles: The Architecture of Four Ecologies.* New York: Harper & Row, 1971.

Benjamin, Asher. *The American Builder's Companion.* (Reprint of 6th edition.) New York: Dover Publications, 1969.

Berry, Wendell. *What Are People For?* San Francisco: North Point Press, 1990.

———. *Home Economics.* San Francisco: North Point Press, 1987.

———. *The Unsettling of America.* San Francisco: Sierra Club Books, 1977.

Blake, Peter. *God's Own Junkyard.* New York: Holt, Rinehart and Winston, 1964.

———. *Form Follows Fiasco.* Boston: Atlantic Monthly Press, 1977.

Bletter, Rosmarie Haag, van Bruggen, Coosje; Friedman, Mildred; Giovannini, Joseph; Hines, Thomas, Viladas, Pilar. *The Architecture of Frank Gehry.* New York: Rizzoli, 1986.

Brooks, Paul. *The View from Lincoln Hill: Man and the Land in a New England Town.* Boston: Houghton Mifflin, 1976.

Browne, Ray B., and Fishwick, Marshall (eds). *Icons of America.* Bowling Green, Ohio: Bowling Green University Press, 1978.

Calthorpe, Peter; Kelbaugh, Doug; et al. *The Pedestrian Pocket Book.* Edited by Doug Kelbaugh. Princeton: The Princeton Architectural Press, 1989.

Calthorpe, Peter, and Van der Ryn, Sim. *Sustainable Communities.* San Francisco: Sierra Club Books, 1986.

Carmen, Harry J.; Ellis, David M.; Frost, James A.; and Syrett, Harold C. *A History of New York State.* Ithaca: Cornell University Press, 1957.

Caro, Robert A. *The Power Broker: Robert Moses and the Fall of New York.* New York: Alfred A. Knopf, 1974.

Council of American Building Officials. *One and Two Family Dwelling Code.* Falls Church: CABO, 1989.

Creese, Walter L. *The Legacy of Raymond Unwin.* Cambridge: MIT Press, 1967.

Curtis, William, J. R. *Le Corbusier: Ideas and Forms.* New York: Rizzoli, 1986.

Davies, Donald Finlay. *Conspicuous Production: Automobiles and Elites in Detroit 1899–1933.* Philadelphia: Temple University Press, 1988.

Downing, Andrew Jackson. *Cottage Residences.* Reprint. New York: Dover Publications, 1981.

Fishwick, Marshall. *Parameters of Popular Culture.* Bowling Green, Ohio: Bowling Green University Press, 1974.

Flink, James J. *The Automobile Age.* Cambridge: MIT Press, 1988.

Golden, Peter. *The Quiet Diplomat: A Biography of Max M. Fisher.* New York: Herzl Press, 1991.

Gravagnuolo, Benedetto. *Adolf Loos, Theory and Work.* New York: Rizzoli, 1982.

Gutman, Robert. *The Design of American Housing.* New York: Publishing Center for Cultural Resources, 1985.

Handlin, David P. *American Architecture.* New York: Thames and Hudson, 1985.

Hawke, David Freeman. *Everyday Life in Early America.* New York: Harper & Row, 1988.

Hayden, Dolores. *Redesigning the American Dream.* New York: W. W. Norton, 1984.

Hegemann, Werner, and Peets, Elbert. *The American Vitruvius.* Edited by Alan J. Plattus. Reprint. Princeton: The Princeton Architectural Press, 1988.

Hine, Thomas. *Populuxe.* New York: Alfred A. Knopf, 1986.

Hiss, Tony. *The Experience of Place.* New York: Alfred A. Knopf, 1990.

Hitchcock, Henry-Russell, and Johnson, Philip. *The International Style.* New York: W. W. Norton, 1932.

Hollevan, Andrew. "The Mouse and the Virgin." *Wigwag Magazine,* August 1990.

Humphries, Lund, ed. *From Schinkel to the Bauhaus.* London: The Architectural Association, 1972.

Jackson, John Brinckerhoff. *Discovering the Vernacular Landscape.* New Haven: Yale University Press, 1984.

Jackson, Kenneth T. *Crabgrass Frontier: The Suburbanization of the United States.* New York: Oxford University Press, 1985.

Johnson, Paul. *The Birth of the Modern.* New York: HarperCollins, 1991.

Kostof, Spiro. *America by Design.* New York: The Oxford University Press, 1987.

Krier, Leon. "L'Achevement de Washington, D.C." Brussells: Archives D'Architecture Moderne. No. 30, 1986.

Lewis, Peirce. "The Galactic Metropolis." From *Beyond the Urban Fringe: Land Use Issues of Nonmetropolitan America.* Edited by George Macinko and Rutherford H. Platt. Minneapolis: University of Minnesota Press, 1983.

Liebs, Chester H. *Main Street to Miracle Mile.* Boston: Little, Brown and Company (New York Graphic Society Editions), 1985.

Luxenberg, Stan. *Roadside Empires: How the Chains Franchised America.* New York: Viking, 1985.

Lynd, Helen M., and Lynd, Robert S. *Middletown.* New York: Harcourt, Brace & World, 1929.

Lynes, Russell. *The Tastemakers.* New York: Harper & Brothers, 1949.

Marx, Leo. *The Machine in the Garden.* New York: Oxford University Press, 1964.

Miller, Donald L. *Lewis Mumford—A Life.* New York: Weidenfeld & Nicolson, 1989.

Morison, Samuel Eliot. *The Story of the Old Colony of New Plymouth.* New York: Alfred A. Knopf, 1956.

Mumford, Lewis. *The City in History.* New York: Harcourt, Brace & World, 1961.

Nairn, Ian. *The American Landscape.* New York: Random House, 1965.

Nash, Roderick. *Wilderness and the American Mind.* New Haven: Yale University Press, 1967.

Portoghesi, Paolo. *After Modern Architecture.* New York: Rizzoli, 1982.

Roth, Leland M. *McKim, Mead & White, Architects.* New York: Harper & Row (Icon Editions), 1983.

Rybczynski, Witold. *Home: A Short History of an Idea.* New York: Viking/Penguin, 1986.

Sargeant, John. *Frank Lloyd Wright's Usonian Houses.* New York: Watson-Guptill, 1976.

Scully, Vincent. *American Architecture and Urbanism.* New York: Henry Holt and Company, 1988.

Shoshkes, Ellen. *The Design Process: Case Studies in Project Development.* New York: Watson-Guptill (Whitney Library of Design Editions), 1989.

Silver, Nathan. *Lost New York.* Boston: Houghton Mifflin, 1967.

Stern, Robert A. M. *Pride of Place.* Boston: Houghton Mifflin (New York: American Heritage), 1986.

Stilgoe, John R. *Borderland.* New Haven: Yale University Press, 1988.

Tischler, William H., ed. *American Landscape Architecture: Designers and Places.* Washington, D.C.: The Preservation Press, 1989.

Tocqueville, Alexis de. *Democracy in America* vols. 1 and 2. New York: Alfred A. Knopf, 1945.

Trollope, Frances. *Domestic Manners of the Americans.* London: Richard Bentley, 1839.

Tunnard, Christopher, and Pushkarev, Boris. *Man-Made America: Chaos or Control?* New Haven: Yale University Press, 1963.

Venturi, Robert, and Scott-Brown, Denise. *A View From Campidoglio.* New York: Harper & Row (Icon Editions), 1984.

Venturi, Robert; Scott-Brown, Denise; and Izenour, Stephen. *Learning from Las Vegas.* Cambridge: MIT Press, 1977.

Viollet-de-Duc, Eugene-Emmanuel. *The Architectural Theory of Viollet-le-Duc.* Edited by M. F. Hearn. Cambridge: MIT Press, 1990.

Warner, Sam Bass, Jr. *The Urban Wilderness.* New York: Harper & Row, 1972.

Wolfe, Tom. *From Bauhaus to Our House.* New York: Farrar Straus Giroux, 1981.

JAMES HOWARD KUNSTLER is the author of eight novels. He has worked as a newspaper reporter and an editor for *Rolling Stone,* and is a frequent contributor to *The New York Times Sunday Magazine.* He lives in upstate New York.